7-6-75

rymyng craftily

Meaning in Chaucer's Poetry

rymyng craftily

Meaning in Chaucer's Poetry

by

Stephen Knight

HUMANITIES PRESS

ATLANTIC HIGHLANDS, N.J.

First published in 1973 by

ANGUS AND ROBERTSON (PUBLISHERS) PTY LTD
102 Glover Street, Cremorne, Sydney
2 Fisher Street, London

Reprinted 1976 by Humanities Press by
arrangement with the original publisher

ISBN: 0-391-00595-2

Printed in the
United States of America

1909016

for my mother and father

Contents

Acknowledgments ix

Introduction xiii

Chapter 1. Anelida and Arcite and The Parlement of Foules 1

Chapter 2. Troilus and Criseyde: Minor Characters and the Narrator 49

Chapter 3. The Knight's Tale 98

Chapter 4. The Manciple's Tale and The Franklin's Tale 161

Chapter 5. The Nun's Priest's Tale 206

Appendix: The Figures of Style 236

Index 243

ACKNOWLEDGMENTS

I thank Oxford University Press for permission to quote from F. N. Robinson's second edition of *The Works of Geoffrey Chaucer* (Oxford, 1957), and the editors of *The Chaucer Review* and *The Teaching of English* for permitting me to re-use some material on 'The Franklin's Tale' and 'The Nun's Priest's Tale' which first appeared in their journals.

Introduction

The idea of writing this book has developed slowly while I have been discussing Chaucer's poetry with university students. Although an increasing amount is written on Chaucer each year, very little of it treats him distinctively as a poet. Yet, in the close examination of his poetry that is a normal feature of teaching, it has become more and more obvious to me that when the Man of Law says of Chaucer:[1]

> he kan but lewedly
> On metres and on rymyng craftily,

this is one of the poet's most extreme pieces of deception. There is great craft in the way he handles 'metres', 'rymyng' and other aspects of the poet's art. The purpose of this study is to show how Chaucer often writes with great attention to the detailed working of the poetry in a passage, and that on many occasions the meaning of the poem is directly created by the nature and the modulation of the poetry.

Within the small body of writers who discuss Chaucer's work as poetry there are several who have been particularly stimulating to me in one way or another. The Cambridge critical tradition of recent decades has produced two of them. John Speirs has written *Chaucer the Maker* and the title implies the book's concerns.[2] His criticism stimulates by being ultimately disappointing, since he rarely explores the working of the poetry, but tends to summarise, as if by intuition entirely, the tone or impact of a passage. These intuitions can be impressive, but even then they seem to be only the beginnings of a thorough critique of the nature—and so the quality—of Chaucer's poetry. A. C. Spearing has written in a more detailed way in *Criticism and Medieval Poetry*, where he gives a thought-provoking account of the style of *The Book of the Duchess*,[3] but he has said little more on this aspect of Chaucer: his editions of separate

Canterbury Tales have a naturally restricted scope, though he still finds room for a number of stimulating comments.

From Oxford, Dorothy Everett has written two very interesting articles about Chaucer's poetic; these, 'Chaucer's "Good Ear" ' and 'Some Reflections on Chaucer's "Art Poetical" ', combine shrewd descriptive comments on features of Chaucer's style with subtle reflections about the topic in general.[4] In her other articles she makes several penetrating *obiter dicta* on this topic, and the quality of her insight makes it only the more sad that she did not live to write more.

Two leading American medievalists have also dealt at a high level with Chaucer as a writer of poetry. E. Talbot Donaldson has written one outstanding article on this topic: in his 'The Idiom of Popular Poetry in "The Miller's Tale" ' he shows how Chaucer uses his knowledge of contemporary poetry to add by stylistic implication a subtle level of meaning to this comic masterpiece.[5] Donaldson's technique in showing how the poetry works is particularly impressive. He indicates in other articles that he is well aware of Chaucer's stylistic powers, but he has not written anything else specifically on the topic. Charles Muscatine has produced the largest body of detailed criticism of Chaucer's poetic; in his book *Chaucer and the French Tradition* he uses a good deal of stylistic discussion to support his thesis that there are two basic elements in Chaucer's work, the bourgeois and the courtly.[6] In the process he gives some excellent criticism, which may well be of more lasting importance than his thesis itself. His analysis of the personalities of Troilus, Criseyde and Pandarus seems to me a model of how this sort of critique can open up a poem and show both why it is so good and how the poet achieves this level of art. However, Muscatine is using this material towards his thesis, not exploring it for itself, and he deals with other poems in a rather different manner, tending there to concentrate on plot and character.

All of these critics have helped to establish the groundwork for a criticism of Chaucer's poetic, and all of them have contributed ideas and techniques to this study—probably more so than I can now recognise. Throughout this book I will be referring to them and to their opinions, and in the process I hope to justify the epitomes given here of the nature of their works. But although their comments are useful and often stimulating, it seems to me that no one book has yet set out to offer a critique of the way Chaucer evolves meaning through his poetry itself.

There are several initial problems which must confront the critic who decides to attempt such a study. The first is that if an analysis of the inter-relationship of the poetry and meaning is to be given, then a description of the nature of the poetry must be an initial step. This description, to be of any use to readers of such a study, must have a good deal of exchange value and not be a purely idiosyncratic or incomprehensible reading. In order to achieve this there must be much careful analysis, and a whole series of terms and notions must be carefully applied. But care and detail seem to me to be all the critic needs; he should not be expected to give a total and totally accurate account of the poetry. Linguists have often faulted literary critics on these grounds; an extremely relevant example is Roger Fowler's castigation of Spearing:[7]

> ... after making great claims for close textural description, that is, practical criticism of the Cambridge sort, [he] deals in unrealities like 'breathless short sentences' which sit neither in the critic's mind nor in the text ...

These are fairly hard words, but in a linguist's terms they may well be justified for they arise from the difference in method between the linguist and the literary critic. Linguists work toward a full and objective account of a passage, but literary critics work toward a full account of what they judge to be of importance in a passage. The linguist analyses all that he observes, the critic begins with an intuition and develops it with detail. The linguist would find 'breathless short sentences' to be inadequately defined and therefore meaningless, but the literary critic would accept it as a development of a thesis about the passage, and though he might prefer it to be more fully and more precisely explained this does not invalidate it as a comment.

One of the results of the linguist's concern with total and objective description is that when linguists use their techniques to move toward literary criticism they seem to achieve little. Thus Fowler's own essays and the similar work of G. N. Leech, Roman Jakobson, Seymour B. Chatman and S. R. Levin operate, in the context of literary criticism, at a rather elementary level, as F. W. Bateson has sharply observed in his debate with Fowler on the topic.[8] This is not because linguists are limited or insensitive people, as many literary critics appear to believe. It is because of the difference between the two techniques; attempting to give a total and reliable account, the linguist works carefully through some of the features of poetry which may be fully described and which are therefore not the most elusive features, while the literary critic, jumping off with an intuition and not feeling the need to base everything on observed data or to give a total account, can deal and usually chooses to deal with the more subtle issues. It is significant of this vital difference that Leo Spitzer, the most far-reaching of the linguistically trained critics, lays out with meticulous care the part intuition plays in his own criticism.[9]

Consequently, in trying to analyse and explain what is going on in a passage of poetic language, the critic does try to give explanation and detail, but this detail is posterior to and explanatory of a decision he has made about what is important in the passage; in the whole process there is a flexible, even a hopeful element, as the critic must depend on the quality of his judgment for the relevance and usefulness of what he is saying. It is this path which I follow here, trying to identify the principal effects in passages of poetry and trying to shape at least the beginnings of a critique of Chaucer's poetic method.

The other great problem that must confront the critic who talks of meaning in poetry, especially if his title uses the expression, is that in many ways the poetry and its meaning may not be divided. It is a well-known issue, but one of such importance that it is necessary to clarify my position. It appears to me axiomatic that in poetry the style and the meaning are not, in fact, separate things: the major concern of this book is to show that this axiom applied in Chaucer. Yet that does *not* mean that the two things may not be discussed separately. The word 'style' and the word 'meaning' are not synonyms and we can grasp the concepts separately, although we may not feel that in function the things are separate. To discuss the nature of a poet's art it seems essential to make this working distinction, in order to see how that same art, fully understood, makes the two elements indistinguishable. After we have conducted such a discussion and found the two indistinguishable, we are wiser about the particular poem and about poetry in general than if we had, in a spirit of logical purity, merely contemplated the poem-object as an indivisible and therefore indescribable complex. On this topic I would refer to Graham Hough's brief but intelligent discussion in his recent book *Style and Stylistics*, where he defends the functional use of the word 'style' and expounds the dangers involved in a study like this one.[10]

The approach here is, as has been implied, exploratory and suggestive. I have chosen to study a small number of poems in depth rather than provide a cursory survey of the whole works, in the hope that this will establish more successfully the elements of Chaucer's meaningful poetic. I have taken poems of different sorts written at different stages for the purposes of contrast, and in two chapters have deliberately set in contrast poems of rather different characters to show how Chaucer's art is various and developing in nature.

The basic method is to analyse the meaningful uses of poetic style, poetic device and poetic modulation in Chaucer. It has often been convenient to use Latin rhetorical terms in referring to some aspects of style or to some poetic devices. These precise terms exist, they belong to the period discussed and though Chaucer rarely refers directly to rhetorical figures he does appear, as I hope to show, to recognise many of them as the figures they are. These terms may initially seem obscure, but to have avoided using them would have imposed a greater obscurity, as either new terms or generally descriptive phrases would then have been employed. An appendix containing a definition and illustration of the figures of style is provided, as nowadays few, if any, of us carry the whole rhetorical corpus in our heads.

I do not argue in this study that all of Chaucer's poetic and his poetic modulation is meaningful; indeed there are long stretches of his work which are straightforward and efficient narrative, though as I am here talking about meaningful poetic I have, I think naturally, not commented widely on such passages. A good example of the variable nature of Chaucer's poetic method is that we can find similar passages, some of which have a simple function and some of which are more complex in effect. In *Troilus and Criseyde* there are a number of short passages which are a series of co-ordinate clauses: each line in the stanza begins with 'And'—a *repetitio*, in the language of the rhetoricians—and each line is similar in its structure and movement—*compar*. Some of these passages are no more than an orderly marshalling of facts, like Pandarus's instructions to Troilus (II.1010–17) or Cassandra's history lesson to Troilus (V.1492–1512). But a number of these passages chart the reactions of Criseyde to some stimulus, often explaining why she will do something later— II.451–56, II.659–65, III.918–21, V.1076–85 are good examples. In these passages the repetition seems a little more obvious, the movement of the sequence a little stiffer in effect, and Chaucer exploits the level, unsubordinated nature of the syntax to suggest how Criseyde makes almost automatic reactions to stimuli, how she lacks a series of cerebral, subordinated arguments behind her actions at crucial moments in the story. The bald syntax and repetitive movement set out her reactions and actions steadily; there is no difference

B

of pause, no sign of a reason and no sense of culminating importance. It is a small but important part of the characterisation of Criseyde as a person who is manipulated by others because of her lack of a firm personality and a clear set of values.

The purpose of this study is firstly to draw attention to Chaucer's power to write poetry of this sort and, secondly, by doing this to argue that in addition to all the other qualities we acknowledge in him we should also recognise him as an extremely subtle and skilful poet, one who masters his form and its potentialities as well as any of the other great poets of the language.

I should like to express my gratitude to The University of Sydney for granting me the year's leave when most of this book was written, and to a number of people whose advice, help and ideas have been greatly responsible for whatever may be of value here: I thank Professor H. L. Rogers, Associate Professors B. K. Martin and W. M. Maidment, Mr D. Anderson and the many students with whom I have discussed Chaucer and his poetry.

NOTES

1. I quote here and throughout this study from F. N. Robinson's edition of *The Works of Geoffrey Chaucer*, second edition (Oxford, 1957).
2. London, 1951.
3. London, 1964, pp. 10–19.
4. Oxford, 1955, see Chapters VI and VII, pp. 139–74.
5. *English Institute Essays*, 1950, ed. A. S. Downer (New York, 1951), pp. 116–40, reprinted in *Speaking of Chaucer* (London, 1971), pp. 13–29.
6. Berkeley and Los Angeles, 1957.
7. *The Languages of Literature* (London, 1971), p. 48.
8. Leech, *A Linguistic Guide to English Poetry* (London, 1969), Nowottny, *The Language Poets Use* (London, 1962), Chatman, *A Theory of Meter* (The Hague, 1965), Levin, *Linguistic Structures in Poetry* (The Hague, 1962), Bateson, 'Literature and Linguistics,' *EC*, XVII (1967), 335–47 and his further comment in *EC*, XVIII (1968), 176–82.
9. See his essay 'Linguistics and Literary History' in *Linguistics and Literary History* (Princeton, 1948), pp. 1–39.
10. London, 1969, see especially pp. 7-9.

1. *Anelida and Arcite and The Parlement of Foules*

The poems that tradition has usually named *Anelida and Arcite* and *The Parlement of Foules* both belong to Chaucer's 'Italian period', and while this seems certain to have followed his 'French period', that is about all that can be said with confidence about its dating.[1] The three rhyme royal poems—*Anelida and Arcite, The Parlement of Foules* and *Troilus and Criseyde* (and perhaps a 'Palamon and Arcite' as well)—may have been spread over fifteen years or more, and there is no certainty that *The Parlement of Foules* was written before *Troilus and Criseyde*, though we usually assume that this is the case. For the same reasons we should not assume that *Anelida and Arcite* and *The Parlement of Foules* are near contemporaries though it seems certain that *Anelida and Arcite* was written first. Nor should the fact that both are short tempt us to see them as generically similar, for *Anelida and Arcite* is a fragment of a projected poem that may have been meant to be of considerable length, and *The Parlement of Foules* is a carefully finished short poem.

It is important to bear these differences in mind, for in this chapter I propose to make some comparisons between the style of the two poems. What emerges is largely a series of contrasts between them, and it should be made clear now that I do not consider them to be companion pieces, but believe that to look at the two poems in juxtaposition is a good way of comprehending their styles. From this comparison it becomes clear that the stylistic pattern of *Anelida and Arcite* is on the whole unsatisfactory and that in *The Parlement of Foules* Chaucer has perfected the subtle and various style typical of the poems that are commonly thought to be his greatest.

I. *Anelida and Arcite*

Although little has been written about this poem, within that amount there is a surprising variety of opinion. Most of the earlier critics of the modern period found something to deplore and also something to praise—the praise usually related to the style of the poem. Manly was perhaps the most severe, finding in the poem what he believed to be Chaucer's early devotion to literary tradition:[2]

> The much discussed and little understood *Anelida and the False Arcite* seems also purely an experiment in versification and is of interest, chiefly if not solely, because the formal Complaint is an even more remarkable *tour de force* in rhyming than the famous translations from Sir Otes de Granson.

Ker interpreted the poem more generously, feeling that 'the fineness of the style in this unfinished poetical essay gives it rank among the greater poems'[3] and Wolfgang Clemen, who also found the poem 'experimental, tentative and unequal' was more explicit in his praise of its style. In the introduction to the narrative he was impressed by '. . . the swift compression from the general to the particular, the conciseness and the abundance of pregnant detail'[4], and in the Complaint he judged that

> . . . it is the voice of genuine human suffering which we hear behind the veil of Chaucer's artistry. His ability to come near to the 'speaking voice' while employing a stanza so rigidly and intricately constructed is astonishing.

Robinson gave a thoughtful introduction to the poem—one of those short pieces which are often overlooked by later writers, but which are models of brief, lucid criticism; he found[5]

> The characterization is poor and conventional; the expression of feeling and sentiment a little more adequate, perhaps because of Chaucer's reading of Ovid.

But while being more restrained than Clemen, he also saw 'the great metrical proficiency' of the Complaint and felt that

> In the introductory story, too, thin as the substance is, there begins to appear the swift and flexible narrative style of Chaucer's later years.

These critics have disagreed over the value and import of elements of the poem, but in general they have seen the same elements: more recently some American critics have argued quite differently about the poem. James I. Wimsatt speaks of its qualities much more highly, finding in it 'delicacy of tone, fineness of expression, and highly-wrought versification' and he concludes his article not only with lofty praise but, bizarrely, with satisfaction that the poem is unfinished:[6]

> As it stands the poem has such fine pathos and polished style that one can hardly wish for a continuation in which the tragedy proves no tragedy and the artifice becomes excessive. It is probably just as well that this poem which has so much in common with the French *dits* of complaint and comfort ends with the complaint.

An equally curious account of the poem is given by Michael D. Cherniss. He suggests that the original 'Palamon and Arcite' may have been meant as the consolation to be offered to Anelida; he then accounts briskly for the apparent inconsistencies (Arcite's different character in the two poems, for example) by suggesting that they were just why the linkage was not made.[7] Logical idiosyncrasy is also found in an article by A. Wigfall Green, who first asserts that 'The story as a whole is well designed' then goes on to confide that 'the story was not completed.'[8] The bulk of his article is an attempt to show the poem to be an ironic comedy, with some unconvincing evidence; in reference to stanza forty (lines 299–307) where one rhyme is used throughout, he says: 'although the material is basically serious the multiplicity of rhyme makes the entire stanza comic.'

These recent American critics are the only ones who have argued that the work is a real success, but the inadequacy of their arguments should not make us dismiss this notion. It would be a mistake to expect the poem to be a failure because it is unfinished, to assume that it is abandoned by the author with relief, especially when the author is Chaucer, who left so many works unfinished (yet, oddly, we still regard him as a level-headed, sensible, untemperamental sort of man). So, in looking at the poem I have tried to start with an open mind, to view its style as objectively as possible and to see which of these critical views is the most sound. There are a number of views to consider because, unusually in Chaucer criticism, a large part of the published opinion on this poem is concerned with style. The reasons for this are not hard to find; the poem's style is often striking, and when a work is so patently unfinished speculation about meaning, plot and character can hardly be very fruitful. It is possible, however, to comment on the style of an unfinished poem, though this too can be dangerous: the effects of a poem's style may depend upon large-scale juxtaposition or developments which occur over long periods and these may not be perceptible in a fragment. But I hope to show that something can be made of the poem's style, that it does have an interest both in itself and as an indication of a stage in Chaucer's poetic career.

The poem begins with an invocation that foreshadows a grim story:

> Thou ferse god of armes, Mars the rede,
> That in the frosty contre called Trace,
> Within thy grisly temple ful of drede
> Honoured art, as patroun of that place;
> With thy Bellona, Pallas, ful of grace,
> Be present, and my song contynue and guye;
> At my begynnyng thus to the I crye.   1–7

The pattern of the stanza is often to be found in Chaucerian invocations in rhyme royal: the name and nature of the deity is elaborated in the bulk of the stanza and the main verb actually invoking the deity comes later.[9] It is an intrinsically ornate structure, for the delaying of the verb creates a sense of build-up, and the amplification of the deity's nature demands figural repetition with variation. This stanza is fairly ornate, for there is a brief *pronominatio* in the first line and striking epithets are used frequently. But in comparison with later passages it is not very ornate: the *pronominatio* quickly turns into a series of descriptive phrases and clauses, and the fine epithets do not have the powerful prosodic support that the same words have in the description of Mars's temple in 'The Knight's Tale' (lines 1970–4).

But to judge this passage by greater ones written later is probably unfair; in the opening lines, at least, it is fluent and striking, ornately honouring the invoked God. A more proper criticism is that in the later part of the stanza the writing seems loose. The phrase 'as patroun of that place' is not very gripping to us, but this is partly because the word 'patroun' is no longer as unusual as it was in Chaucer's time;[10] the phrase has an alliterative ornateness as well, linking with 'Pallas' in the next line. But little can be said for the lagging effect of the sixth line; it unfortunately combines with the word 'contynue' to imply a long and tedious continuation. The last line seems an afterthought: its simple nature may be meant to show a descent in style as the narrator begins to recount his poem, but it has an obviousness in meaning that combines with its tacked-on syntax to bring the stanza to a disappointing close; later invocations (especially in *Troilus and Criseyde*) will make the rhyme royal stanza a more united entity, often by saving the main verb till the last line.

A simpler style is adopted for the explanatory second stanza:

> For hit ful depe is sonken in my mynde,
> With pitous hert in Englyssh to endyte
> This olde storie, in Latyn which I fynde,
> Of quene Anelida and fals Arcite,
> That elde, which that al can frete and bite,
> As hit hath freten mony a noble storie,
> Hath nygh devoured out of oure memorie. 8–14

The opening lines have that easy demotic movement that we associate so much with Chaucer; it is a relaxed, firm progress in which no element seems to jump out at us, and in which nothing seems redundant. Just as before, though, there seems some trouble in filling out the stanza, for in the last three lines the organisation is complicated without seeming subtle, and the unsophisticated repetition of 'frete' emphasises this. It would be harsh to call these last three lines unsuccessful, but they do slow and disturb the forceful flow that is established by the first four lines.

After this straightforward stanza there is a rise in tone for a second invocation:

> Be favorable eke, thou Polymya,
> On Parnaso that with thy sustres glade,
> By Elycon, not fer from Cirrea,
> Singest which vois memorial in the shade,
> Under the laurer with that may nat fade,
> And do that I my ship to haven wynne.
> First folowe I Stace, and after him Corynne. 15–21

Again the opening is polished; here the invocatory verb comes first and this is a pleasing variation on the delayed verb of the first stanza, a directness of invocation that seems to respond to the more direct style of the second stanza, and while the second and third lines have the delaying, qualifying note of the first stanza, the fourth and fifth have the fine flow of the second stanza. They are justly famous lines, rich in imagination and expression—'memorial' is first used here, and only used once by Chaucer, and 'laurer' also has some ornateness: Chaucer is the second to use it, and then only in formal contexts. The sixth line effectively uses a familiar narrator's metaphor in a poised monosyllabic line to end the whole invocation. But the fine judgment of these six lines, moving as they do with supple ease makes much worse the effect of the bathetic final line. It limply communicates a fact of little vitality, it has no relation with what has gone before and the assonance in 'him Corynne' does not help its dignity at all; the final name seems tacked on to provide the rhyme, just as the whole line is attached to complete the stanza. It is a line that the author of 'Sir Thopas' might well have looked back at with a blush.

This invocation is mixed in a number of ways. It opens with a reasonably ornate stanza and the fact that Chaucer later wrote ones more ornate should not lead us to think that here he only seeks to touch a middle style. The high first stanza is followed by the simple second and then both are skilfully resolved in the mixed pattern of the third, at first complex in movement and then flowing easily. The effect of this skilled mixture of styles is to prepare us for a poem of mixed style and, to a certain extent, this expectation will be fulfilled. But cutting across this careful plan for the invocation is the real failure to round off the stanzas successfully; it is tempting to suggest that this is a first attempt at the rhyme royal stanza by Chaucer, for here the stanza seems too hard for him, and I can think of no other reason to explain this phenomenon. What in later poems will be an instrument of marvellous subtlety here seems to have him groping for final lines. So this invocation at once illustrates the boldness of the poet's mind, the great skills which he controls, and yet it shows a certain falling short as well.

In the opening part of the story the deeds and honour of Theseus are described; it is the topic of the opening sequence of 'The Knight's Tale', and the style Chaucer uses also resembles that poem. We first find the packed narrative that he will use to describe the busy scenes before the tournament:

> When Theseus, with werres longe and grete,
> The aspre folk of Cithe had overcome,
> With laurer corouned, in his char gold-bete,
> Hom to his contre-houses is he come;
> For which the peple, blisful al and somme,
> So cryeden that to the sterres hit wente,
> And him to honouren dide al her entente.   22–8

The short phrases and the forceful epithets that characterise Chaucer's denser style are visible here; it is a vigorous stanza and, though the last line is a little weak and the last phrase in the fifth line rather slack, it is more successful as a whole than the stanzas of the invocation. The movement of it is direct; it is by no means ornate in style, and when we compare this stanza with its source in Statius (the first three lines of the Latin passage, spelt in the medieval way, stand as an epigraph) we can see how faithfully Chaucer has presented the vigorous and solid tone of the Latin:

Iamque domos patrias Scythicae post aspera gentis
proelia laurigero subeuntem Thesea curru
laetifici plausus missusque ad sidera vulgi
clamor et emeritis hilaris tuba nuntiat armis.

The paraphrasing of the Latin seems to give to Chaucer's verse a much firmer form than is achieved when he translates from French in *The Romaunt of the Rose*, and this may have been an important stage in the development of his style for, as I frequently argue in this study, one of Chaucer's subtlest skills is his ability to make the movement of his poetry seem at times dense and slow and at other times open and swift.

The honour that the people give to Theseus is acted out in the next stanza, where we find the poised, balanced style that is to be so characteristic of the finer passages of 'The Knight's Tale':

Beforn this duk, in signe of victorie,
The trompes come, and in his baner large
The ymage of Mars; and, in token of glorie,
Men myghte sen of tresour many a charge,
Many a bright helm, and many a spere and targe,
Many a fresh knyght, and many a blysful route,
On hors, on fote, in al the feld aboute.   29–35

Repetitio, the use of overt repetition, and *compar*, the balancing of lines and phrases, are frequently used by Chaucer to imply the poise and grandeur of chivalric display. It is true that the rhythms in lines five and six are rather tripping compared with the more sonorous tone to be struck so often in 'The Knight's Tale', and this does detract from the effect here, but the stanza profits from the fact that the last line is well attached, and that overall it has an impressive movement, pausing, repetitive and implying a sense of conclusion.

As the poet moves on he continues to describe the scene in an amplified manner, but the movement, like that of the opening stanza, is still direct, for the elaboration comes from epithets and from relative clauses rather than from the rhetorical elaboration briefly used in the second stanza:

Ipolita his wif, the hardy quene
Of Cithia, that he conquered hadde,
With Emelye, her yonge suster shene,
Faire in a char of gold he with him ladde,
That al the ground about her char she spradde
With brightnesse of the beaute in her face,
Fulfilled of largesse and of all grace.   36–42

The hyperbole, or *superlatio*, in lines five and six is attractive and stands out from the even progress of the stanza, couched in a middle style as it is. This shows well the poet's ability to elevate and elaborate his material, but the next stanza makes it clear that his main purpose is not to honour Theseus's court:

> With his tryumphe, and laurer-corouned thus,
> In al the flour of Fortunes yevynge,
> Let I this noble prince Theseus
> Toward Athenes in his wey rydinge,
> And founde I wol in shortly for to bringe
> The slye wey of that I gan to write,
> Of quene Anelida and fals Arcite.   43–9

The material about Theseus has only been introductory and the way in which it is cut off communicates a sense of drive at this point. The sharp change from amplified description to a brisker narrative follows up the invocatory promise of a mixed style. But now, as at several later points, the poem seems to lose its way. Instead of pressing on with a plain narrative about Anelida it offers us several more historical stanzas. They are only marginally relevant to Anelida and Arcite themselves and they seem to be here only to pad the poem out so that Anelida can appear at line seventy-one. The poem is divided into seventy-line segments and at this point the preorganised structure of the poem seems to dominate its style and meaning. It is always possible, we must recall, that in the finished poem these stanzas would have leapt into relevance: I frankly doubt it, and even if this were so there would still be a flaw in having several prosodically undistinguished stanzas dissipating the poem's onward movement before its heroine appears. As the poem stands, in these stanzas the reader drifts along, noting only that the rhyme royal form now seems mastered, for the stanzas are satisfactory units, though some rather clumsy repetitions are used to bring this about:

> For when Amphiorax and Tydeus,
> Ipomedon, Parthonope also
> Were ded, and slayn proude Campaneus,
> And when the wrecched Thebans, bretheren two,
> Were slayn, and kyng Adrastus hom ago,
> So desolat stod Thebes and so bare,
> That no wight coude remedie of his care.   57–63

When we come to the magic line seventy-one, the opening words give the poet away, for any writer may ruefully recognise in them the general phrase, that hopeful device by which he tries to make organisation materialise where there has been none:

> Among al these Anelida, the quene
> Of Ermony, was in that toun dwellynge,
> That fairer was then is the sonne shene. 71–3

Not only is the opening unhappily loose; the third line is slackly reminiscent of many a lovely lady, and the 'quene/shene' rhyme has already been used in lines 36 and 38.[11] The stylistic change at lines 45–9 led us to expect a plainer style when the heroine appears, but this is beyond plainness—it is flat and dull. The rest of the stanza is quite smooth, but rather lifeless; its rhythms merely repeat the even movement of the unexciting third line, the caesura falls monotonously and there is no vivacity in thought or in style:

> Thurghout the world so gan her name springe,
> That her to seen had every wyght likynge;
> For, as of trouthe, is ther noon her lyche,
> Of al the women in this worlde riche. 74–7

There is a flatness here that would not be surprising in Gower, where we expect a smooth unvarying line (though he can sometimes startle us), but compared with other Chaucerian poetry where so much is done with variation of pause and rhythm, the stanza is poor. The next stanza continues this muted and rather mechanical note:

> Yong was this quene, of twenty yer of elde,
> Of mydel stature, and of such fairenesse,
> That Nature had a joye her to behelde;
> And for to speken of her stidfastnesse,
> She passed hath Penelope and Lucresse;
> And shortly, yf she shal be comprehended,
> In her ne myghte no thing been amended. 78–84

The repetitive phrasing of the opening two lines does not solidify into *compar*, rather it seems like an uninventive list. The matter of fact tone in lines 4 and 6 is used with great effect in the 'General Prologue' to discuss some rather ordinary people in a cutting way (cf. the ends of the descriptions of the Monk, Merchant and Man of Law), but when it is used to praise a classical heroine it can only communicate bathos. The stanzas are dull, they do not convince us of their rather hackneyed praises; the heroine is not made interesting and as a result the poem is labouring badly.

Arcite is now introduced in a stanza which seems more interesting, though not because its movement is more subtle—it, too, is repetitive —but because it does recount action, in a general way:

> This Theban knyght eke, soth to seyn,
> Was yong, and therwithal a lusty knyght,
> But he was double in love and no thing pleyn,
> And subtil in that craft over any wyght,
> And with his kunnyng wan this lady bryght;
> For so ferforth he gan her trouthe assure
> That she him trusted over any creature.   85–91[12]

The repetition of 'knyght' in the first two lines is far from felicitious, but the first lines have a varied rhythm and there is some action, so the stanza seems to achieve a little more than the previous ones. Perhaps the poet feels the need for a stimulus, for in the next stanzas there is some gesture towards emotion. He begins:

> What shuld I seyn? she loved Arcite so
> That when that he was absent any throwe,
> Anon her thoghte her herte brast a-two.   92–4

The forceful opening is followed by a rather flat account of heartbreak, and any residual excitement is then swallowed up by a quite remarkable sequence of slow-moving monosyllabic lines:

> For in her sight to her he bar hym lowe,
> So that she wende have al his hert yknowe;
> But he was fals; hit nas but feyned chere,—
> As nedeth not to men such craft to lere.   95–8

The clipped beginning to line 97 just does not surface above the dull weight of the complicated syntax and dragging movement of the lines; the last line, detached, slow and rather enigmatic, hangs heavily around the stanza's neck. The same thing happens in the next stanza, where the narrator again uses a short exclamation to whip up enthusiasm but again swamps it with a sage, sententious enigma:

> Alas, the while! for hit was routhe and synne,
> That she upon his sorowes wolde rewe;
> But nothing thinketh the fals as doth the trewe.   103–5

Throughout this seventy-line sequence expounding Anelida's miserable situation the style is very flat. It seems to set out to be simple and direct in diction and movement, but falls quickly into the dangers of the plain style, becoming the 'meagre', a 'dry and bloodless kind of style'.[13] The quoted stanzas show this happening, and, as the last stanza of the sequence will illustrate, even when action occurs the effect is still a flat one:

> When she shal ete, on him is so her thoght,
> That wel unnethe of mete tok she kep;
> And when that she was to her reste broght,
> On him she thoghte alwey til that she slep;
> When he was absent, prevely she wep:
> Thus lyveth feire Anelida the quene
> For fals Arcite, that dide her al this tene.   134–40

The stanza is well-balanced; the first four lines move in pairs and the fifth line is divided equally, but the evenness of the stanza is achieved through a total lack of contour, not through any balancing of forceful units. As the end of a long sequence of dull stanzas it does not transcend their effect in any way, and where the first seventy line segment seemed padded to reach its length, this one seems to have little vigour at all. It is, of course, quite conceivable that this was in part deliberate. The poet may well have meant this sequence to be plain—the invocation and lines 45–9 would support such an interpretation. Anelida's character is later described as 'lowly' (line 142) and 'meke' (line 200), and this could therefore be a prosodic creation of her character. It could also be made plain to highlight the Complaint to come. The former explanation seems speculative, for only rarely in this poem does the poet modulate his style to imply character, and this would be a long and rather uncertain example of such modulation—most of the examples of this poetic art discussed in this study are fairly clearly signalled by the poet. I would be more confident in explaining this plain sequence as a contrast to the fine Complaint, for the next seventy-line segment shows something of a climb up the register of style, but I cannot believe that for either of these reasons Chaucer meant to write badly in this sequence. Rather it seems that at this stage he was unable to master the delicate variations of rhythm and pause that can make a plain style interesting; quite often his syntax becomes awkward, rather than plain, in order to fit the stanza form and, while a simple diction is obviously appropriate, he too often creates a clumsy effect by repeating words. To criticise the sequence is to judge Chaucer by his own standards, and in particular I believe that *The Parlement of Foules* shows how Chaucer later learnt to write plainly but to create a constantly interesting surface to the poem. So far in this poem it is the more ornate passages which have been the more successful, and as the style of the poem now begins, rather uncertainly at first, to ascend, we might hope to find more of this impressive work.

Arcite's unfaithfulness is recounted in action:

> This fals Arcite, of his newfanglenesse,
> For she to him so lowly was and trewe,
> Tok lesse deynte of her stidfastnesse,
> And saw another lady, proud and newe,
> And ryght anon he cladde him in her hewe—
> Wot I not whethir in white, rede, or grene—
> And falsed fair Anelida the quene.   141–7

As before, the movement is straightforward and the rhythm of each line tends to repeat that of the previous one, but there are some signs of life. There are a few pauses, the action of the stanza does give it forward movement and though the sixth line seems a strained one, at least it does offer a rhyme for 'quene' other than 'shene'. The narrator's incursion here varies the nature of the narration and this is pursued, for in the next stanza he comments further on the action:

> But neverthelesse, gret wonder was hit noon
> Thogh he were fals, for hit is kynde of man,
> Sith Lamek was, that is so longe agoon,
> To ben in love as fals as evere he can;   148–51

It is quite an interesting comment, but still the rhythm is dull: the caesura falls in exactly the same place in each line and the stanza is heading for a boring effect—but this changes as soon as the rhythm varies, as soon as a delayed caesura and enjambement invigorate the movement:

> He was the firste fader that began
> To loven two, and was in bigamye;
> And he found tentes first, but yf men lye.   152–4

The pause after 'fader' is late, and this gives more emphasis to the phrase 'To loven two'. The irregularity of caesura is somewhat arresting, and the same happens in the last line here: the clause 'but yf men lye' follows another late caesura and it has emphasis; it projects the crisp note that we associate with the Chaucerian narrator, cutting across his material with a shrewd, dry voice. Where before the narrator's voice seemed as stodgy as the movement of the poem, rhythmic variation gives it an immediate bite. It does not indicate a sharp change of style, however, for the next stanza moves off with the level drone that we have now seen so much:

> This fals Arcite, sumwhat moste he feyne,
> When he wex fals, to covere his traitorie,
> Ryght as an hors, that can both bite and pleyne;   155–7

The lines break in the same place, and the opening two lines are quite flat; as a result the familiar epithet 'fals', used frequently of Arcite, seems derived more from a lack of imagination than from the formulaic epithets of epic tradition. The third line, however, is given some stimulus by beginning with a strong syllable, and this provides support to the fairly vigorous simile it embodies.

In the beginning of this sequence, then, we have seen some signs of life where before there were hardly any, but this does not mean that the verse has changed radically. We have seen some good effects which do not manage to struggle free of the unsuccessful context, and as the seventy-line segment moves on this is continued. In the next stanza the narrator essays a small apostrophe:

> Alas! what herte myght enduren hit,
> For routhe or wo, her sorwe for to telle?
> Or what man hath the cunnyng or the wit?
> Or what man mighte within the chambre dwelle.
> Yf I to him rehersen sholde the helle
> That suffreth fair Anelida the quene
> For fals Arcite, that dide her al this tene.   162–8

The opening lines move well; they are not very ornate but offer an *exclamatio* neatly developed with *repetitio* and this opening *exclamatio* is skilfully married into the last three lines. But the last line is in itself not strong, slackly repeating what has been forcefully stated before, and it is an exact repetition of line 140 without any ironic meaning being implied by the repetition.

The following stanza expounds more fully Anelida's grief, so that we find the *exclamatio* the more convincing (the mature Chaucer would probably have done it the other way round, so that our emotions would be aroused with the narrator's):

> She wepith, waileth, swowneth pitously;
> To grounde ded she falleth as a ston;
> Craumpyssheth her lymes crokedly;
> She speketh as her wit were al agon;
> Other colour then asshen hath she noon;
> Non other word speketh she, moche or lyte,
> But 'merci, cruel herte myn, Arcite!'   169–75

The sharp *articulus* of the first line both asserts the depth of her grief and also implies the dramatic, breathless way in which it found expression. The stanza as a whole seems to take its cue from this line, for the first five lines are heavily end-stopped, each one stating one aspect of her grief-stricken behaviour. It is a dramatic device, and I think we should recognise this as an effort to mould the style of the poetry to the meaning—and a largely successful one, though not one that Chaucer uses again. He frequently uses *articulus* to express grief, but does not extend it in this way—when he describes Dorigen's grief in 'The Franklin's Tale' (lines 817–21) the poetry is not as mannered as it is here. In my judgment this mannered quality is something of a fault, though it may well be a part of the build-up in style to the very mannered Complaint which is to follow. If that were so then the fault would be that here the build-up is too sharp, for this elaborate stanza stands in the middle of a sequence which is the opposite of mannered. So far the rise in style has been rather gradual; there were signs of increasing complexity in the style of the first three stanzas of this sequence (lines 141–61) and then the poet began to deploy rhetorical figures. However the step from a slight decoration to the formality of this stanza is an abrupt one, and it seems to me an artistic failure, though this judgment, like several others made here, is guided by the very skilful modulation from one tone to another which is found in Chaucer's later poems.

After this heightened couple of stanzas the rise in the poem's style is more assured; the continuing narrative is clearly more elaborate than before—a middle style, perhaps, for the diction is richer and figures of comparison now appear quite frequently:

> And thus endureth, til that she was so mat
> That she ne hath foot on which she may sustene;
> But forth languisshing ever in this estat,
> Of which Arcite hath nouther routhe ne tene.
> His herte was elleswhere, newe and grene,
> That on her wo ne deyneth him not to thinke;
> Him rekketh never wher she flete or synke.   176–82

The movement is more varied than in the plain style sequence before—even the straightforward first two lines cannot be read as iambic pentameters, and their slight irregularity is skilfully bound up with the enjambement. The diction is to a certain extent richer than before, for 'endureth', 'languisshing' and, 'deyneth' have some ornateness.[14] Metaphor, the 'difficult ornament' of *translatio* appears in 180 and 182. This level of style is maintained, and the heightened

style and finer sweep of the next passage is exemplified by the fact
that it runs on and it is necessary to quote ten lines, not seven:

> His newe lady holdeth him so narowe
> Up by the bridil, at the staves ende,
> That every word he dredeth as an arowe;
> Her daunger made him bothe bowe and bende,
> And as her liste, made him turne or wende;
> For she ne graunted him in her lyvynge
> No grace, whi that he hath lust to singe,
>
> But drof hym forth, unnethe liste her knowe
> That he was servaunt unto her ladishippe;
> But lest that he were proud, she held him lowe.   183–92

There are some things here that would appear clumsy in *Troilus and
Criseyde*—the repetition in lines 186 and 187 seems unimaginative
and stops the movement of the sequence, and line 192 seems an un-
necessarily obvious summing-up. At the same time, though, the
confident placing of 'No grace' and the way the stanza swings on to
the dramatic 'But drof hym forth' are well up to the standard of
Chaucer's later work and the vigorous similes and metaphors are
similar in ironic effect to the animal metaphors used of Troilus in
Book I of *Troilus and Criseyde*.

The style continues to be fairly elaborate:

> Thus serveth he, withoute fee or shipe;
> She sent him now to londe, now to shippe;
> And for she yaf him daunger al his fille,
> Therfor she hadde him at her owne wille.   193–6

Indeed, the clustering of metaphors here might well make the style
nearer high than middle, in Chaucerian terms at least, and the *rime
riche* in lines 193–4 adds a further polish. The way in which through
these last few stanzas the style has been enlivened is well shown by
the varying movement and brisk attack of the narrator's summary
of all this:

> Ensample of this, ye thrifty wymmen alle,
> Take her of Anelida and Arcite,
> That for her liste him 'dere herte' calle,
> And was so meke, therfor he loved her lyte.
> The kynde of mannes herte is to delyte
> In thyng that straunge is, also God me save!
> For what he may not gete, that wold he have.   197–203

c

The caesura varies from line to line; where before the couplet in lines four and five of the stanza tended to thump down, here the run-on of line five makes the effect much subtler. Where an isolated last line was often before a drag on the stanza, here it is an unrepetitive and balanced summary of the stanza, slowing the whole thing down well; in the context of vigorous poetry like this a slow, even line, which might have seemed dull when there was no contrast, can have a real point as we see when the next stanza comes to a steady and expectant end:

> She caste her for to make a compleynynge,
> And with her owne hond she gan hit write,
> And sente it to her Theban knyght, Arcite. 208–10

The poem is about to change its nature quite radically with Anelida's Complaint. The high style of this will contrast vividly with the plain evocation of her situation, though the middle style of the sequence from line 140 to 210 has made a bridge between the two. In the stanzas of the invocation the poem presented a mixed style and in its development so far we have found first a very plain style and then a rather more decorated style. It is to move on to use as high a style as Chaucer writes. In this poem, then, Chaucer seems clearly aware of the possibilities of poetic variation, but any consideration of his success at large must wait until we have looked at the Complaint in detail. At the moment what can be said is that the planning seems too ambitious for the execution. Chaucer's art here seems too limited to produce a plain style without falling into banality, the seventy-line segments seem at times to overtax his invention, the rhyme royal stanza is not always mastered, especially early in the poem and, while there are passages that are in the fullest sense Chaucerian, they are often marred by some adjacent clumsiness.

The opening sentence of the Proem to Anelida's Complaint proclaims the elaboration of what is to follow:

> So thirleth with the poynt of remembraunce
> The swerd of sorwe, ywhet with fals plesaunce,
> Myn herte, bare of blis and blak of hewe,
> That turned is in quakyng al my daunce,
> My surete in awhaped countenaunce,
> Sith hit availeth not for to ben trewe; 211–16

The syntax is complicated and its progress is held up by phrases in apposition and by qualifying clauses and phrases. The diction is quite elaborate, especially in the rhymes, and alliteration makes the opening lines the more ornate. But the most striking effect is the elaborate metaphor that opens the sentence, and which is followed by further metaphor in 'bare', 'blak of hewe' and 'daunce'. As we have seen, the poet had started to use metaphor in the preceding stanzas, but the complexity of the initial metaphor here is quite new. Chaucer's use of metaphor and simile, the two forms of *collatio* as the rhetoricians describe them, has not received nearly enough attention; he only rarely uses the extended metaphor and then largely when he is translating. In general, simile seems to come more naturally to him (though it is scorned by Geoffrey of Vinsauf[15]), and he never extends a metaphor for more than a few lines; when he uses them he tends to shift to another metaphor quite soon, as in the invocation to Book II of *Troilus and Criseyde* or in Troilus's love song (Bk. I, 415–20). This is a fairly rare moment, then, and worth looking at.

If we think about the way later poets use metaphor, what is most striking here is the immediate specification of the metaphor—the meaning of the sword, of its point and why it is sharp are all made clear at once. This is so in Chaucer's other major metaphors,[16] and in poetic terms the effect is to make the metaphor a decoration of the poetry, rather than the vehicle of the poetry itself, as it so strikingly is in a poem like Wyatt's 'My galy charged with forgetfulnes' or Shakespeare's 'That time of year thou mayst in me behold'. Familiar as he seems to have been with Petrarch, Chaucer does not follow him into making the metaphor a main part of his poetic strategy.[17] The metaphor here stands out as a device of fine elaboration, a conceit to be admired and a means of arousing feeling, but the metaphor does not communicate more than this; where later poets will transmit all their meaning through their images, here the explanation of Anelida's elaborate agonies is couched in literal language:

> For whoso trewest is, hit shal hir rewe,
> That serveth love and doth her observaunce
> Alwey til oon, and chaungeth for no newe.   217–19

Elaborate syntax and a certain courtliness in the diction are still required to express the basis of Anelida's grief, but metaphor is not: here, as elsewhere, it is not an essential to Chaucer.

The ornateness of the Complaint, as the Strophe begins, rests partly on a sense of formal balance and partly on the rich effect created when only two rhyme sounds are used in a stanza now nine lines long:

> I wot myself as wel as any wight;
> For I loved oon with al myn herte and myght,
> More then myself an hundred thousand sithe,
> And called him myn hertes lif, my knyght,
> And was al his, as fer as hit was ryght;
> And when that he was glad, then was I blithe,
> And his disese was my deth as swithe;
> And he ayein his trouthe hath me plyght
> For evermore, his lady me to kythe.   220–8

As before when Anelida was described, the movement is simple, the lines are end-stopped and, apart from line 225, the caesura falls in the same place; here though the patterning of the words makes this into *repetitio* with *compar*, that method of organisation which Chaucer uses so often when he wishes to imply nobility. The speaking voice of Anelida is being created, it seems.

The complaint settles down into a fluent, even statement of woe; there is some rhythmical variation and some sign of rhetorical flourish, but it can at times be dangerously close to the hum-drum repetitive rhythms found before:

> Now is he fals, alas! and causeles,
> And of my wo he is so routheles,
> That with a word him list not ones deyne
> To bringe ayen my sorowful herte in pes,
> For he is caught up in another les.   229–33

After the opening stress of 'Now' and the pause on 'alas!' this runs very evenly indeed, but in general these stanzas find enough rhetorical elaboration and rhythmical variation to have verisimilitude as the statement of an emotionally disturbed, though still dignified heroine:

> And shal I pleyne—alas! the harde stounde—
> Unto my foo that yaf myn herte a wounde,
> And yet desireth that myn harm be more?
> Nay, certis, ferther wol I never founde
> Non other helpe, my sores for to sounde.   238–42

This has a dramatic impact; *exclamatio* and *correctio* are the vehicles of feeling and they are neatly emphasised by pauses. Here the opening metaphor of a wound is well worked into the statement; it is not given an embellished air, but rather deepens the sense of emotion in the stanza. There is formality here, but there also seems to be a successful characterisation of the suffering woman. The last of these four opening stanzas in the Strophe continues this note; a certain rhythmical variation works against the formal balance to save it from a sense of artificality, and the fairly elevated diction continues to assert the nobility of the woman and her feelings:

> Alas! wher is become your gentilesse,
> Youre wordes ful of plesaunce and humblesse,
> Youre observaunces in so low manere,
> And your awaytyng and your besynesse
> Upon me, that ye calden your maistresse,
> Your sovereyne lady in this world here?
> Alas! is ther now nother word ne chere
> Ye vouchen sauf upon myn hevynesse?
> Alas! youre love, I bye it al to dere.   247–55

After the assertive and rather melodramatic metaphor that began the Complaint we have now had a series of finely-wrought stanzas that have built up a satisfying portrait of the heroine. The poem appears to be unfolding in a clear direction; the narration seems mimetic and within that mode it is quite successful—only by Chaucer's later standards could we find Anelida's speech so far a little bland. But at this point the poet makes a sudden change of direction, and one of the moments which disturb this uneven poem occurs as Anelida goes on:

> Now, certis, swete, thogh that ye
> Thus causeles the cause be
> Of my dedly adversyte,
> Your manly resoun oghte hit to respite,
> To slen your frend, and namely me,
> That never yet in no degre
> Offended yow, as wisely he,
> That al wot, out of wo my soule quyte!   256–63

This is very supple and skilful, the springing rhythms in the opening lines give way to a more sombre note in the longer lines, and thus make a love-lyric form into a lament. The quality of the poetry in itself must be recognised. But we must also note the change this has on the poem as a story. Anelida was described as 'lowly' and 'meke' and though her Proem seemed uncharacteristically florid her first stanzas did not conflict with this picture: they were dignified and not overwrought, and it seemed as if a stylistic characterisation of her was in process, continuing the simple tone of her presentation in line 71–140 which had increased its elevation as her passion rose without losing a dignified straightforwardness. But suddenly she has become a mouthpiece for metrical virtuosity, and the evolving 'real' character disappears. This stylish stanza links with the poetically self-assertive metaphors of the Proem and the reader is now confused about the very nature of the poem. The next stanza confirms this confusion; it reverts to nine lines, basically five-stressed, but it too has metrical virtuosity:

> My swete foo, why do ye so, for shame?
> And thenke ye that furthered be your name
> To love a newe, and ben untrewe? Nay!
> And putte yow in sclaunder now and blame,
> And do to me adversite and grame,
> That love yow most—God, wel thou wost—alway?   272–7

The internal rhyme is skilful—though the fourth and sixth lines are not quite as easy and convincing as the others—but, especially as it concludes the Strophe, this stanza supports the tone of the previous one and further confirms the generic confusion here. The point is not to say that a poem which can be called a 'metrical exercise' is a poor one, or worse than another sort of poem (such an evaluative comparison of different genres seems pointless to me); what happens here is that the poem wavers between two genres, between Clemen's 'voice of genuine human suffering' and 'the experiment in versification' that Manly thought it to be. Consequently the poem is without an identifiable personality, and such a confusion must be a major flaw.

In the Antistrophe we will find a similar duality, for it—naturally enough—echoes the structure of the Strophe. It opens frankly, showing that little new argument is to be expected:

> Lo! herte myn, al this is for to seyne,
> As whether shal I preye or elles pleyne?
> Which is the wey to doon yow to be trewe?   281–3

The tone is similar to the beginning stanzas of the Strophe; the ideas are conventional ones, and the verse gives no new life to them:

> For either mot I have yow in my cheyne,
> Or with the deth ye mote departe us tweyne;
> Ther ben non other mene weyes new.
> For God so wisely upon my soule rewe,
> As verrayly ye sleen me with the peyne;
> That may ye se unfeyned on myn hewe.   284–9

The stanza appears flat partly because the tone and theme have already been developed, but even if this stanza had started the Strophe its level movement and the matter of fact last line would have deprived it of any real force. As the Antistrophe continues, a certain amount of elaboration is employed as in the Strophe, though not all the devices are the same, for here *articulus* is interwoven with *repetitio* and *compar*:

> For sorowe and routhe of your unkyndenesse
> I wepe, I wake, I faste; al helpeth noght;
> I weyve joye that is to speke of oght,
> I voyde companye, I fle gladnesse.   292–5

It is mobile and dramatic; the effect is powerful but, coming as it does in a second sequence of lament and after such prosodic display at the end of the Strophe, the lines hardly have the force of a dramatic revelation of the character; rather they compound the confusion, for the reader is unsure whether to take them as the 'real' voice of Anelida—they are rather elaborate for that—or as sheer display—they are rather dramatic for that. Yet, within this tonal and structural disorder, there is a clear sign of the poet's power and a suggestion of what a fine poem this could have been if its organisation and point of view had been better handled. We find formal patterning invigorated with a direct force of language, and now some of the prosodic fireworks do seem to create meaning:

> And shal I preye, and weyve womanhede?
> Nay! rather deth then do so foul a dede!
> And axe merci, gilteles,—what nede?
> And yf I pleyne what lyf that I lede,
> Yow rekketh not; that knowe I, out of drede;
> And if that I to yow myne othes bede
> For myn excuse, a skorn shal be my mede.
> Youre chere floureth, but it wol not sede;
> Ful long agoon I oghte have taken hede.   299–307

This is a fine and powerful stanza; it moves strongly, having both rhetorical elevation and the disturbed movement of passion. The confident placing of 'what nede?' and 'Yow rekketh not' shows that this poet handles verse dialogue with masterful ease and, contrasting strongly with the Proem of the Complaint, the metaphor in the penultimate line seems to be from the speaker's emotions, not from a school-book.[18] Similarly the prosodic skill in using a single rhyme throughout here works in the meaning of the poem, not as display:

it communicates the intensity, even the introversion of her grief as the same rhyme-sound beats out in line after line.

The following stanza is also forceful, though not as tight and dramatic:

> For thogh I hadde yow to-morowe ageyn,
> I myghte as wel holde Aperill fro reyn,
> As holde yow, to make yow be stidfast.
> Almyghty God, of trouthe sovereyn,
> Wher is the trouthe of man? Who hath hit slayn?
> Who that hem loveth, she shal hem fynde as fast
> As in a tempest is a roten mast.
> Is that a tame best that is ay feyn
> To renne away, when he is lest agast?   308–16

To a modern taste the last three lines will look rather like a mixture of metaphors (though there is no sign that medieval people would have found this disturbing) and the third line seems rather slack, but the force of the opening couplet and the moving sweep from 311–14 are very fine; here the repetition of 'trouthe' has a real meaning in the stanza, where other repetitions in the poem have seemed to come from an impoverished vocabulary.

These stanzas, in my view the finest in the poem in that their fluency develops an emotion-laden meaning, make us believe again in the speaker as a wretched woman of noble birth; she speaks finely, but with a stricken passion. This effect changes the direction of the poem again: once more it seems a dramatic poem, creating characters, and the sequence looks forwards to some of Chaucer's greatest triumphs. But this poem continues its erratic course as in the next lines verse of almost Skeltonic sound cuts across the verisimilitude of the previous stanzas:

> Now merci, swete, yf I mysseye!
> Have I seyd oght amys, I preye?
> I noot; my wit is al aweye.   317–19

Just as the speaker here draws back from the passion of the two previous stanzas, so the poem again changes its tone and reduces the force of the speech from dramatic self-revelation to a skilled *amplificatio*. We do, of course, have our own preconceptions about metres and it may be that for Chaucer and his audience the shorter metre did not seem such a sing-song as it does to us. The great French poets had used it and Chaucer had written *The Book of the Duchess* and *The House of Fame* in it and they are by no means lightweight. But in those poems he uses only couplets, not multiple rhymes, and he seems to take some trouble to avoid a metre as tripping as this.[19] The lyric quality of the form must have been present to some extent and in any case the contrast between this style and that preceding it must have heightened the display element in this faster moving, more decorative poetry.

As before, a stanza of internal rhyme follows the stanza of shorter lines, confirming the assertion of the poet's persona over that of the poem:

> The longe nyght this wonder sight I drye,
> And on the day for thilke afray I dye,
> And of al this ryght noght, iwis, ye reche.   333–5

The Complaint comes to an end with a stanza of conclusion, stately in movement and skilfully taking up the note of the opening stanza:

> Then ende I thus, sith I may do no more,—
> I yeve hit up for now and evermore;
> For I shal never eft putten in balaunce
> My sekernes, ne lerne of love the lore.
> But as the swan, I have herd seyd ful yore,
> Ayeins his deth shal singen his penaunce,
> So singe I here my destinee or chaunce,
> How that Arcite Anelida so sore
> Hath thirled with the poynt of remembraunce.   342–50

The last of the poem's extant seventy-line segments is ended as it began; the prosodic artifice of this is clear, but the fineness of the stanza makes it also work as a lyric statement of passion. This stanza, like several others, shows how good the poem is in parts, how a great dramatic poet emerges in a poetic structure better suited to formal display.

The most notable thing about the poem is its uneveness, and this is intrinsic to the poem as it stands, not the result of its being incomplete. It would be foolish to suggest that the uneveness caused Chaucer to leave the work unfinished, as this would be the merest speculation. What is of more profit is to reflect on the poem's varied quality. It shows many of Chaucer's abilities, but it also shows failings that contradict the praises of the recent American critics, and it toys with techniques like division into even segments and a mixture of stanza styles that Chaucer never again—in his surviving works— employs as a basic pattern. The qualities are equally easy enough to identify; those that are later to flower are the ability to set convincing self-expression in a difficult stanza form, to combine a real formality of structure and mode with a driving force of language and meaning, and the ability to model detailed style to detailed meaning; these, the last the least frequently, are found in the invocation, to some extent in the opening discussion of Theseus, intermittently in the sequence from line 141 to 210 and, most strikingly, at certain points in the Complaint.

On the other hand we find a curious failure to dominate the rhyme royal stanza in the early parts of the poem, a real flatness in the style in lines 71–140 and occasional dullness in the Complaint. But the failure that is most notable is that here the point of view and the tone shift without apparent reason. In later poems Chaucer is to juxtapose tones and viewpoints with great success, but here, if that is what he is trying to do, he fails to suggest that there is a pattern beneath the complication. The invocation promises a mixed style and the segments of the poem do seem to follow this, though rather crudely: 71–140 plain, 141–210 mixed, 211–80 high. But the poverty of the plain style and the infelicities that appear in the middle style damage the poem's effect badly, and the contradictions of tone and genre which become overt in the Complaint only confirm this failure. Above all, as we read the poem we lack that essential confidence that the narrator and poet (and here they seem the same throughout) knows where he is going; the poetic infelicities shake our faith, of course, and no clear directions come to restore our confidence. There is a lot in the poem to please as well as to disappoint, and many a poet would have been happy to have written *Anelida and Arcite* at the height of his powers, let alone as an early and abandoned piece. But in the canon of Chaucer's work it is a failure and a study of its style shows us the principal reason: at this time the poet's technique was not fully developed and in consequence he made errors in the detailed writing of his stanzas and in the larger organisation of the poem as a whole.

II. *The Parlement of Foules*

One of the many differences between *Anelida and Arcite* and *The Parlement of Foules* is that while a good deal has been written about *The Parlement of Foules* little has been said about its style. The important accounts of the poem given by Robert W. Frank Jr. and Charles O. McDonald in articles, by J. A. W. Bennett in his book and by D. S. Brewer in his edition all concentrate on the meaning that is to be drawn out of the poem's complex pattern of reference and juxtaposition.[20] Bennett does observe that the poem has a 'tight verbal texture'[21] and Brewer goes further than this when he assesses the effect of oral performance on the poem's nature.[22] The only detailed critique of the poetry is a study by F. W. Bateson of the opening stanzas.[23] Like these references, other critical comments on the poem's style are restricted to a discussion of specific points, rather than the more general assessments which have been made of *Anelida and Arcite*. Consequently I have not tried to give a resumé of critical opinion here, but have made use of such comments as do exist when they become relevant in the course of this study of the poem's style.

The opening stanza of the poem is the only one that has been fully discussed in terms of its style:

> The lyf so short, the craft so long to lerne,
> Th'assay so hard, so sharp the conquerynge,
> The dredful joye, alwey that slit so yerne:
> Al this mene I by Love, that my felynge
> Astonyeth with his wonderful werkynge
> So sore, iwis, that whan I on hym thynke,
> Nat wot I wel wher that I flete or synke.   1–7

Many critics have remarked on the flurry of rhetorical figures of style in the opening three and a half lines where, to quote Bennett, '*contentio, oxymoron, sententia, chiasmus, suspensio*, all play their parts'.[24] But for a thorough analysis of the stanza we must look to Bateson. He asks 'what is the literary function of this rhetorical density?' and 'Why in particular does the rhetoric run out at the end of the third line?' and further states that:[25]

> A metrical analysis seems to confirm the deliberateness of the stylistic reversal. It will be noticed that the first three lines of the stanza are all end-stopped and with the caesura in exactly the same place each time. . . With l.4, however, pronounced enjambement sets in, the caesura moves, and the iambic and syllabic regularity breaks down. . .
>
> In other words the metre of the first three lines of the stanza demands a slow and incantatory enunciation, with a pause at the caesuras and the end of each line; the last four lines, on the other hand, 'want' to be spoken almost as prose, slowly and emphatically at first and then with a rush which only slows down as it reaches the semi-comic last line.

Bateson suggests that this change may be partly due to the variety of Chaucer's audience, the opening being for 'a sophisticated minority' and the rest for those who 'may well have preferred stronger meat' and partly due to the author's wish to prepare 'the way in these lines for a return to this favourite role in the longer poems of comic nincompoop'.[26] The first reason is too simplistic an explanation of a mixed style (not that Batson offers it with absolute confidence), but the second is a shrewd comment. The narrator starts with an aphoristic firmness based on his learning. This fades, as Bateson excellently shows, into something much less certain as the narrator speaks about his own experience. The development seen here will be acted out through the poem, as the narrator finds himself unable to transform the confident message of his books into a private sureness of his own. At the same time, in terms of structure, the first stanza employs several rhetorical devices of balance and enigma and so it also provides the stylistically dominant note of the poem: throughout its length, experiences, speeches and descriptions are to be placed in an enigmatic balance.

In these ways the nature of the opening links with the poem to follow. The mixture of styles in the opening is not greatly different from that in the invocation to *Anelida and Arcite* (though it is poetically more assured) but here the changing of style acts out a dramatic presentation of the narrator's apparently confident, but actually uncertain personality; whereas the earlier poem's opening was attractive in a static way, this has real attack and pitches us straight into the stylistic and conceptual tension that permeates the whole poem.

The narrator moves on quickly and elaborates his puzzlement in an even, four-line sequence:

> For al be that I knowe nat Love in dede,
> Ne wot how that he quiteth folk here hyre,
> Yit happeth me ful ofte in bokes reede
> Of his myrakles and his crewel yre. 8–11

The balance of the two divisions under 'For' and 'Yit' and the smooth flow of the lines seem to set out the dilemma in an undisturbed manner, for his bookish experience is at hand to resolve his problems. But the following lines suggest that this calm analysis will not help him personally:

> There rede I wel he wol be lord and syre;
> I dar not seyn, his strokes been so sore,
> But 'God save swich a lord!'—I can na moore. 12–14

The structure here is complex, so much so that a good deal of discussion has worried over the meaning and punctuation of the lines, but this version seems to be the best.[27] The disturbed rhythm of the lines and their wrenched syntax acts out the narrator's uncertain reaction to love (it is one of the things that mark this poem off from *Anelida and Arcite* that we can identify the persona of a narrator); the dramatic nature of the verse and the overt discussion of his problems work together in this. These two elements, style and thought interwoven, are continued as the next stanza begins:

> Of usage—what for lust and what for lore—
> On bokes rede I ofte, as I yow tolde.
> But wherfore that I speke al this? Nat yoore
> Agon, it happede me for to beholde
> Upon a bok, was write with lettres olde,
> And therupon, a certeyn thyng to lerne,
> The longe day ful faste I redde and yerne.   15–21

The movement of this stanza is extremely varied: the pauses fall differently in each line and only the last line is without a pause. In *Anelida and Arcite* we quite often found stanzas with a number of pauses and the effect was sometimes to suggest that the poet was labouring with his verse-form—the internal-rhyme stanzas are notable examples. But here the lines move with such colloquial ease—something like prose, as Bateson says of stanza one—that we can have no failure of confidence in the poet's ability. Rather than struggling with his stanza, he is creating a mobile demotic style which has none of the stable confidence of an even rhyme royal stanza: the unease of the narrator's mind is excellently presented. His style is not all unease, though; in stanza one he set out his learning in an orderly way and then expressed his failure to come to a conclusion in disordered lines, and now this contrastive device is used again, for after this shifting stanza the narrator offers us and himself a comforting *sententia*; it advocates book learning and is delivered in an even, balanced voice, just as were the earlier remarks which drew their authority from learning. The style helps to create the notion that the narrator here at least finds solid ground beneath his feet:

> For out of olde feldes, as men seyth,
> Cometh al this newe corn from yer to yere,
> And out of olde bokes, in good feyth,
> Cometh al this newe science that men lere.   22–5

With this to bolster his confidence, he moves on briskly to his topic:

> But now to purpos as of this matere; 26

This introduction shows, then, a highly complex use of contrastive styles of poetry; the sage and even disposition of book learning in lines 1–3, 8–11 and 22–5 contrasts sharply with the shifting movement and colloquial phrasing of the narrator's own attempt to approach the complexities of love. The writing is extremely tight, compared with *Anelida and Arcite*; nothing seems padded or inexpert, the thought is densely packed and meticulously argued out and—the principal difference between this poem and the other—the style is setting up implications of meaning in itself. And yet this is done without prosodic or rhetorical pyrotechnics. Though we can, and probably should use rhetorical terms to describe much of what is done here, the figures used have clearly a function in terms of the poem not, as it often seemed in *Anelida and Arcite*, merely being representations of themselves and indications of the poet's technical expertise.

After this opening—one that I find the more artful and powerful the more I read it—the first major sequence of the narrative follows from line 27 to 91; the divisions are not as schematised here as in *Anelida and Arcite*.[28] This sequence gives the gist of the particular book the narrator has been reading, and it is introduced in a direct way:

> To rede forth hit gan me so delite,
> That al that day me thoughte but a lyte.

> This bok of which I make mencioun
> Entitled was al thus as I shal telle:
> 'Tullyus of the Drem of Scipioun.' 27–31

This strikes a new tone in the poem, neither stylishly balanced nor nervous in movement; in the first four lines the movement is even, the caesura falls regularly and no pauses break up the lines. It is an easy plain style, but where in *Anelida and Arcite* this plain style was allowed to fall into a dull repetitiveness, here a certain surface variation is soon brought in after the regular, confident beginning; the last line begins with a strong stress and there seem only three other stresses in the line. As the narrator goes on, prosodic variation is maintained:

> Chapitres sevene it hadde, of heven and helle
> And erthe, and soules that therinne dwelle,
> Of whiche, as shortly as I can it trete,
> Of his sentence I wol yow seyn the greete. 32–5

In the first line the initial foot is reversed and a smooth enjambement runs this line into the second; the next two lines have an early caesura and then the last line moves with a contrastive and conclusive smoothness to the close of the stanza. This is in no way ornate—the style is as simple as the narration is transparent, for the narrator is always present before us. No attempt is made to complicate the process by suspending disbelief or by raising the style, but a subtle prosodic variation maintains variety and interest in the surface of the poetry. Six stanzas follow, each beginning with a firm reminder that this is reported reading: the first is 'Fyrst telleth it' and then there follow: 'Than telleth it', 'Than axede he', 'Thanne shewede he', 'Than bad he', 'Thanne preyede hym'.

This succession gives a certain organisation to the sequence, but there is no rhetorical formality in the pattern, and in the body of each stanza the simplicity of the passage is maintained:

> Fyrst telleth it, whan Scipion was come
> In Affrike, how he meteth Massynisse,
> That hym for joie in armes hath inome;
> Thanne telleth it here speche and al the blysse
> That was betwix hem til the day gan mysse,
> And how his auncestre, Affrycan so deere,
> Gan in his slep that nyght to hym apere.   36–42

There is a clear enjambement after the first line, a muted one after the fourth; the second line has an early caesura, and then in the fifth and sixth lines there is one more syllable before the break, and this changes the rhythm subtly. It is by no means a highly worked stanza; rather it is the easy, varied rhyme royal stanza that in this poem and in others (notably *Troilus and Criseyde* and 'The Prioress's Tale') Chaucer seems to be able to produce without strain—but which often seemed beyond his ability or ambition in *Anelida and Arcite*. Of these stanzas the one nearest to being flat has a similar, though less obvious modulation:

> Thanne shewede he hym the lytel erthe that here is,
> At regard of the hevenes quantite;
> And after shewede he hym the nyne speres,
> And after that the melodye herde he
> That cometh of thilke speres thryes thre,
> That welle is of musik and melodye
> In this world here, and cause of armonye.   57–63

The first two lines effectively underline the contrast of heaven and earth, the uneven rhythms of the first parts of the two lines throwing into prominence their contrasting second parts. The rest of the stanza is not so impressive, for there is a repetitive note about lines three to five, and the organisation of the last two lines seems a little awkward, but any awkwardness dissolves in the rich final word 'armonye', a Chaucerian neologism.

The last of these expository 'Thanne' stanzas embodies the beginning of Scipio's moral in a style at first sight as direct and forceful as the whole exposition:

> And he seyde, 'Know thyself first immortal,
> And loke ay besyly thow werche and wysse
> To commune profit, and thow shalt not mysse
> To comen swiftly to that place deere
> That full of blysse is and of soules cleere. 73–7

Yet within this plain style there is a whisper of artifice; the alliterative phrase 'werche and wysse' we might discount as insignificant were it not for the artful assonance of 'To commune' and 'To comen', that confirms a note of rising elaboration. The next stanza shows that this does herald a change in tone and an increase in emphasis, for there is no 'Thanne seyde he' to begin it, but with a sense of urgency it sweeps on with the speech:

> 'But brekers of the lawe, soth to seyne,
> And likerous folk, after that they ben dede,
> Shul whirle about th'erthe alwey in peyne,
> Tyl many a world be passed, out of drede,
> And than, foryeven al hir wikked dede,
> Than shul they come into this blysful place,
> To which to comen God the sende his grace.' 78–84

The syntax is more extended than before, for the verb comes in the third line—and it is the dramatic verb 'whirle'—and the length of the sequence is stressed by the lateness of the caesura in the third line; this more emotional note is maintained by the brief 'And than' and by the repetition of 'Than' in the next line. There is, then, an injection of dramatic force into Affrycan's words to stress the importance of his message. The stanza stands out from this plain sequence by virtue of these slight changes of style and makes both a structurally effective ending to it and one totally in accordance with its elevated meaning.

The narrator sums up simply in that style that all readers of Chaucer recognise as his characteristic voice: it is easy and yet forceful, in no way jerky, but the words cannot be glided over unthinkingly as we can often glide over a passage of Gower. The stresses align with firm nouns and verbs and we hardly notice the alliteration that gives the stanza added backbone:

> That day gan faylen, and the derke nyght,
> That reveth bestes from here besynesse,
> Berafte me my bok for lak of lyght,
> And to my bed I gan me for to dresse,
> Fulfyld of thought and busy hevynesse;
> For bothe I hadde thyng which that I nolde,
> And ek I nadde that thyng that I wolde.   85–91

His summary of the situation in the last two lines is a balanced enigma; balance was used before when the narrator relied on his book-learning, but here such a balance only expresses doubt. The narrator has lost his early confidence it seems, although he has been experiencing some lucid and much respected literary material. With a fine poetic irony Chaucer uses the same prosodic pattern to express first the narrator's confidence and then his doubt. Before, the firm style was undermined by being juxtaposed to a disturbed style; now it is itself a vehicle of uncertainty. It makes the narrator's opening aphorisms seem rather foolish, and we will see more of this aspect of him.

The poet now sleeps, and his sleep and dream are introduced in an unobtrusive manner; there is no formal opening to the dream at first, but this beginning of the new sequence is presented in the quiet manner that typified the first narrative sequence of the poem:

> But fynally, my spirit at the laste,
> For wery of my labour al the day,
> Tok reste, that made me to slepe faste,
> And in my slep I mette, as that I lay,
> How Affrican, ryght in the selve aray
> That Scipion hym say byfore that tyde,
> Was come and stod right at my beddes syde.   92–8

The lack of poetic flurry and elaboration as the narrator sleeps is typical of the muted style of this poem so far and makes a good tonal link between these two sentences; but this does not mean that the whole poem is to be in the unadorned style, for in the very next stanza we find something markedly more formal, a series of balanced *sententiae* about the relation between daytime activity and dreams:

D

> The wery huntere, slepynge in his bed,
> To wode ayeyn his mynde goth anon;
> The juge dremeth how his plees been sped;
> The cartere dremeth how his cartes gon;
> The riche, of gold; the knyght fyght with his fon;
> The syke met he drynketh of the tonne;
> The lovere met he hath his lady wonne.   99–105

The repetition gives a formal note, but the poet takes care to vary the rhythm a little: lines three and four have the same cadence as each other and lines six and seven match are alike each other and are similar to the previous pair, but line five strikes a different note—Chaucer normally introduces some variation into a repetitive sequence like this, as is clearly seen in *Troilus and Criseyde*.[29] In the next stanza the poet debates the motivation of his own dream and introduces his dream interlocutor:

> But thus seyde he: 'Thow hast the so wel born
> In lokynge of myn old bok totorn,
> Of which Macrobye roughte nat a lyte,
> That sumdel of thy labour wolde I quyte.'   109–12

This has not responded to the raising of style in the previous stanza, for here the simple demotic manner is continued; Affrycan treats the narrator as a friend, calls him 'Thow' and speaks in a familiar way. But this does not mean that the previous stanza is isolated; rather it seems that, allowing for Affrycan's cheerfully egalitarian style, this whole sequence is pitched at a higher note, for now we find an invocation:

> Cytherea! thow blysful lady swete,
> That with thy fyrbrond dauntest whom the lest,
> And madest me this sweven for to mete,
> Be thow myn helpe in this, for thow mayst best!   113–16

The pattern is that of a middle style invocation; there is no *pronominatio* or *interpretatio*, but some elaboration is brought in by relative clauses,[30] and the verb is delayed to the end of this short sequence. The poet's plea for assistance is similarly only a little ornate, for the *collatio* it contains is straightforward in form, however obscure its meaning is to modern readers:

> As wisly as I sey the north-north-west,
> Whan I began my sweven for to write,
> So yif me myght to ryme and ek t'endyte.   117–19

Bennett has remarked that it is quite common to find an invocation in this position in medieval writing.[31] This is no doubt true, but it is not common to find one in this position in a Chaucerian poem: the invocation to *The Hous of Fame*, for example, is much more prominent. This is partly caused by the late beginning of the dream here, making this much more like *The Book of the Duchess* in form, although that poem lacks an invocation. The effect here is almost as muted as that of *The Book of the Duchess* and through this we see that while Chaucer recognises the pressure for certain decorous formal elements in a poem on love, he also seems determined to limit them, to stop them dictating the tone of the poem as a whole. He observes the forms but, as usual, alters them; the praises of love in stanza one were skilfully turned into a study of the narrator's mind at work, and the invocation is used to raise the style of the poem from the orderly recounting of the narrator's reading to his dream itself.

As the dream begins, there is a certain formality in the style, and the 'verses' over the gate have a stately movement:

> 'Thorgh me men gon into that blysful place
> Of hertes hele and dedly woundes cure;
> Thorgh me men gon unto the welle of grace,
> There grene and lusty May shal evere endure.
> This is the wey to al good aventure.   127–31

The message of the other side is similarly formal yet, having a grim meaning as it does, it is without the calm balance of this stanza; a subtle difference in movement underlines the difference in import:

> 'Thorgh me men gon,' than spak that other side,
> 'Unto the mortal strokes of the spere
> Of which Disdayn and Daunger is the gyde,
> Ther nevere tre shal fruyt ne leves bere.   134–7

The conflicting messages put the narrator back into a state of uneasy equipoise:

> For with that oon encresede ay my fere,
> And with that other gan myn herte bolde;
> That oon me hette, that other dide me colde:
> No wit hadde I, for errour, for to chese,
> To entre or flen, or me to save or lese.   143–7

Once again the narrator's state of mind is described with a balanced style setting out the equal tensions in his mind. As Bateson observed, there is some humour implicit in the narrator's transition from his opening aphoristic confidence to his present dithering and Chaucer takes the opportunity to make the comedy explicit. The narrator uses an ornate little figure to describe himself and almost seems to be revelling in his indecision, when brusque action is taken:

> Right as, betwixen adamauntes two
> Of evene myght, a pece of yren set
> Ne hath no myght to meve to ne fro—
> For what that oon may hale, that other let—
> Ferde I, that nyste whether me was bet
> To entre or leve, til Affrycan, my gide,
> Me hente, and shof in at the gates wide,   148–54

The fine comedy derives largely from the skill with which the poet leads the stanza up in little, precise clauses and phrases which characterise the meticulous, scholarly narrator ('my gide' is perhaps the finest, with its finicky redundance) until he is finally forced into action. The crisp phrasing of 'Me hente' and 'shof' shows the verbal judgment of a great writer. To a certain extent the stanza is by-play, part of the Chaucerian self-deprecation that he so often locates in his narrators, but it has other functions as well. The dazzling poetic skill, breathing fluency and confidence, makes us trust the poet completely; the comic *persona* of the narrator engages our sympathy and, most important of all, the assertion that the narrator has no answers alerts our intelligence. If we want to know what is going on, we realise that we must pay attention to the poem; the teller cannot interpret it for us. He needs all sorts of reassurance, and we perhaps feel a little superior to him as he tags after the forceful Affrycan:

> With that myn hand in his he tok anon,
> Of which I confort caughte, and wente in faste.   169–70

As the narrator begins to describe the park he enters the poetry is at first relaxed and fluent, epithets and simile having a familiar, but not hackneyed effect:

> For overal where that I myne eyen caste
> Were trees clad with leves that ay shal laste,
> Ech in his kynde, of colour fresh and greene
> As emeraude, that joye was to seene.   172–5

It is a pleasant, mobile type of verse, promising congenial experiences, but its easy rhythms are at once interrupted by the more overtly artful structure of the next stanza, a formal catalogue of trees:

1909016

> The byldere ok, and ek the hardy asshe;
> The piler elm, the cofre unto carayne;
> The boxtre pipere, holm to whippes lashe;
> The saylynge fyr; the cipresse, deth to playne; 176–9

The repetitive rhythm is sterner, and the baleful aspects of some of the trees seem to cut across the pleasant impression sketched by the previous stanza.[32] But both the sound and implication of this sequence is allowed to pass for the moment, and the description flows easily on in the next stanza:

> A gardyn saw I ful of blosmy bowes
> Upon a ryver, in a grene mede, 183–4

This graceful poetry reaches a climax in the stanza which introduces animal life:

> On every bow the bryddes herde I synge,
> With voys of aungel in here armonye;
> Some besyede hem here bryddes forth to brynge;
> The litel conyes to here pley gonne hye;
> And ferther al aboute I gan aspye
> The dredful ro, the buk, the hert and hynde,
> Squyrels, and bestes smale of gentil kynde. 190–6

The musical movement is achieved by a constantly shifting caesura, a strong stress to begin lines three and seven and an enjambement leading into the firm movement of line six; the alliteration on *b* in the first three lines assists the melodic effect. In sound, as well as in meaning, the stanza stresses the 'armonye' and 'gentil kynde' of the scene and its inhabitants. The narrator sums up:

> Th'air of that place so attempre was
> That nevere was ther grevaunce of hot ne cold;
> There wex ek every holsom spice and gras;
> No man may there waxe sek ne old; 204–7

But a harsher note now enters, picking up the implication of the 'trees' stanza, for in this seeming earthly paradise there are weapons: Will tempers Cupid's arrows so that:

> . . . after they shulde serve
> Some for to sle, and some to wounde and kerve. 216–17

And the narrator regretfully has to notice imperfection here:

> Tho was I war of Plesaunce anon-ryght,
> And of Aray, and Lust, and Curteysie,
> And of the Craft that can and hath the myght
> To don by force a wyght to don folye—
> Disfigurat was she, I nyl nat lye;   218–22

The last line is strikingly incursive; it breaks the rhythm of the stanza, the word 'Disfigurat', with its ugly connotations, is placed most prominently and the reluctant words with which the narrator closes the last line seem to have an extra stress that slows down further their monosyllabic movement. Ugliness has cut into this world, and as the passage goes on it becomes clearer that as well as beauty we must consider the wretchedness of love.

The dual nature of the park is elaborated in a fluent style that observes without a ripple, as it were, both benign and malign elements of Venus's world:

> I saw Beute withouten any atyr,
> And Youthe, ful of game and jolyte;
> Foolhardynesse, Flaterye, and Desyr,
> Messagerye, and Meede, and other thre—
> Here names shul not here be told for me—
> And upon pilers greete of jasper longe
> I saw a temple of bras ifounded stronge.   225–31

Because we see these unpleasant characteristics cut through the flowing verse, when we finally come to Venus herself we have a cautious attitude towards her, so that her beauty seems dangerous; the narrator certainly finds her attractive, but we have already learnt to doubt his judgment and the last line of his descriptive stanza has an almost sniggering tone:

> Hyre gilte heres with a golden thred
> Ibounden were, untressed as she lay,
> And naked from the brest unto the hed
> Men myghte hire sen; and, sothly for to say,
> The remenaunt was wel kevered to my pay,
> Ryght with a subtyl coverchef of Valence—
> Ther nas no thikkere cloth of no defense.   267–73

The dangers of Venus's sort of love are finally asserted in a list of stricken lovers, the formality of which must remind us of the list of trees:

> Semyramis, Candace, and Hercules,
> Biblis, Dido, Thisbe, and Piramus,
> Tristram, Isaude, Paris, and Achilles,
> Eleyne, Cleopatre, and Troylus,
> Silla, and ek the moder of Romulus:
> Alle these were peynted on that other syde,
> And al here love, and in what plyt they dyde. 288–94

This remorseless list is rhythmically harsh, heavy with stresses and, particularly in lines two and three, with reversed feet. The metrical effect is one with the meaning of the passage, and the dreamer's experience of Venus's sort of love ends on this sombre note.

The list of trees had a harsh aspect, in style and in meaning, but it also had benign qualities; the meaning of this sequence about Venus largely lies in the fact that though much of it has been fluent and beautiful, it closes by stating only the ugliness that was suggested in the ambivalent opening set-piece, and the style of the end exaggerates the sternness of the rhythms of the trees passage into a real harshness. In the following climactic sequence of the poem we will see a similar development working in the opposite direction, for there through a similarly fluent and vivid style the emphasis is steadily placed on the benign aspect of the created world. Bennett has written well on Venus and Nature as opposed elements of love,[33] and the poetry supports this view. Venus and Nature are given similar introductions, but the ending of their scenes are, as we shall see, quite different, characterising their different values. And even in the opening of the scenes the superiority of Nature is implicit, for Nature's is finer, suggesting a greater value. As the narrator walked into the park he saw the lovely surroundings and the trees, varied in kind. Here he sees similar things:

> And in a launde, upon a hil of floures,
> Was set this noble goddesse Nature.
> Of braunches were here halles and here boures
> Iwrought after here cast and here mesure;
> Ne there nas foul that cometh of engendrure
> That they ne were prest in here presence,
> To take hire dom and yeve hire audyence. 302–8

It is poised and beautiful; the diction is somewhat higher than that used of Venus and this is fitting, for in the light of the whole poem Venus is shown to be inferior to this 'noble emperesse'. Where one stanza described the trees of the park, here we find a grandly

formal list of birds extending through five stanzas. As before, the
list represents a whole range of activities, beneficent and maleficent:

> The sparwe, Venus sone; the nyghtyngale,
> That clepeth forth the grene leves newe;
> The swalwe, mortherere of the foules smale
> That maken hony of floures freshe of hewe;
> The wedded turtil with hire herte trewe;
> The pekok, with his aungels fetheres bryghte;
> The fesaunt, skornere of the cok by nyghte;   351–7

The formality is presented in lines of varying rhythm; the easy
skill that is right through the poem is nowhere better illustrated
than in this stanza where the poet achieves at the same time an
interesting variety of rhythm and also a sense of formal regularity.
The richness and order of the created world is brilliantly suggested
by the sequence and in the following narrative we see the multi-
fariousness of medieval society reflected in the birds as they debate
whom the formel eagle should take as her mate. As the list of birds
has shown, there is blood-letting and conflict in the natural world
and the action to follow will show a good deal of disagreement.
Yet this is all located within a scene which opens and closes with
harmonious poetry. Chaucer implies, that is, that in the natural
world the prevailing quality is of order and harmony: conflict is
within that system. In Venus's world, on the other hand, the
development was from the formal images of *The Romaunt of the Rose*
to a harshly expressed list of human disasters. The visually static
quality of the Venus scene and the mobile richness of the Nature
scene is another important contrast, as is the stilted personification
of the former against the vivid naturalism of the latter.

At the opening of her scene, Nature's greatness and essential
superiority to Venus are finely expressed in a passage that is similar
to the great invocation of Book III of *Troilus and Criseyde*, where
Chaucer also characterised the divine force of love:

> Nature, the vicaire of the almyghty Lord,
> That hot, cold, hevy, lyght, moyst and dreye
> Hath knyt by evene noumbres of acord,   379–81

This great power is here shown to be resident in the birds: it is
they, not Nature, who make the important decisions in the scene
and it is their practices and views which are central. Nature is the
abstracted essence of their natures, and they typify the whole
creation. As they conduct their business Chaucer rises excellently

to his opportunity, creating a whole series of attitudes and speech styles, a miniature of *The Canterbury Tales* as has often been observed. In this well-known sequence, to many modern tastes the most attractive in the poem, the 'royal tersel' eagle is the first to speak, declaring his love for the formel resting on Nature's hand. Nature has introduced him with a very formal, balanced style:

> 'The tersel eagle, as that ye knowe wel,
> The foul royal, above yow in degre,
> The wyse and worthi, secre, trewe as stel,'   393–5

And his speech is suitably poised:

> 'Unto my soverayn lady, and not my fere,
> I chese, and chese with wil, and herte, and thought,
> The formel on youre hond, so wel iwrought,
> Whos I am al, and evere wol hire serve,
> Do what hire lest, to do me lyve or sterve;'   416–20

In this classical statement of *fin amor* the deliberate pauses convey a sense of tentativeness, of extreme *politesse* before his lady, but do not appear breathless (as do Aurelius's words in 'The Franklin's Tale', cf. pp. 199–200) because the argument keeps moving steadily. His language is elevated and judicious, the stanzas are finely modelled, shaping an ornate, deliberate vow that conveys in language and form its seriousness:

> 'And if that I to hyre be founde untrewe,
> Disobeysaunt, or wilful necligent,
> Avauntour, or in proces love a newe,
> I preye to yow this be my jugement,
> That with these foules I be al torent,
> That ilke day that evere she me fynde
> To hir untrewe, or in my gilt unkynde.   428–34

The formel's reaction to this is embarrassment, but the expression emphasises the stateliness of her reaction:

> Ryght as the freshe, rede rose newe
> Ayeyn the somer sonne coloured is,
> Ryght so for shame al wexen gan the hewe
> Of this formel, whan she herde al this;   442–5

The second eagle speaks less grandly, in accordance with his 'lower kynde':

> 'That shal nat be!
> I love hire bet than ye don, by seint John,
> Or at the leste I love hire as wel as ye,
> And lenger have served hire in my degre,
> And if she shulde have loved for long lovynge,
> To me ful-longe hadde be the guerdonynge.
>
> 'I dar ek seyn, if she me fynde fals,
> Unkynde, janglere, or rebel any wyse,
> Or jelous, do me hangen by the hals!   450–8

He is more monosyllabic than the first eagle, and his lines flow
less smoothly—lines 454–5 have an especially slow, almost turgid
movement; when he uses pauses, as in line 457, there is a jarring
quality in them which was absent in the first eagle's speech. The
whole is in keeping with his lower rank and sketches a less noble
personality for him—just as the death he suggests is less grandiose
than that the first eagle seeks.

When the third eagle speaks Chaucer continues to differentiate
them; this eagle seems to be more intellectual than the others for
he uses a more complex syntax and a more elaborately structured
argument:

> 'Of long servyse avaunte I me nothing;
> But as possible is me to deye to-day
> For wo as he that hath ben languysshyng
> This twenty wynter, and wel happen may,
> A man may serven bet and more to pay
> In half a yer, although it were no moore,
> Than som man doth that hath served ful yoore.   470–6

Where the first eagle was a true courtier, the second sounded more
like a straightforward country eagle, and this one seems to have
spent some time in the schools.

As the poem moves on the other birds are similarly characterised
by the nature of their speech:

> The noyse of foules for to ben delyvered
> So loude rong, 'Have don, and lat us wende!'
> That wel wende I the wode hadde al toshyvered.
> 'Com of!' they criede, 'allas, ye wol us shende!   491–4

The unobtrusive alliteration of the narrator's reflection in line 493
expresses the peace that is shattered by the sharp alliteration on

k in the next line, as the birds cry out, and this motif is amplified in the next stanza:

> The goos, the cokkow, and the doke also
> So cryede, 'Kek kek! kokkow! quek quek!' hye,
> That thourgh myne eres the noyse wente tho.   498–500

The effect is not very subtle, but it is skilful and swift: the noise of the first two lines makes us assent readily to the narrator's statement in line 500. The poet's skill continues to create verisimilitude as, in the following sequence, the poet gives brief characterisations of a number of the birds. The cuckoo is assertive:

> 'And I for worm-foul,' seyde the fol kokkow,
> For I wol of myn owene autorite,
> For comune spede, take on the charge now,
> For to delyvere us is gret charite.'   505–8

The aggressive 'For' at the beginning of the last three lines, strengthened by the alliteration on *f* in the first line, catches well the confident, bossy character of the cuckoo. The 'turtel' speaks in a calm manner, using some fine diction:

> 'I am a sed-foul, oon the unworthieste,
> That wot I wel, and litel of connynge.
> But bet is that a wyghtes tonge reste
> Than entermeten hym of such doinge,
> Of which he neyther rede can ne synge;
> And whoso hit doth, ful foule hymself acloyeth,
> For office uncommytted ofte anoyeth.'   512–18

In the well-judged movement of her speech, her subtle language[34] and the thoughtful *sententia* in the last line, the 'turtel' shows herself far from ignorant, and her humble sensitivity stands out against the other rowdy birds.

When the tercelet speaks for the 'foules of ravyne', he has a clear-headed, legal style:

> 'Ful hard were it to preve by resoun
> Who loveth best this gentil formel heere;
> For everych hath swich replicacioun
> That non by skilles may be brought adoun.
> I can not se that argumentes avayle:
> Thanne semeth it there moste be batayle.'   534–9

The eagles interrupt and, still like a lawyer, he rebukes them for not waiting till the end of his meticulous argument:

> 'Nay, sires,' quod he, 'if that I durste it seye,
> Ye don me wrong, my tale is not ido!   541–2

The goose, ironically described as having a 'facound gent', speaks fittingly:

> And for these water-foules tho began
> The goos to speke, and in hire kakelynge
> She seyde, 'Pes! now tak kep every man,
> And herkneth which a resoun I shal forth brynge!
> My wit is sharp, I love no taryinge;
> I seye I rede hym, though he were my brother,
> But she wol love hym, lat hym love another!'   561–7

The phrase 'tak kep' picks up excellently the sound and sense of 'kakelynge' and her jerky utterance goes well with her down-to-earth advice: it is a social vignette, and Chaucer follows it up to show this little society in swift action and reaction when the nobler sparrowhawk speaks sharply, but with some knowledge of rhetorical matters:

> 'Lo, here a parfit resoun of a goos!'
> Quod the sperhauk; 'Nevere mot she thee!
> Lo, swich it is to have a tonge loos!
> Now, parde! fol, yit were it bet for the
> Han holde thy pes than shewed thy nycete.   568–72

The use of 'Lo', the rather complex organisation of the last two lines and the use of the rare word 'nycete'[35] all point to a speaker from a higher social position.

The turtle-dove speaks again and her voice and actions both suit the tradition of love poetry:

> 'Nay, God forbede a lovere shulde chaunge!'
> The turtle seyde, and wex for shame al red.
> 'Though that his lady everemore be straunge,
> Yit lat hym serve hire ever, til he be ded.   582–5

But across her affirmation of love cuts the duck's magnificent interruption:

> 'Wel bourded,' quod the doke, 'by myn hat!
> That men shulde loven alwey causeles,
> Who can a resoun fynde or wit in that?   589–91

The coarse aggression of the first line is easy to see, but equally effective is the way in which the rhyming phrase 'or wit in that' follows a pause in its line and makes a subtle echo of 'by myn hat', emphasising its comic force and the jerky, bathetic utterance of the duck. These lines have tremendous vigour, and the stanza ends on a similarly high comic note:

> Ye quek!' yit seyde the doke, ful wel and fayre,
> 'There been mo sterres, God wot, than a payre.' 594–5

Again a second brief phrase, 'God wot', echoes the broad comedy of the first, 'Ye quek!' The whole sequence begs to be read aloud by an actor or actress who can fully demonstrate how skilfully the writing creates the loud-mouthed plainness of the duck.

The logical tercelet follows up fittingly, crisply dismissive:

> 'Now fy, cherl!' quod the gentil tercelet,
> 'Out of the donghil cam that word ful right!
> Thow canst nat seen which thyng is wel beset!
> Thow farst by love as oules don by lyght:
> The day hem blent, ful wel they se by nyght. 596–600

The cuckoo comments less forcefully than before, but is still blunt enough:

> Lat ech of hem be soleyn al here lyve!
> This is my red, syn they may nat acorde;
> This shorte lessoun nedeth nat recorde.' 607–9

And the merlin rounds on the cuckoo with a finely lofty piece of abuse:

> 'Thow mortherere of the heysoge on the braunche
> That broughte the forth, thow rewthelees glotoun!
> Lyve thow soleyn, wormes corupcioun!
> For no fors is of lak of thy nature—
> Go, lewed be thow whil the world may dure!' 612–16

Nature calls a halt to this cacophonous parliament, and she speaks with a stately control as she invites the formel to make her choice:

> 'But as for conseyl for to chese a make,
> If I were Resoun, certes, thanne wolde I
> Conseyle yow the royal tercel take,
> As seyde the tercelet ful skylfully,
> As for the gentilleste and most worthi,
> Which I have wrought so wel to my plesaunce,
> That to yow hit oughte to been a suffisaunce.' 631–7

The stanza is one intricate sentence, the diction is quite elaborate and the whole style bespeaks Nature's nobility and controlling power. The formel makes her reply quietly:

> With dredful vois the formel tho answerde,
> 'My rightful lady, goddesse of Nature!
> Soth is that I am evere under youre yerde,
> As is everich other creature,
> And mot be youres whil my lyf may dure,
> And therfore graunteth me my firste bone,
> And myn entente I wol yow sey right sone.'   638–44

The movement of her speech is very simple, co-ordinate where Nature's was elaborately subordinated, and the evenness of the last three lines fits very well with the notion of her 'dredful vois'. So, right to the end of the scene Chaucer varies the speaking style of the birds, transmitting a dramatic effect by the nature of his poetry. The sequence is not, perhaps, greatly subtle in its poetic effects: to make briefly appearing characters speak differently is not one of the narrative artist's highest skills—though Chaucer is an innovator here, and among the poets only Shakespeare can match his skill. But apart from our pleasure in the wit and vigour of the scene, the verisimilitude of the birds' impromptu parliament is an important element of the poem. The mimetic force of the poem compels us to take seriously the curious chain of experiences the narrator receives, and consequently urges us more strongly so see in them the pattern the narrator cannot himself discern. In this complex process the apparently straightforward art of the birds' characterisations is a vital element.

Nature dismisses the birds in a fairly simple way:

> A yer is nat so longe to endure,
> And ech of yow peyne him in his degre
> For to do wel, for, God wot, quyt is she
> Fro yow this yer; what after so befalle,
> This entremes is dressed for yow alle.'   661–5

It is not a plain style for we have enjambement here and at least one rare word in 'entremes',[36] but the syntax is not as intricate as before when Nature spoke and the speech does not have the same stateliness. This may be because Chaucer has relaxed his attention, but it may have another function, for now the poem comes to an end in a quite straightforward style, reminiscent in several ways of the simple style in the beginning of the poem, and this last speech of Nature seems to quieten down the poem. After this the narrator closes the action in his easy plain style:

> And whan this werk al brought was to an ende,
> To every foul Nature yaf his make
> By evene acord, and on here way they wende.   666–8

As the birds leave, they sing the closing roundel, and its style is extremely simple:

> 'Now welcome, somer, with thy sonne softe
> That hast this wintres wedres overshake,
> And driven away the longe nyghtes blake!   680–2

The multiple rhyme of the roundel could in another context seem ornate but combined with the simple repetitive language of the song its effect is to round off the long and elaborate dream with a calm and graceful coda that contrasts vividly with the harsh repetitions at the end of Venus's scene. The mellifluous effect of the rhymes is made more marked when we see that in the stanza from lines 666–72 one of the roundel's rhymes was used and that in the next stanza the final couplet, 678–9 uses again the rhyme of 671–2. There is a deliberate tying up of the rhymes at the end, to stress the harmony that Nature imposes on the creation. The poetic skill is obvious enough: what is the more remarkable here is to see how the different verse-form of the roundel arises out of the plot of the poem and how the rhyme effect serves a specific function in the structure and the meaning of the poem. It is a great advance on the less meaningful use of poetic skills in *Anelida and Arcite*.

But the finality that is given here is the finality of the dream; the poem itself does not have so final an end, for the narrator speaks one more stanza:

> And with the shoutyng, whan the song was do
> That foules maden at here flyght awey,
> I wok, and othere bokes tok me to,
> To reede upon, and yit I rede alwey.
> I hope, ywis, to rede so some day
> That I shal mete som thyng for to fare
> The bet, and thus to rede I nyl nat spare.   693–9

The dramatic touch of the early caesura in 'I wok' is as effectively emphatic as the other examples of this device we have seen in the poem, but the most notable effect of the stanza is its nervous movement. There are several short phrases here, and a good deal of enjambement. The first and fifth lines run on to some extent, but line six has a strong enjambement and it creates an odd effect: we do not get a last line of any finality, no sequence of confident lines flows to the end here as they do so well in, for example, *Troilus and Criseyde*. The nervous movement of the stanza is very like that of several early stanzas in the poem where the narrator expresses his uncertainty. It is clearly a deliberate way of ending the poem and of returning the problem of its meaning to the reader; the narrator has not been an authoritative guide, merely a puzzled reporter of his experiences and finally he gives no sign that he has learned 'a certeyn thyng' but returns to his books, hopeful that here he will 'fare The bet'.

The narrator's unresolved final stanza is a measure of his failure to master his experience and a measure of the challenge to the reader. At the beginning the narrator's reading was briefly presented to us in a balanced style, and the dream of Scipio—a sort of reader's epiphany—has an ordered plain style. But the narrator's disordered statements at the end and early on in the poem show that he fails to understand both his book learning and Affrycan's direct statement in terms of the created world: as a result he is in a disorder of mind and speech when the dream that should have advised him has ended in a harmonious resolution. I have argued elsewhere in detail about this firm backbone of Christian meaning in the poem;[37] the point here is that the narrator fails to see the balance that is in creation and this failure is created and reflected in the poem's style. To study the poem's tytle is not only to find all sorts of subtleties and delights; it also helps us to see more clearly the main line of meaning, and ultimately to see how inextricably interwoven are the poetic style and poetic meaning of this subtle and beautiful poem.

Above I suggested that *Anelida and Arcite* was without poetic subtlety in that the surface of the poem often fell flat because of its rhythmic simplicity, the personalities were not dramatised consistently by the poetry and the movement of the verse did not help us towards the poem's meaning: when a direction seemed to appear it was soon contradicted. From what has been said here about *The Parlement of Foules* it is clear that I would argue that all these subtleties of poetry are to be found in it; I believe that however closely we look at this poem, however seriously we take each nuance, there is something to be discovered. In *The Parlement of Foules* the failures of *Anelida and Arcite* are forgotten; the execution triumphantly fulfils the complex planning and the poem is at once a sign that

Chaucer has mastered the most complex problems of poetry and is also, in its own terms a substantial and satisfying work of art.

NOTES

1. For a summary of the dating issue see Robinson, pp. xxviii–xxx, 788 and 791 and D. S. Brewer, *The Parlement of Foulys* (London, 1960), pp. 2–3.
2. 'Chaucer and the Rhetoricians', *Proceedings of the British Academy*, XII (1926), 95–113; see p. 98.
3. *Essays on Medieval Literature* (London, 1905), p. 83.
4. *Chaucer's Early Poetry* (London, 1963), pp. 201 and 206.
5. P. 304, both references.
6. '*Anelida and Arcite*: a Narrative of Complaint and Comfort', *CR*, V (1970–1), 1–8.
7. 'Chaucer's *Anelida and Arcite*: Some Conjectures', *CR*, V (1970–1), 9–21.
8. 'Meter and Rhyme in Chaucer's "Anelida and Arcite"', *Studies in English* (University of Mississippi), II (1961), 155–63; see p. 55.
9. Cf. other rhyme royal invocations in *TC*, III. 1–7, IV. 22–8, V. 1835–7; *The Parlement of Foules*, 113–16; 'The Prioress's Tale', 467–73; 'The Second Nun's Tale', 29–35 and the extended one, 36–63; 'The Clerk's Tale' is, not surprisingly, without a formal invocation.
10. The word 'patroun' is first recorded in *Sir Gawain and the Green Knight*, then in Wyclif; it only appears twice in Chaucer, here and in the 'Mars'.
11. This last fault is particularly noticeable in a poem where such care has been given to the rhyming; Wimsatt argues that Chaucer tries to avoid the same rhyme-couplet appearing twice, see p. 6 of his article.
12. Robinson inserts '[Arcite]' after 'knyght in the first line', but I cannot see the need for it; it is in none of the MSS and the line does not seem unduly irregular without it.
13. Brian Vickers translates *Ad Herrenium* IV. X: 15–16 in this way, see *Classical Rhetoric in English Poetry* (London, 1970), p. 74; most of the rhetoricians repeated this warning.
14. The words 'endureth' and 'deyneth' are reasonably common in the fourteenth century and Chaucer uses them about a dozen times, but both are clearly more elevated than the preceding diction; 'languisshing' is also quite common but is only used by Chaucer in the context of *fin amor*.
15. Geoffrey regards metaphor or *collatio occulta* as the more stylish—'longe solemnior usus', *Poetria Nova*, 263.
16. The two famous metaphors from *Troilus and Criseyde* mentioned above are good examples; this does not seem to be true when the metaphors have a proverbial flavour, cf. *TC*, I.353–5 and 507–9.
17. He does use traditional metaphor about love—fire and ice, etc., usually when translating from Italian—but his strength lies in simile, as the descriptive material in *The Canterbury Tales* shows, though he may well have judged metaphor too ornate a figure for the General Prologue. However, Chaucer's use of simile can be very subtle and suggestive, as in the description of Alisoun, where it takes on the power more commonly associated with metaphor. This is obviously too large a topic to be enlarged here, and I hope to treat it more fully elsewhere.
18. That such material could come from school books is shown by J. J. Murphy in 'A New look at Chaucer and the Rhetoricians', *RES*, n.s. XV (1964), 1–20.
19. As is the case with most of the poems discussed in this study, the styles of *The Book of the Duchess* and *The Hous of Fame* have received little attention. Robinson remarks that 'In both works the verse has something of the roughness or irregularity of the traditional English accentual type' (p. 280). It seems to me an open question whether this irregularity is native to Chaucer or an artful contrivance (*Anelida and Arcite* suggests the latter), but through it Chaucer avoids the sort of jingling effect that regular octosyllabics can create, which is to be found in *The Romaunt of the Rose* and is sometimes used with great effect in *Sir Orfeo*.

E

20. Frank, 'Structure and Meaning in the *Parlement of Foules*', *PMLA*, LXXI (1956), 530–9; McDonald, 'An Interpretation of Chaucer's *Parlement of Foules*', *Speculum*, XXX (1955), 444–57; Bennett, *The Parlement of Foules: An Interpretation* (Oxford, 1957); Brewer, see note 1 above.

21. P. 55.

22. Pp. 49–51.

23. In his Editorial Appendix to Brewer's 'English in the Universities III. Language and Literature', *EC*, XI (1961), 255–63.

24. P. 26.

25. P. 258

26. Pp. 259 and 260.

27. The passage has been discussed in detail by Mahmoud Manzalaoni, *EC*, XIII (1963), 221–3; he argues convincingly for Robinson's reading.

28. There are, however, 699 lines in the poem and if the editors repeated line 682 after 686, as I believe the sense and shape of the roundel demand, the poem would be 700 lines—or 100 stanzas—long. I cannot see any other numerological elements in the poem, but others better versed in the subject might do so.

29. See the similar passages discussed below, p. 91–3.

30. The invocation spoken by Arcite in 'The Knight's Tale' similarly uses relative clauses and phrases instead of *pronominatio* and I argue below (p. 121) that this denotes a lower style than that of Palamon and Emily, who do use *pronominatio*.

31. P. 61.

32. The effect seems very similar to the use of *repetitio* and *compar* in the negative stanzas at the end of *Troilus and Criseyde*, see pp. 91–3 below.

33. See Chapter III, 'Nature and Venus', pp. 107–33.

34. Only 'uncommytted' is a Chaucerian neologism, but Chaucer's use of several of these words suggests elevation: 'uncommytted' and 'acloyeth' only appear here; 'annoy' is used more often, but basically in *Boece*, *The Romaunt of the Rose* and 'The Parson's Tale'—a curiously common pattern for words that seem to have a learned or elaborate connotation; 'entermeten' is mostly used in *The Romaunt of the Rose* and even 'office', though quite common, usually has a weighty connotation. Particularly in its context, the diction of the stanza seems quite high.

35. In the sense of 'wantonness', 'nicety' is used by Langland and the Gawain-poet, probably before this poem was written, but Chaucer is the first recorded user in the senses of 'folly, lust, coyness'. Presumably the first is the sense here; Chaucer uses it a dozen times, which suggests the word is not outstandingly rare, but has some quality of unusualness—which would seem just right for this context.

36. The word is not new in Chaucer, for it does appear elsewhere in the fourteenth century, though not very freely; but its unusualness is clear from the fact that Chaucer only uses it here and once in *The Romaunt of the Rose*.

37. 'The Meaning of *The Parlement of Foulys*', *Southern Review* (Adelaide), II (1967), 223–9.

2. *Troilus and Criseyde: Minor Characters and the Narrator*

In his book *Chaucer and the French Tradition* Charles Muscatine has written at some length on the part the style of *Troilus and Criseyde* plays in creating the characters of Troilus, Pandarus and Criseyde.[1] He has demonstrated how Troilus and Pandarus have radically different styles of speech and how Criseyde, that complex and varying character, uses both styles. This exposition of *Troilus and Criseyde* is the only one to show how the force and meaning of this great poem arises from its poetry, and in this chapter I intend to go further into this topic. Not only the major characters are shaped by poetic modulation: in this work Chaucer's care and skill extends so far that the nature and significance of even the minor characters and the narrator himself are created by the poetry that presents them.

By their nature, minor characters are restricted in scope and effect, but within these limits they tend to be more clearly defined than major characters. This seems especially true of minor characters created by those masters of naturalism who direct their fictions towards moral issues. The First Gravedigger, Kent, Mr Collins, Mrs Weston, Joe Gargery and Christopher Casby are all powerful representations of one particular morality in action, and against them the leading figures of the fictions in which they appear work out their complex moral destinies. I would think Chaucer's naturalistic powers and moral concern similar to those of Shakespeare, Austen and Dickens, and so it is not surprising that he provides examples of the same process in *Troilus and Criseyde*, the work where his naturalistic presentation of character is most developed. Here I will discuss the minor characters Calchas, Ector, Antigone and Diomede; each represents one aspect of human activity and attitude, and in each characterisation Chaucer's poetic skills have an important part. Little criticism has been written about these figures and none of it refers to the poetic style that presents them; there is no previous comment to epitomise at the beginning of this discussion, then, but such critical comments as are in any way relevant will be referred to *passim*.

I. *Calchas*

Calchas makes two major appearances in the poem, once when he is reported as leaving Troy in Book I and once in Book IV when he asks for a prisoner to exchange for Criseyde. He is referred to by other characters and he does make other brief appearances in Book V, but at none of these times does he occupy the poem's attention for more than a few lines. In Book I he is introduced as 'a lord of great auctorite, A gret devyn' (I.65–6) and the action of his leaving Troy is recounted in three stanzas; the reaction of the Trojans is then given in one stanza (I.85–91) and the story moves on to Criseyde and how this affects her. Within this brief account there are some curious poetic effects that suggest an attitude towards this 'gret devyn'. The first of these has been widely observed. The narrator says:

> So whan this Calkas knew by calkulynge, I.71

And as Paull F. Baum remarks of the pun, 'this has been missed by no one'.[2] In his note on the line Robinson says that puns are relatively rare in Chaucer, but recent studies have disagreed. Baum and Helge Kökeritz have both given lists of Chaucerian word-play.[3] Some of their examples are *significationes*, i.e. *double entendres*, but most are verbal play of the sort seen here, based on verbal repetition— Kökeritz classifies them as *traductio* when the word is unchanged and as *adnominatio* when it is altered to some extent, as here. But nothing seems to have been said about the literary impact of these devices, though a verbal figure of this arresting nature clearly may have an effect on the tone of the poetry, locally at least. When such a figure appears on its own there is perhaps no effect other than to convince us of the author's ingenuity. Yet in the case under discussion, some belittling effect seems implicit, as no one regards obvious plays on his name as complimentary (I speak from tedious experience). It is true that the pun can be a serious revelatory device in medieval literature, as B. F. Huppé shows in his well-known article on *Piers Plowman*,[4] but here the pun merely links the man's name with 'calkulynge', one of the techniques of the medieval scholar. It would, though, be tendentious to identify with confidence a belittling or 'sinking' effect here,[5] unless there were other evidence. But this does exist: there is plenty to suggest that Chaucer deliberately establishes a jingling note in the poetry of this passage, and the whole effect seems clearly intended to belittle Calchas.

Before we have come to this pun, we have been told of Calchas:

> . . . that he
> Knew wel that Troie sholde destroied be,   I.67–8

This is clearly some sort of word-play; it could be taken as an accident or a momentary quibble, for both possible sources use the same construction (though in neither French nor Italian does it amount to word-play),[6] and the phrase is hardly as strained a play as the 'Calkas/calkulynge' pun. But Chaucer does not let us slip over the phrase in this way, for after the play on Calchas's name it recurs:

> For wel wiste he by sort that Troye sholde
> Destroyed ben,   I.76–7

The earlier word-play is repeated with 'Destroyed' in a prominent position. If by now the reader had any doubt that Chaucer was deliberately making word-play a tonal motif in this passage, the rest of line 77 should convince him:

> . . . ye, wolde whoso nolde.

The forceful jingle 'sholde/wolde/nolde' is hard to miss, especially as it ends the stanza and is involved in the rhyme. After the effect of these lines the opening of the next stanza becomes suspect:

> For which for to departen softely
> Took purpos ful this forknowynge wise,   I.78–9

I cannot believe that a poet so convincingly described by Dorothy Everett as having a 'good ear' would have missed the fact that the repetition of 'for' in line 78, emphasised by the pause after 'which', is made obtrusive by the stressed 'for' in the next line, itself emphasised by alliteration with the firmly stressed 'ful'.

Within fifteen lines there has been a number of jingling effects which give the passage a tone rather like that of a nursery rhyme. This contrasts sharply with the sober presence expected of 'a lord of gret auctorite, A gret devyn' and in the light of the lines which follow that description the repetition of the word 'gret' itself sounds dangerously like a parroted convention rather than just a stressed epithet. Calchas's asserted greatness is diminished by the sound of the poetry which describes him. The effect is a subtle one (similar to the way in which Spenser implies with jingling alliteration that Archimago is not the simple holy man he claims to be, cf. *The Faerie Queene*, I.1.xxix–xxx) and because of it we are persuaded towards a critical judgment of Calchas—though we may not extend the judgment as far as the Trojans do:

> . . . he and al his kyn at-ones
> Ben worthi for to brennen, fel and bones.   I.90–1

To describe the passage in this way is not to assume that any jingle or word-play must be sinking in its effect. There are quite a lot of jingles in Chaucer, and Kökeritz has commented on the phenomenon:[7]

> This artifice sang itself into Chaucer's ears as he was reading his French masters. He learned it quickly and practised it several times and not without success, particularly in his earlier poems.

In these earlier poems it is often a device of ornamentation (cf. *The Book of the Duchess*, 265–6 and 1123–4) and there are apparently neutral instances of it in *Troilus and Criseyde*. When Troilus is in the depths of despair we read:

> And forth I wol of Troilus yow telle.

> To Troie is come this woful Troilus,
> In sorwe aboven alle sorwes smerte,   V.196–8

There is a stanza break between the first and second lines here, but for all that the repetition of the 'Troi-' syllable and of 'sorwe' is pointed. But nothing in the context suggests that the device here is belittling; rather it seems a rhetorical stressing of Troilus's sorrow and, perhaps, a linking of his fate with that of Troy. But at another place in the poem another verbal jingle does seem to have a trivialising note, when Pandarus says:

> 'Nece, alle thyng hath tyme, I dar avowe,
> For whan a chaumbre afire is, or an halle,
> Wel more nede is, it sodeynly rescowe
> Than to dispute, and axe amonges alle
> How this candele in the straw is falle.
> A, *benedicite*! for al among that fare
> The harm is don, and fare-wel feldefare!   III.855–61

Pandarus is stressing the notional danger to Troilus and is trying to calm Criseyde's fear at the same time. The lightness and speed of the last two lines demonstrate subtly his skill, for the threat is sweetened with a pleasing jingle: the context makes quite clear the nature of the effect of the last two words of the stanza.

In the context of Calchas's betrayal and in view of the emphasis on verbal jingles in this early scene, it seems plain that here Chaucer is modulating his style to imply an attitude towards Calchas. The passage is not, of course, spoken by Calchas: it is in the narrator's voice. But Calchas does speak in his second important appearance, and it is very satisfying to see that then Chaucer uses the same type of poetic characterisation in direct speech and description as he used before when the narrator alone was speaking.

As Calchas's second appearance begins, the motif of verbal jingle is immediately reintroduced, for the first line uses again one of the more striking effects from Book I:

> Whan Calkas knew this tretis sholde holde,
> In consistorie, among the Grekes soone
> He gan in thringe forth with lordes olde, IV.64–6

The 'sholde holde/olde' jingle is the marked one, but in its shadow there are minor effects of assonance—'in thringe' and 'lordes olde'. On their own these would attract no attention, but in the context of such a dominant major jingle anything with a mildly repetitive sound keeps the sing-song tone going. At the end of the stanza more jingles appear:

> And with a chaunged face hem bad a boone,
> For love of God, to don that reverence,
> To stynte noyse, and yeve hym audience. IV.68–70

The phrase 'bad a boone' is alliterative and bouncy, and then in lines 69 and 70 the rhyme words of 68 and 69 are picked up internally—'boone/don,' 'reverence/yeve'. It is a complex piece of poetry, no doubt largely dependent on oral reading for its full effect, but its nature and purpose are by now quite clear.

Calchas receives his 'boone' and embarks on a long speech. This is larded with jingles of various sorts, and as the point now seems not to need labouring in detailed analysis, I quote the best examples:

IV. 71   'Lo, lordes . . .

72   Troian, as it is knowen . . .

76–7   . . . thorugh yow shal in a stownde
Ben Troie ybrend, and beten down to grownde.

81–4   This knowe ye, my lordes, as I leve.
And, for the Grekis weren me so leeve,
I com myself, in my propre persone,
To teche in this how yow was best to doone,

86 Right no resport, to respect of youre ese.

87–8 . . . and to yow wente,
Wenyng in this . . .

93–8 . . . whanne out of Troie I sterte.
O sterne, O cruel fader that I was!
How myghte I have in that so harde an herte?
Allas! I ne hadde ibrought hire in hire sherte!
For sorwe of which I wol nought lyve to-morwe,
But if ye lordes rewe upon my sorwe.

100–1 Hire to delivere, ich holden have my pees;
But now or nevere, . . .

105–12 Syn I thorugh yow have al this hevynesse.
'Ye have now kaught and fetered in prisoun
Troians ynowe; and if youre willes be,
My child with oon may han redempcioun,
Now, for the love of God and of bounte,
Oon of so fele, allas, so yive hym me!
What nede were it this preiere for to werne,
Syn ye shul bothe han folk and town as yerne?

113 'On peril of my lif, I shal nat lye,

115–16 I have ek founde it by astronomye,
By sort, and by augurye ek, trewely,

117–19 . . . the tyme is faste by,
That fire and flaumbe on al the town shal sprede,
And thus shal Troie torne to asshen dede.

125–6 Bycause he nolde payen hem here hire,
The town of Troie shal ben set on-fire.'

These examples all seem clear enough in their nature and in the effect they have on the tone; to tie it all up Chaucer produces a last stanza of remarkable complexity, with patterns of half-rhyme and assonance that would please the ear of any lover of *cynghanedd*:

127–33 Tellyng his tale alwey, this olde greye,
Humble in his speche, and in his lokyng eke,
The salte teris from his eyen tweye
Ful faste ronnen down by either cheke.
So longe he gan of socour hem biseke
That, for to hele hym of his sorwes soore,
They yave hym Antenor, withouten moore.

It is important to realise that Calchas is not shown to be a skilled rhetorician in spite of the complex surface of much of this poetry. The language that describes him and the language he uses is only distinguished by a crude sort of word-play. There are some examples of *traductio* and *adnominatio* (as Kökeritz distinguishes them) in the opening part of his first appearance but in the rest of that sequence and, very notably in his own speech, they are absent. *Significatio* does not appear and there is only one example of *rime riche* (IV.81–2), a verbal pattern we might have expected if there is a lot of repetition about.[8] The verbal complexity does not create any figures of style or of thought: the tone is jingling and tricky, not rhetorically admirable or skilful. By this means Chaucer states in poetic terms the attitude his poem takes towards Calchas. Critics have observed well in general the way Chaucer sees him. In terms of the historical development of the figure R. M. Lumiansky says that:[9]

> There is to be observed, however, something of a progressive downgrading of Calchas's character by the four writers: Guido is less respectful of him than Benoit, and Chaucer is more biting towards him than Boccaccio.

Tatlock summarises Chaucer's presentation:[10]

> Calchas is an abject; a great and skilled lord whose compliance with the will of the gods learned from his science does not save him from the degeneration caused by violation of human honor, or from his daughter's disrespect.

What has been seen here is the way in which the stylistic treatment of Calchas helps to create the 'biting' tone and the 'abject' note. The verbal complexity catches exactly Calchas's slippery intellectualism, and the stylistic presentation seems very like a full extension of a remark by Diomede:

> 'And but if Calkas lede us with ambages,
> That is to seyn, with double wordes slye,
> Swich as men clepen a word with two visages,   V.897–9

The sharp-witted Diomede distrusts Calchas and his words here provide an explicit internal co-relative for the tone of the passages that show us this learned traitor. The whole presentation of him echoes with 'double wordes slye' and the total effect is a remarkably thorough and successful piece of characterisation by style. Chaucer's poetry works strongly here, but as we have already seen in *The*

Parlement of Foules and will see again in other poems, when he moulds
style to create meaning he does not only work by creating a tonal
character in a scene, he also creates contrasts with other scenes. The
case of Calchas gives a good example of this: as a figure he contrasts vividly with Ector. They each have two scenes and Ector's
follow closely after Calchas's. In and around Ector, Chaucer
creates a sharply contrasting style and personality.

II. *Ector*

After her father's departure Criseyde kneels before Ector 'Wel neigh
out of her wit for sorwe and fere,' (I.108). Ector's reaction is
stated simply in three end-stopped main clauses:

> Now was this Ector pitous of nature,
> And saugh that she was sorwfully bigon,
> And that she was so fair a creature;   I.113–15

These strong measured lines introduce us to Ector, the rock-like
figure of simple nobility. He is exactly what Criseyde needs. He is a
source of reassurance and strength; his speech is imperative in
construction as one might expect of a clear-headed, decisive prince.
It is slow-moving and heavily stressed, confident in tone:

> And seyde, 'Lat youre fadres treson gon
> Forth with meschaunce, and ye yourself in joie
> Dwelleth with us, whil yow good list, in Troie.   I.117–19

The first two lines differ from those immediately preceding in that
they are not end-stopped. In the characterisation of Calchas Chaucer
sometimes used enjambement to stress a word-play (I.67–7, IV.106–
7) or to help the speed of the passage (I.90–1, IV.76–7), but it was
never a dominant feature. In the opening lines of this speech,
however, the enjambement is obtrusive because the run-on is
composed of heavy stresses falling together—'gon Forth' and 'joie
Dwelleth'. This gives a weighty tone to the passage; the general
effect is that the lines almost seem to be broken up into prose; the
fall of stresses and pauses gives the poetry a deliberate, even a
rugged tone. The firm note is continued in Ector's few remaining
lines here:

> 'And al th'onour that men may don yow have,
> As ferforth as youre fader dwelled here,
> Ye shul have, and youre body shal men save,
> As fer as I may ought enquere or here.'   I.120–3

This is not totally monosyllabic, but the large number of mon-syllabic stresses and half-stresses, especially in lines 120, 122 and 123, gives the four lines a slow, certain movement. There is no enjambe-ment here, though: after the prose-like beginning to the speech Ector's reassuring quality resolves itself in heavy single lines. And it is not only the poetic style which is here rather dense and slow-moving. The meaning of these lines is at times quite knotty and the reader has to go slowly to get the full meaning out of the passage. This is strikingly shown by the fact that Root, who does not often translate lines, sensibly addressing himself to readers for whom Chaucer's 'language is no longer a serious barrier,' here feels the need to gloss lines 117, 118, 119, 121, 125 and 126.[11]

The poetic pattern does not stop with the end of Ector's speech, for Criseyde's behaviour indicates in the style of its presentation that she is reassured:

> And she hym thonked with ful humble chere,
> And ofter wolde, and it hadde been his wille,
> And took hire leve, and hom, and held hir stille.   I.124–6

Criseyde, who is so liable to persuasion in so many ways throughout the poem, is here persuaded to calm by Ector. As has been shown above,[12] her reaction to stimuli is quite often portrayed in a paratac-tic *repetitio* filled with *compar*. Here at least that reaction is fully in key with the stimulus, and unlike most of the other instances there seems no possible suggestion that her reaction is unwise. Ector's strength has been communicated to her, and the steadiness, even the bluntness of the poetry which presents him is in striking contrast to the mobile, almost flippant poetry which presents Calchas: Ector's poetry has the note of a true paternal strength. And just as in the presentation of Calchas, the poetic implications of the early scene are pressed home in the later scene.

When Ector appears again, shortly after Calchas has appeared for the second time, the bluntness is there from the beginning:

> Ector, which that wel the Grekis herde,
> For Antenor how they wolde han Criseyde,   IV.176–7

Here there is no complexity in language, merely a careful setting out of the facts. Just as Ector's name has firmly started the stanza, the third line gives his reactions strongly:

> Gan it withstonde, and sobrely answerde: IV.178

Like all really skilful writers, Chaucer does not use the summing up epithet until we have seen enough of the character to accept it. It is the action and the poetry which inform us about Ector, not merely the adverb 'sobrely'. The sobriety of his answer is similarly self-expressed:

> 'Syres, she nys no prisonere,' he seyde;
> 'I not on yow who that this charge leyde,
> But, on my part, ye may eftsone hem telle,
> We usen here no wommen for to selle.'   IV.178–82

The opening words of each line are heavy and a forceful personality comes across from them, just as it does in the opening lines of 'The Wife of Bath's Prologue', where almost every line begins strongly, many of them with a reversed foot.[13] In that case, though, there is speed in the body of the lines to create a more mobile characterisation; here there are some pauses, Ector's statements are straightforward, dogmatically clipped and the general impact is monosyllabic and end-stopped. Against this certitude the simile of the people's opposition is all the more suggestive of chaos:

> The noyse of peple up stirte thanne at ones,
> As breme as blase of straw iset on-fire;   IV.183–4

And because Ector's sobriety has been so convincing we assent readily to the proleptic judgment in lines 185–6:

> For infortune it wolde, for the nones,
> They sholden hire confusioun desire.

In the previous scene, when he calmed Criseyde, Ector was a source of good advice and peace of mind; here too he would have been, had the people listened but, as the narrator says:

> . . . cloude of errour lat hem nat discerne
> What best is.   IV.200–1

Ector is cried down. He resists, and it is most fitting that the last we hear of him is stubborn but monosyllabic:

> Altheigh that Ector 'nay' ful ofte preyde.   IV.214

In these brief passages a style of speaking and presentation is created for Ector. He has none of Troilus's fluency and rhetoric, none of the persuasive drive of Pandarus and Diomede. He speaks in a simple, blunt fashion. That this is a deliberate stylistic characterisation is clear if we compare Ector's style in these instances with that of his brother Deiphebe. He too is a noble prince, and one accustomed to command, but his speech is more fluent than Ector's:

> 'Of Ector, which that is my lord, my brother,
> It nedeth naught to preye hym frend to be;
> For I have herd hym, o tyme and ek oother,
> Speke of Cryseyde swich honour, that he
> May seyn no bet, swich hap to hym hath she.
> It nedeth naught his helpes for to crave;
> He shal be swich, right as we wol hym have.   II.1450–6

This is a whole stanza; Ector nowhere speaks a whole stanza. It moves easily, has one speedy enjambement and has a touch of formal repetition in lines 1451 and 1455. The stanza is not particularly distinctive in terms of style—it could also have been spoken by Troilus, Pandarus or Criseyde. It is a mobile, graceful rhyme royal stanza. But it is quite different from the style of Ector's speech and the description of him, and this shows that for this little-seen but quite important figure of plain authority Chaucer has taken the trouble to sketch in a characteristic style. We hear of Ector that he is 'wise, worthi' (III.158) and that:

> In al this world ther nys a bettre knyght
> Than he, that is of worthynesse welle;   II.177–8

His speech and the style of his description are full of straightforward knightly worthiness, he is a man Criseyde can find comfort in and a man who defends the honourable customs of Troy. To look more widely, there is advantage to the plot of the poem in his limited powers: had he been a speaker of persuasive force perhaps Criseyde would not have been exchanged. The inarticulacy of true honour and the articulacy of those whose manipulations lead to disaster can be taken as a thematic motif, though a small one, in the poem, and this suggests an added dimension to the appropriateness of Chaucer's stylistic characterisation of Ector.

III. *Antigone*

Antigone is another character who appears rarely, but she has one scene of considerable importance. Chaucer not only gives her a name (as he gives names to several other minor figures in the poem, including an owl[14]) but he also gives her a song of great beauty and creates around her and Criseyde a scene of real sublety and complexity.

Criseyde has been reflecting whether she should take Troilus as a lover; she is divided between fear of possible consequences and attraction towards Troilus and the whole idea. She is in a state of some tension:

> And after that, hire thought gan for to clere,
> And seide, 'He which that nothing undertaketh,
> Nothyng n'acheveth, be hym looth or deere.'
> And with an other thought hire herte quaketh;
> Than slepeth hope, and after drede awaketh;
> Now hoot, now cold; but thus, bitwixen tweye,
> She rist hire up, and wente here for to pleye.   II.806–12

After this description Criseyde walks down into the garden where her nieces are at play, and the garden is described in four lines, just as her state of mind was described. The two descriptions are also similar in that they use *contentio* and *commutatio*, devices of formal juxtaposition, but the effect of the two descriptions is quite different. The passage about Criseyde's feelings juxtaposes contrasting notions —'hope' and 'drede', 'hoot' and 'cold'—and so the poetry's meaning makes the balance of the lines a nervous one, showing Criseyde being pulled in two directions at once. The second descriptive passage, however, offers complementary ideas in juxtaposition, and so a sense of restful balance is created:

> This yerd was large, and rayled all th'aleyes,
> And shadewed wel with blosmy bowes grene,
> And benched newe, and sonded all the weyes,
> In which she walketh arm in arm bitwene,   II.820–3

The first line is a syntactic *commutatio*; the second and third lines begin with exactly the same syntactic construction—it is a brief *repetitio*. The ends of the second and third lines do not balance precisely, though each is a firm descriptive phrase, but as Kökeritz has pointed out, the third line is in Chaucerian pronunciation something very close to an elaborate *rime riche* with the first line.[15] And in the fourth line this sense of formal balance is given a physical co-relative as they walk together down the paths of the formal garden. The grace and poise of the passage suggests excellently the quality of the garden; its restfulness is especially striking after the almost schizoid effect of the preceding description of Criseyde, and the poetry makes us feel that here the disturbed woman will find assurance. There is not only the ease of ordered beauty here, however: the garden is given a direct voice to bring further ease and assurance to Criseyde:

> Til at the last Antigone the shene
> Gan on a Troian songe to singen cleere,
> That it an heven was hire vois to here.   II.824–6

The song that follows is beautiful and richly worded. Chaucer has worked on it with great care, for though it derives from Machaut's *Le Paradis d'Amour* it is heavily rewritten for this context—Kittredge calls it 'an example of adaptive mastery.'[16] The opening expresses in complex form a self-dedication to the God of Love:

> She seyde: 'O love, to whom I have and shal
> Ben humble subgit, trewe in myn entente,
> As I best kan, to yow, lord, yeve ich al,
> For everemo, myn hertes lust to rente.   II.827–30

The word-order and syntax are richly complex but the verse flows gracefully, and here too there is a strong sense of balance in each line, though it is not as marked as in the preceding description. The song gains richness as the lover is described in the high formality of *interpretatio* and *pronominatio*, the list evenly balanced to form *repetitio*:

> 'As he that is the welle of worthynesse,
> Of trouthe grownd, mirour of goodlihed,
> Of wit Apollo, stoon of sikernesse,
> Of vertu roote, of lust fynder and hed,
> Thorugh which is alle sorwe fro me dede,
> Iwis, I love him best, so doth he me;
> Now good thrift have he, wherso that he be!   II.841–7

Antigone sings regularly in full stanzas; not every one is as fully and evenly balanced as this, but throughout the song there is an even opposition of poetic units and of ideas:

> 'And whoso seith that for to love is vice,
> Or thraldom, though he feele in it destresse,
> He outher is envyous, or right nyce,
> Or is unmyghty, for his shrewednesse,
> To loven; for swich manere folk, I gesse,
> Defamen Love, as nothing of him knowe.
> Thei speken, but thei benten nevere his bowe!   II.855–61

The first two lines are answered by the next two; the statement in lines three and four does run over into line five, it is true, but the first four lines are so full of balances and alternatives that this seems only a slight irregularity. And even this short enjambement is then balanced by the phrase 'I gesse' at the end of the fifth line. The last two lines are in almost exact equipoise, the one a colloquial version of the other.

The tonal motif of the song, then, is balance; Criseyde's mind was disturbed, pulled two ways at once, and then she stepped into a garden of even balance. The equipoise of the song seeks to offer her confidence and mental equilibrium, and this is stated overtly in the last two lines of the song—naturally, a finely balanced couplet:

> Al dredde I first to love hym to bigynne,
> Now woot I wel, ther is no peril inne.' II.874–5

Antigone's song is a careful answering of the doubts Criseyde has felt, as Sister Borthwick has shown.[17] But it does not entirely satisfy Criseyde as a rational answer. After the song Criseyde questions Antigone and Antigone reasserts the quality of love, but the debate is unfinished:

> Criseyde unto that purpos naught answerde,
> But seyde, 'Ywys, it wol be nyght as faste'. II.897–8

There is no rational, spoken end to the discussion. But there is an end of a different sort, for Criseyde thinks on:

> But every word which that she of hire herde,
> She gan to prenten in hire herte faste,
> And ay gan love hire lasse for t'agaste
> Than it did erst, and synken in hire herte,
> That she wex somwhat able to converte. II.899–903

This seems to me an important and most subtle moment. Borthwick sums up by saying of Criseyde 'She is never really convinced by Antigone, but she allows the words of the girl to work upon her, softening her in her attitude toward love'.[18] This is broadly true, but it is the beauty of the song, its balanced confidence, that has affected Criseyde so. The balanced garden, so carefully though so briefly described, is an expansive image here and in her song Antigone has taken Criseyde arm in arm, as it were, down ways that seem beautiful, smooth and delightful. At this stage of the scene it would be dangerous to say that these ways do only *seem* satisfying, and are in fact illusory. But as the poem goes on, this implication is made.

The narrator tells us that night is coming:

> The dayes honour, and the hevenes ye,
> The nyghtes foo—al this clepe I the sonne—
> Gan westren faste, and downward for to wrye, II.904–6

This curious passage can only be read as a piece of counter-rhetoric, similar to that in 'The Franklin's Tale'.[19] I take the example there as, at the most, an assertion of the Franklin's personality. Here though, it is harder to take the trope so lightly. It imitates the *interpretatio* and *pronominatio* that has just provided the rhetorical climax in the beautiful song, and then snaps it off with *praecisio*: the effect has an irresistibly mocking tone. I can only see this as a warning from the narrator that beautiful words can obscure as well as adorn, a reminder that we should not be swept away by Antigone's rhetoric as Criseyde has been. In a mood of heightened awareness we read on:

> As he that hadde his dayes cours yronne;
> And white thynges wexen dymme and donne
> For lak of lyght, and sterres for t'apere,
> That she and alle hire folk in went yfeere.   II.907–10

It is a charming and poised description of the coming of dusk; in the light of the narrator's previous sharp tone, however, it is tempting to read this as another expansive image. Antigone has been described as 'the shene'; she too would grow dim and dark now. It is unwise to be dogmatic about a scene as suggestive as this short one, but I think it would be an insensitive reader who did not feel that this darkening, coming so soon after the jolting tone of line 905, does not imply in some way the inauspicious aspect of what Criseyde is considering. It is tempting to link it with the phrase 'wordes white,' meaning 'specious words' in III.901, since the narrator seems to imply here a specious quality in Antigone's rhetoric. There may also be a link between this ominous darkening and the fact that the consummation is in the dark of the moon; further, when Criseyde is at a similar crisis in the Greek camp, considering whether to give herself to Diomede, her mood seems to be affected crucially by the artificial brightness of her father's tent. There may well be a motif of darkness and of true and illusory light in the poem; the prohemium to Book III would be relevant here—'O blisful light'—and P. M. Kean has an interesting article touching this topic.[20] This should perhaps be regarded as the fullest development of the meaning of this scene, arising ultimately from the unease conveyed here. As the scene goes on, this unease does not vanish.

Criseyde hears a nightingale sing; Antigone's song made her 'able to converte' and this conversion now takes place as the song lifts her heart:

F

> A nyghtyngale, upon a cedir grene,
> Under the chambre wal ther as she ley,
> Ful loude song ayein the moone shene,
> Peraunter, in his briddes wise, a lay
> Of love, that made hire herte fressh and gay.   II.918–22

He sings in 'his briddes wise' under the 'moone shene'; it is hard to avoid the notion that this is a bird's version of Antigone's beautiful song—as beautiful, but even more devoid of rational content. Its melody completes Criseyde's revival, though it has no message at all. After this she is able to dream of an exchange of hearts. The dream features a fierce eagle, though she feels no pain as he tears out her heart. I do not think the ferocity of the dream has any ironic meaning, any prolepsis of the torments they will finally feel: Troilus is, after all, a warrior, and the eagle might seem a suitable animal counterpart. But the fact that these two incidents, the dream and this second 'lay Of love', both involve birds might give us pause. The animal-imagery of the poem does seem ironic, especially with regard to Troilus, and some of the hunting metaphors have a suggestive force.[21] But the nightingale and the eagle are noble creatures, unlike 'Bayard' or the snail, to both of which Troilus is likened (I.218–22 and 300), and I would hesitate to press this issue strongly as a major cause of unease in this scene.

Borthwick also feels that though Antigone's song is all for love, 'Indirectly, however, a note of disapproval is sounded'. She hears this note in the fact that the song speaks of those who oppose love and the fact that it contains Christian elements.[22] It is true that there is a reference to the heavenly nature of love by the narrator (II.826) and, obliquely, by Antigone (II.894–5), yet both of Borthwick's arguments seem to depend entirely on ironies which are only in the reader's eye. This is the Robertsonian assumption that such ironies *should* be present, and this view has, of course, been fully criticised by Kaske and Donaldson and, most recently, by Paul Piehler.[23] I also think the song is questioned, but I would argue that in the narrator's comments we are given an internal tonal key to this. He implies an unease with the 'rhetoric' and also suggests that time darkens all things. The two are linked: Criseyde has exorcised her worries in an affective manner, not in rational discourse, and time, we feel, will show her worries to have been too easily laid aside in the context of beauty. For before being placated by a beautiful song and a nightingale she has said a lot of things which are to come terribly true:

'For love is yet the mooste stormy lyf,
Right of hymself, that evere was bigonne;
For evere som mystrust or nice strif
Ther is in love, som cloude is over that sonne.   II.778–81

Chaucer's skill here is in hinting to us by stylistic modulation and suggestive irony that these remarks will come true, that the beauty-inspired confidence will die away. His touch is delicate enough to show how easy it is to be swayed by such moving poetry, while reminding us by changes of tone that this is not wise. The scene's fullest meaning links up with the overall meaning of the poem, stated by the narrator at the end of Book V, in verse even finer than that of this scene.

IV. *Diomede*

The last of the four minor characters I look at here also works upon Criseyde for her ultimate ill; indeed, the more we look at the minor characters the more we see how Chaucer has assembled influences around his heroine: only the inarticulate Ector stands for her good. Diomede is the most openly malevolent influence on her, and in his characterisation Chaucer employs some elegant stylistic modulation, making him a convincingly persuasive villain.

Diomede is briefly mentioned in the prohemium to Book IV, but does not appear till early in Book V:

Ful redy was at prime Diomede,
Criseyde unto the Grekis oost to lede,   V.15–16

These two lines have a crisp, almost aggressive tone. The more we see of Diomede the more appropriate we will find it that the first words about him are the peremptory ones 'Ful redy'—he is always ready for action. The lines suggest that he will not be waiting around, dithering; the two names, Diomede and Criseyde, are juxtaposed and this itself conveys a pressing note. The next we see of Diomede is action; the narrator says of Troilus:

For ire he quook, so gan his herte gnawe,
Whan Diomede on horse gan hym dresse,   V.36–7

The second line has three stresses falling closely together in 'horse gan hym' (Root reads 'hors' and so makes the emphasis stronger), and this catches well the effect as Diomede acts briskly while Troilus stands lamenting. The contrast is made overt when, in the next stanza, Troilus apostrophises his inaction:

> 'Whi nyl I make atones riche and pore
> To have inough to doone, er that she go?
> Why nyl I brynge al Troie upon a roore?
> Whi nyl I slen this Diomede also?
> Why nyl I rather with a man or two
> Stele hir away? Whi wol I this endure?
> Whi nyl I helpen to myn owen cure?'   V. 43–9

A repetitive rhetoric, *interrogatio* and *repetitio* the dominant figures, is Troilus's response to the situation. He remains honourable, for the narrator tells us that his inaction is caused by his concern for Criseyde's safety. In some ways he is a figure to pity beside the silent, busy 'Ful redy' Diomede. The contrast is to be enlarged later, but it is perhaps never as sharply present as it is here.

Diomede observes the farewells, and draws the right conclusions:

> With that his courser torned he aboute
> With face pale, and unto Diomede
> No word he spak, ne non of al his route;
> Of which the sone of Tideus took hede,
> As he that koude more than the crede
> In swich a craft, and by the reyne hire hente;
> And Troilus to Troie homward he wente.   V. 85–91

The words 'koude' and 'craft' present a new notion about Diomede: he is perceptive, we see. The description of him and his actions here is suggestively monosyllabic—Troilus has most of the polysyllables in the stanza, though there are not many. The next stanza presses home this brusque aspect of Diomede's personality:

> This Diomede, that ledde hire by the bridel,
> Whan that he saugh the folk of Troie aweye,
> Thoughte, 'Al my labour shal nat ben on ydel,
> I that I may, for somwhat shal I seye.
> For at the werste it may yet shorte oure weye.
> I have herd seyd ek tymes twyes twelve:
> "He is a fool that wole foryete hymselve." '   V. 92–8

Diomede is still leading her; his relation with Criseyde is fore-shadowed by the first three verbs used to link them—'lede', 'hente' and 'ledde'. As soon as they leave, he plans, and plans for his own profit. He has a callously cheerful self-concern—he may as well have a go at her, is his feeling. His limited, maxim-ridden thoughts are phrased in simple, forceful language. The last three lines are notably monosyllabic and the two disyllables 'twyes' and 'foryete' are both words of Old English origin. Craft and brusqueness are the two characteristics sketched in so far, and these are amplified in the next stanza, when he advises himself to be roundabout:

> . . . if she have in hire thought
> Hym that I gesse, he may nat ben ybrought
> So soon awey; but I shal fynde a meene,
> That she naught wite as yet shal what I mene.' V.102–5

This is a curious stanza. Its diction, syntax and word-order are simple and direct, just like the three previous stanzas. But there is an element of complexity toward the end of the stanza: lines 102–3 and 103–4 are run-on, though there do seem to be slight pauses at the end of each line, and the final couplet shows *rime riche*. It is a skilful transitional stanza, in fact, for in the next lines the style fully shows the change to a roundabout approach as Diomede searches for a 'meene' to trap Criseyde:

> This Diomede, as he that koude his good,
> Whan this was don, gan fallen forth in speche
> Of this and that, and axed whi she stood
> In swich disese, and gan hire ek biseche,
> That if that he encresse myght or eche
> With any thyng hire ese, that she sholde
> Comaunde it hym, and seyde he don it wolde. V.106–12

At the end of line 107, the very point when the narrator drops into *oratio obliqua*, enjambement runs on much more quickly than it did in the previous stanza. It occurs again at the end of line 108. Both Root and Robinson place a comma at the end of line 109, so I will not say that it is run-on; but if the comma were removed the line would run on very well and make better sense, I feel—a pause here sounds rather strange. Lines 110 and 111 are obviously run-on strongly. As well as this spectacular piece of fluency we have a sudden rush of terms from the courtly lover's phrasebook—'disese', 'encresse', 'ese' and 'comaunde'. The effect is subtle and powerful, acting out Diomede's cunning. In the next stanza the tone is not quite the same: rather it is steady, reassuring:

> For treweliche he swor hire, as a knyght,
> That ther nas thyng with which he myghte hire plese,
> That he nolde don his peyne and al his myght
> To don it, for to don hire herte an ese. V.113–16

Here the verse is not as supple; it is fairly simple in movement and the last two lines contain a lot of straightforward repetition. Is this not a tone of reassurance, the calming of a nervous lady which accompanies the courtly 'meene' that he has found? It is suggestively different from the more rugged, honest reassurances she has earlier received from Ector.

This smooth reassurance is the tone of the next stanzas as he promises her kindnesses among the Greeks; the craft that is typical of him is still obvious. He skilfully introduces the notion of friendship:

> 'And by the cause I swor yow right, lo, now,
> To ben youre frend, . . .   V.127–8

This 'frend' is a word of dual meaning in Middle English; it can be 'friend' as in Modern English, but it can also mean 'lover'. He at first specifies the former sense:

> 'And that ye me wolde as youre brother trete;
> And taketh naught my frendshipe in despit;   V.134–5

But when in the next stanza he goes on to speak of the 'god of Love' he seems to have shifted the semantic context of 'frend' and his own style becomes that of an appealing lover:

> O god of Love in soth we serven bothe.
> And, for the love of God, my lady fre,
> Whomso ye hate, as beth nat wroth with me,
> For trewely, ther can no wyght yow serve,
> That half so loth youre wratthe wold disserve.   V.143–7

The *commutatio* in the first two lines is stylishly brought off, but it is not only a pretty piece of rhetoric—it also obscures whether he is talking about God or about Love, and the same devious effect is attained by the stylish *rime riche* and tricky argument of the last two lines. Diomede is moving along with nuance, suggestion and a steady introduction of amorous topics. The next stanza states his service to her in a manner distinctly unbrotherly:

> Yeve me youre hond; I am, and shal ben ay,
> God helpe me so, while that my lyf may dure,
> Youre owene aboven every creature.   V.152–4

And the following stanza, while formally being a declaration that his heart is virgin, in fact finally specifies the relationship he is proposing:

> I lovede never womman here-biforn
> As paramours, ne nevere shal no mo.   V.157–8

The rest of the speech expresses undying love and ends on as lilting a couplet and as touching a theme as any lover could devise:

> So lowely ne so trewely yow serve
> Nil non of hem, as I shal, til I sterve.' V.174–5

The stylistic range of this scene presenting Diomede has been from the crispest and plainest of monosyllabics to this saccharine conclusion. He is a fine moulder of phrases and a great insinuator. Throughout this lengthy passage Chaucer is working all the time to model his verse to the requirements of each stanza, creating changes of tone with remarkable delicacy and point. In Diomede he shapes, for the first time in the poem, a person who generally speaks in a manner quite different from the way in which he thinks. Pandarus's manipulative skills are meant for the best and seem honest beside this firework display of persuasion. Chaucer's controlling mind and sense of drama remain acute, though, for he tells us that Criseyde has heard little of this; Diomede's attack has largely been in vain, for she has not taken in the insinuations, unless we are to regard their effect as subliminal. Instead:

> . . . she thonked Diomede
> Of al his travaile and his goode cheere,
> And that hym list his frendshipe hire to bede;
> And she accepteth it in good manere,
> And wol do fayn that is him lief and dere,
> And trusten hym she wolde, and wel she myghte,
> As seyde she; and from hire hors sh'alighte. V.183–9

It is another of those passages where Criseyde, in a regular series of main clauses, reacts to people without giving reasons or conditions, where she is shown as plastic for others to mould. But as she has been, we presume, too disturbed to listen properly, the full effect of Diomede's speech is lost, and she takes the word 'frend' in its modern sense: perhaps he was not so shrewd an observer after all. But at least, she now trusts him and will do his will, as the narrator ominously reports. We have seen Diomede's persuasive skills and self-centred determination, and we cannot believe that he will not try again. Next time, as we shall see, he will not merely declare love; he will be less gentle, and less straightforward in his approach.

Just like Calchas and Ector, Diomede in his second appearance confirms the impressions created in the first part of his characterisation, and the same types of stylistic modelling operate as before. Once again we see him at first reflecting to himself. The language is sharp and simple and his vision of the whole business is as unsubtle and as businesslike as it had been previously:

> This Diomede, of whom yow telle I gan,
> Goth now withinne hymself ay arguynge
> With al the sleighte, and al that evere he kan,
> How he may best, with shortest tariynge,
> Into his net Criseydes herte brynge.
> To this entent he koude never fyne;
> To fisshen hire, he leyde out hook and lyne.   V.771–7

The narrator feels that Diomede's own blunt fishing metaphor is the only appropriate one for this crude process; as the account continues it is clear that Diomede's thought processes are at the same low level as before, for the limit of his cerebration still seems to be a simple proverb:

> He nyst how best hire herte for t'acoye.
> 'But for t'asay,' he seyde, 'it naught ne greveth;
> For he that naught n'asaieth, naught n'acheveth.'   V.782–4

The flat rhythms, the end-stopped lines, the simply repetitive language—a jingling note appears here too—all stress the triteness of the thought. Chaucer continues to strike this note at the end of each of the following two stanzas. In the next we read:

> I may wel wite, it nyl nat ben my prow.
> For wise folk in bookes it expresse:
> 'Men shal nat wowe a wight in hevynesse.'   V.789–91

This poverty-stricken monologue is concluded with more threadbare maxims at the end of the next stanza:

> And right anon, as he that bold was ay,
> Thoughte in his herte, 'Happe how happe may,
> Al shoulde I dye, I wol hire herte seche!
> I shal namore lesen but my speche.'   V.795–8

Ida L. Gordon has argued in her book *The Double Sorrow of Troilus* that proverbs are used in the poem with an ironic effect. She feels they are so patently inadequate devices, in cerebral and rhetorical terms, that we are to look critically on anyone who uses this *prosecutio cum proverbiis*.[24] There is a lot in this, though the context must be noted: I cannot agree that the narrator's maxims in the prohemium to Book II have this adverse effect, and a lot of Pandarus's proverbs are harmless cheering-up devices aimed at the prostrate Troilus. But in the case of Criseyde the fact that she often thinks in maxims as well as talking in them (as Lumiansky has shown in an interesting article)[25] is surely meant as a comment on her shallow conceptual powers, and a partial explanation of why she is so easily moulded to the will of others. Here too we see the poverty-stricken nature of Diomede's mind, but we also see the contrast between the words he actually speaks to himself and the glossy front he can erect in verbal play upon Criseyde. This intensifies our feeling of his dishonesty: the plain verse style and the lame conceptual nature of his own thought contrast so strongly with his public manipulative utterances to Criseyde that a judgment is invited. He contrasts vividly with Troilus, for Troilus may at times seem helpless, as at the beginning of Book V, but he is noble; his thoughts are often subtle and the inner and outer man are the same. It is from this powerful contrast, one in which style and meaning are interwoven, that we arrive at the judgment that Diomede is, as Speirs aptly remarks 'a shop-soiled Troilus',[26] a shoddy replica of that noble prince, and there arises a real gloom as we see Criseyde accepting this debased version of her princely lover.

But before she will accept him he has to besiege her with arguments, demonstrating his full manipulative powers in a long final sequence. The narrator delays this by giving us brief sketches of Diomede, Criseyde and Troilus. The location of these *effictiones* may seem odd: it is late in the poem to treat the hero and heroine in this way, but the effect is to stress very strongly the contrast between the two men. Of Diomede we learn that he is a great soldier—the description has a Homeric ring:

> With sterne vois and myghty lymes square,
> Hardy, testif, strong, and chivalrous
> Of dedes, lik his fader Tideus.
> And som men seyn he was of tonge large;
> And heir he was of Calydoigne and Arge.   V.801–5

The rugged *articulus* of line 802 catches well the nature of the man, powerful and forbidding; there is another fine effect too, as we hear that he is 'chivalrous'—a grand quality—but the run-on line minimises the description: his chivalry is only 'Of dedes'. As we have seen already and will again his 'tonge large' signifies more than Homer's epithet meaning 'of the loud war-cry,' and this characteristic is not used in chivalrous manner but to further the desires of his hard, grasping personality.

Troilus is quite different. He too is a warrior, but his qualities reach further; he is 'complete formed' (V.828) and:

> Yong, fressh, strong, and hardy as lyoun;
> Trewe as stiel in ech condicioun;
> Oon of the beste entecched creature
> That is, or shal, whil that the world may dure.   V.830–3

This glowing description does not tail off in anticlimactic comments as Diomede's seems to do—it is a full and admiring account. Criseyde's description, sandwiched ominously between Diomede first and Troilus second, testifies to her beauty but ends with the fading, revealing close:

> Ne nevere mo ne lakked her pite;
> Tendre-herted, slydyng of corage;
> But trewely, I kan nat telle hire age.   V.824–6

We have seen these characteristics in Criseyde before, and when Diomede attacks again they lead her to yield to him. In this way these descriptions gather up the characteristics of the three. They tell us nothing new, but they clarify our views of the characters as the story moves towards its last sequence and thus they emphasise the dramatic wretchedness that is to come before the changing tone of the poem's end.

Diomede now comes to Criseyde full of dishonesty and in the guise, the narrator's simile implies, of a lover:

> This Diomede, as fressh as braunche in May,
> Com to the tente, ther as Calkas lay,
> And feyned hym with Calkas han to doone;
> But what he mente, I shal yow tellen soone.   V.844–7

Diomede begins flowingly; his 'tonge large' is demonstrated as he addresses Criseyde. The narrator, to give an account of it, uses a diction which is often polysyllabic and Romance in origin; enjambement is often present and the lines flow smoothly along:

> He gan first fallen of the werre in speche
> Bitwixe hem and the folk of Troie town;
> And of th'assege he gan hire ek biseche,
> To telle hym what was hire opynyoun.
> Fro that demaunde he so descendeth down
> To axen hire, if that hire straunge thoughte
> The Grekis gise, and werkes that they wroughte;   V.855–61

The verb 'descendeth down' etches sharply the fact that he is following a planned course. He speaks directly to her now, and as he does so the language and movement of the poetry are simplified—a direct, plain and manly appeal seems to be his stalking horse:

> . . . O lady myn, Criseyde,
> That syn I first hond on youre bridel leyde,
> Whan ye out come of Troie by the morwe,
> Ne koude I nevere sen yow but in sorwe.   V.872–5

In the next stanza this simplification of style becomes more of a hardening:

> 'Kan I nat seyn what may the cause be,
> But if for love of som Troian it were,
> The which right sore wolde athynken me,
> That ye for any wight that dwelleth there
> Sholden spille a quarter of a tere,
> Or pitously youreselven so bigile;
> For dredeles, it is nought worth the while.   V.876–82

The reversed foot at the beginning of line 880 brings a roughness into the poetry and the last line, with its firm pause and its bluntly dismissive final phrase, intensifies this tougher note. The reason for this becomes quite clear in the next stanza; Diomede, knowing she loves a Trojan, savagely tells her to forget it:

> 'The folk of Troie, as who seyth, alle and some
> In prisoun ben, as ye yourselven se;
> Nor thennes shal nat oon on-lyve come
> For al the gold atwixen sonne and se.
> Trusteth wel, and understondeth me,
> Ther shal nat oon to mercy gon on-lyve,
> Al were he lord of worldes twies fyve!   V.883–9

As in the previous stanza the fifth line opens with a heavy stress, disrupting the rhythms and making them harsh, and here this strong effect is supported by a clipped monosyllabic diction that drives home the cruelty of the statement. Diomede rephrases the message of despair in the following stanzas, and though none is quite as brusque as this one has been, the argument is relentless and vigorously phrased:

> 'What! wene ye youre wise fader wolde
> Han yeven Antenor for yow anon,
> If he ne wiste that the citee sholde
> Destroied ben? Whi, nay, so mote I gon!

> He knew ful wel ther shal nat scapen oon
> That Troian is; and for the grete feere,
> He dorste nat ye dwelte lenger there.   V. 904–10

Thus with harsh, crisp stanzas he creates in her a state of high anxiety; then with the mobility of a good manipulator he adopts a different persona and becomes the gentle lover, able to offer a way out to this disturbed and abandoned woman. The technique is just that of an interrogator, breaking a prisoner by being hard and then soft:

> 'And thenketh wel, ye shal in Grekis fynde
> A moore parfit love, er it be nyght,
> Than any Troian is, and more kynde,
> And bet to serven yow wol don hys myght.   V. 918–21

All the right phrases are here; he offers her emotional refuge and support—and speedily too, for the double-edged phrase 'er it be nyght' implies immediate comfort for her and a different type of satisfaction for him. After this short speech as a lover, Diomede acts out lover-like behaviour with great facility:

> And with that word he gan to waxen red,
> And in his speche a litel wight he quok,
> And caste asyde a litel wight his hed,
> And stynte a while; and afterward he wok,
> And sobreliche on hire he threw his lok,
> And seyde, 'I am, al be hit yow no joie,
> As gentil man as any wight in Troie.   V. 925–31

The stanza is rather formal; all but the last line is *repetitio* and 926–8 is a fairly exact piece of *compar*. The effect is a mannered one, and in the context that is precisely appropriate. Meech remarks that here Chaucer:[27]

> . . . permits Diomede the blushing, tremolo and averted gaze recorded by Boccaccio, trusting presumably that the private cynicisms which he has attributed to the Greek will lead the reader to take some of this as play-acting.

The context is certainly important, but the tone of the stanza is also important evidence that the action is 'an empty travesty' as Meech also says.[28] In the light of all Diomede's other stylistic changes this is plainly an elaborate piece of acting, elaborately portrayed. His assault on Criseyde goes further than the 'threat and boast' which Donaldson identifies here,[29] for he is careful to offer the right amorous appearances as well as undermining her, and so allows Criseyde to maintain some front while she yields.

He keeps up the attack, but the narrator has had enough; with a note of disgust he says:

> What sholde I telle his wordes that he seyde?
> He spak inough, for o day at the meeste.
> It preveth wel, he spak so that Criseyde
> Graunted, on the morwe, at his requeste,
> For to speken with hym at the leeste,
> So that he nolde speke of swich matere. V.946–51

Criseyde copes as well as she might; she defends her honour and position, and makes at last a pathetically null statement:

> 'I say nat therefore that I wol yow love,
> N'y say nat nay; but in conclusioun,
> I mene wel, by God that sit above!' V.1002–4

After the power and fluency of Diomede's two assaults, and the malign skill of the second in particular, it is with a sense of inevitability that we see her alone, thinking just the thoughts that Diomede has put into her head. It is a mobile, simple stanza, ending with a simple and final statement:

> Retornyng in hire soule ay up and down
> The wordes of this sodeyn Diomede,
> His grete estat, and perel of the town,
> And that she was allone and hadde nede
> Of frendes help; and thus bygan to brede
> The cause whi, the sothe for to telle,
> That she took fully purpos for to dwelle. V.1023–9

We assent fully to the adjective 'sodeyn' for it sums up excellently what Chaucer has shown us. As when the narrator drew attention to Ector's sobriety and Diomede's 'tonge large' the direct description only summarises what has been demonstrated in action, meaning and the tone of the poetry. In Diomede Chaucer has created a man of limited cerebral powers and little morality, but a man expert at manipulating a weaker personality already in a distressed state. The original conception of Diomede was much simpler; as A.M. Hill says, in Benoit, Diomede's '. . . self-confidence and the precipitate character of his suit form a sharp contrast to the humbleness of Troilus.'[30]

But, as Meech continues the story, in Chaucer's work 'The new

Diomede convicts himself of insincerity in love as the old did not and thus comes to stand in more explicit opposition to the hero.'[31]

The critics who have discussed him have seen the basic character of Diomede clearly enough, but they do not see clearly his great fluency. Neither Meech or Tatlock remarks on this, unless it is assumed when Tatlock talks of 'his cool technique as a seducer'.[32] But it emerges from a close analysis of the encounters between him and Criseyde that Diomede's verbal fluency and his cunning insight together bring off the deal—as he might see it. The dishonesty of his speech and the overt cupidity of his mind are skilfully exposed. It should, however, be noted that one critic sees none of this, for Paul E. Edmunds has said '. . . there is no valid reason for believing that Chaucer intended an indictment of Diomede.'[33]

And he goes so far as to claim 'Well may it be said that Diomede was also "a verray gentil, parfit knyght" [*sic*].' The misquotation perhaps weakens further a view to which few would assent; other critics and all readers I have known agree that Diomede is a villain of some sort. But, in assessing just how villainous he is, not enough notice has been taken of the poetic skill which Chaucer devotes to this character; the more attention that is paid to his subtle language the more inevitable it seems that someone who is truly 'tendre-herted, slydyng of corage' will be a victim to his assault. As a moral being, Diomede diminishes the more closely his style is studied.

As in the characterisations of Calchas, Ector and Antigone, Chaucer here modulates his style with an easy skill. In all four cases diction, rhythm, syntax, word-order and stanza-form all create differing tonal patterns to give to the poetry a force which shapes the full meaning of the passages, making meaning and mood grow together. In terms of literary technique alone it is an impressive achievement. In terms of our understanding of the poem as a whole, studying the style of these passages makes it clearer why the poem is so convincing. We are convinced of Calchas's crafty badness, of Ector's inarticulate and ultimately ineffectual nobility, of Antigone's sheer and insubstantial loveliness, and of Diomede's manipulative power; and so we see very plainly the pressures at work on Criseyde's emotional personality. The force of Chaucer's poetry consequently leads us to believe in the poem, to understand its moral drift and also to feel sympathy for the heroine. It is a remarkable achievement.

V. *The Narrator*

A good deal of recent criticism has discussed the figure of the narrator: the main concerns have been to establish to what extent he is separable from Chaucer and to what extent his views are valid or invalid in the light of the poem as a whole.[34] Little of this discussion has used the nature of the poetry as evidence. Talbot Donaldson and Robert O. Payne sometimes comment on the tone of a passage as well as its content,[35] but in general the criticism of the narrator has concentrated on the semantics of the poem. Also, this criticism has dealt mostly with the comments of the narrator within the body of the narrative, paying surprisingly little attention to the occasions when he speaks directly to the audience in his prohemia and at the close of the work. Dorothy Everett has said that 'Most of the rhetorical introductory passages are designed to prepare us for the action to follow',[36] but she does not study the passages in any detail. In this study I intend to concentrate on these prohemia, since I believe they offer, in varying degrees, valuable evidence towards an understanding of this great and often difficult poem; the narrator's formal speeches suggest the attitude in which we should read the narrative to which they are attached, and they also make implications about the varying and much-discussed relationship between the narrator and the poet.[37]

When we first meet the narrator he is in business-like mood; the first stanza of the poem opens with a line notable both for its reminiscence of the Iliad and for its crisp attack:

> The double sorwe of Troilus to tellen,
> That was the kyng Priamus sone of Troye,
> In lovynge, how his aventures fellen
> Fro wo to wele, and after out of joie,
> My purpose is, er that I parte fro ye.   I.1–5

The syntax is quite complex; the opening four lines are a good example of the unusual word-order the rhetoricians call *hyberbaton*, but the purpose of this, of the relative clause in line 2 and of the apposition in lines 3–4, appears to be to obtain a bold opening line. The stanza is not in any other way ornate; the diction is fairly simple and the last line of this opening sentence has a note of plainly-stated purpose: it has taken four packed lines to sketch briefly the topic of the poem, and the narrator's manly determination may well seem appropriate for the large task he has begun. As a whole this opening is neither plain nor ornate in tone, and in the following lines the poem's first invocation continues this note. It is an apostrophe to a divine figure, but it is a brisk one, using to the full the firm and final effect that is characteristic of the couplet that closes the rhyme royal stanza:

> Thesiphone, thow help me for t'endite
> Thise woful vers, that wepen as I write.   I.6–7

This note is typical of the whole prohemium. It is less complex than those to Books II and III, as we shall see. Its business is to make with dignity at a middle style the preliminaries appropriate to a love-tragedy on the large scale. The narrator invokes divine aid in stanza two and states his inadequacy in stanza three: but these formal commencing gestures, *invocatio* and *dubitatio*, do not hold the poem up, for there is a reasonably swift forward movement visible, as the last couplets of stanzas one and three raise the issues to be dealt with in the following stanza. These first three stanzas also have a firm repetitive pattern: in each case the opening four lines develop an issue (stanza one, topic; stanza two, *invocatio*; stanza three, *dubitatio*) and then the fifth line changes the movement, beginning with a short sequence of words followed by a pause. The exact articulation of the three stanzas at this point is different, but each then goes on to end with a firm couplet. There is regularity here, but it is not ornate *repetitio*; rather it suggests a competent and methodical movement through the necessary early stages of a long poem.

After these three stanzas of business, the prohemium continues to its end with one structural sequence. This passage is to an extent modelled on a bidding prayer, as Root observes in his note, and in this prayer the narrator asks his audience of lovers to intercede for all those connected with love, right down to the narrator himself. The prayer is the bulk of the prohemium, and its meaning is rarely examined in the light of the poem at large.[38] But, especially when the more common topics of opening prohemia are dealt with briskly, it must have importance, and I shall return to this when looking at the narrator's last speech to us. The importance of the prayer is mostly stressed by its position; it is not in high style—it shows, rather, a fluent middle style. There is some *repetitio* in the frequent imperatives but this is not obtrusive and if, as Kökeritz suggests, there is *adnominatio* between 'despeired' and 'apeired' in the sixth stanza it has little force.[39] The stanzas of the prayer flow evenly; the first two do not break at the fourth line, thus changing the deliberate note of the first three stanzas of the poem, but then stanzas six and seven return to this pausing form. Notably, stanza seven runs on into stanza eight, so making the more prominent the pause before line 52 where the narrator gathers himself for his closing remarks.

The prohemium exhibits the sorts of poetic skill and variation for effect that we find in most passages of Chaucerian narrative. But this is not stylistically obtrusive; the diction is not ornate and indeed the most striking single effect in the prohemium is the firm monosyllabic *sententiae* which appear, like:

> For wel sit it, the sothe for to seyne,
> A woful wight to han a drery feere,
> And to a sorwful tale, a sory chere.   I.12–14

or like:

> . . . thynketh how that ye
> Han felt that Love dorste yow displese,
> Or ye han wonne hym with to gret an ese.   I.26–8

But even this effect does not assault us to any great extent, for it can be combined with the flowingly polysyllabic, as in:

> . . . to shewe, in some manere,
> Swich peyne and wo as Loves folk endure,
> In Troilus unsely aventure.   I.33–5

In this prohemium, then, the narrator is able and informed, but he does not strike us forcibly with any one particular style; he is not brutally frank with us, nor does he have time to play with fancies. The prohemium uses no simile and no metaphor, except that embedded in words like 'instrument' in line 10. There is no prominent use of rhetorical device—*prosecutio* is the term to describe the overall effect. The relative simplicity of the prohemium is a muted and appropriate lead up to the vigorous beginning of the narrative of the poem: the narrator gets his action under way with four brisk, aggressive lines:

> Yt is wel wist how that the Grekes, stronge
> In armes, with a thousand shippes, wente
> To Troiewardes, and the cite longe
> Assegeden, neigh ten yer or they stente,   I.57–60

Disturbed in movement, dominated by heavy stresses, this passage uses enjambement not to create an intricate, delicate effect as we sometimes see, but to begin the lines with crisp clipped phrases.

The major purpose of this prohemium has been to provide a reasonably unobtrusive introduction to this action, but when we compare this prohemium with the effects of later ones this very neutrality becomes a distinctive quality. Here the narrator is a restrained and shadowy figure, not asserting himself through his style but merely stating his charitable concerns for lovers and opening his long poem modestly.

G

The prohemium to the second book begins differently, on a genuinely high note:

> Owt of thise blake wawes for to saylle,
> O wynd, o wynd, the weder gynneth clere;
> For in this see the boot hath swych travaylle,
> Of my connyng, that unneth I it steere.
> This see clepe I the tempestous matere
> Of disespeir that Troilus was inne;
> But now of hope the kalendes bygynne.   II.1–7

Here we find a large *translatio* of the sea; the metaphor is allowed to grow until the third line and then, in the next three lines, the narrator clarifies the referent of the metaphor without abandoning the metaphor itself. This leads to another *translatio* in line 7: here the metaphor lies in 'kalendes', and though the idea is new in this stanza there is a reasonable consistency between a metaphor of sea-storms and one derived from the calendar. These metaphors are not original, of course (see Root's note on this passage), but neither are they entirely derivative; even if they were, the quality of the style would give them life, for it is rich and vivid.

The opening line addresses us firmly, building itself around the powerful phrase 'blake wawes', and in the second line the poet uses *conduplicatio* to add power to his *exclamatio* in 'O wynd, o wynd.' The syntax is fairly complex at times, notably in the placing of the two phrases 'Of my connyng', and 'of hope', and this prevents the stanza from ever becoming predictable. The language is lofty— 'travaylle', 'tempestous' and 'disespeir' are the obvious examples— and, from within the second metaphor, the learned term 'kalendes' strengthens this aspect of the stanza. As a whole, then, the stanza has a forceful and lively richness that transmits vividly the dramatic metaphors and gives us an expectation of a high-style prohemium.

The following stanza seems to question this expectation, for it scarcely maintains the pitch of its predecessor:

> O lady myn, that called art Cleo,
> Thow be my speed fro this forth, and my Muse,
> To ryme wel this book til I have do;
> Me nedeth here noon othere art to use.
> Forwhi to every lovere I me excuse,
> That of no sentement I this endite,
> But out of Latyn in my tonge it write.   II.8–14

This stanza is very interesting, for in it the narrator rejects the artistry he has just shown in the first stanza. He invokes the muse of history, that factual subject, and asks her in a simple manner to help him 'ryme wel this book, til I have do'. He needs 'noon othere art' than that of the competent historian, for this is no personal testimony; the poem is not written out of 'sentement' and, as Root remarks in his note, 'sentement' here means 'experiential knowledge'. The narrator is distancing himself from the activities and emotions he is reporting—he merely copies his material out of 'Latyn', he claims. But the stanza does not only state the objective position of the narrator; it also establishes a fitting stylistic medium for this objectivity. The opening lines are clearly opposed to the rich rhetoric of the first stanza. The first line opens with a fairly simple *exclamatio*, but the following material in no way supports even this moderate ornamentation. The second and third lines are notably monosyllabic, simple in word-order and syntax, and there is no metaphor here. The stanza does not only oppose the high style of the first with its own plain style, but the exact import of the lower style is also made clear within it. The narrator says, basing his line on two reasonably elevated French words:

> That of no sentement I this endite,

And then he clarifies what he does do in a line without one word even slightly elaborate:

> But out of Latyn in my tonge it write.

King Alfred himself could have written that line, in terms of vocabulary at least. These two lines act out the tension of the first two stanzas, where the narrator juxtaposes the high ornate style of personal feeling and the strong plain style of objective reporting—and chooses the latter.

The movement of these two fine stanzas dramatises stylistically the attitude of the narrator at this stage. He is aware that his topic has histrionic potential—hence his first stanza—but his attitude is to be quite different; he himself does not accept the high-flown passion, he keeps himself disengaged from the course of the action and the issues that are concerned in it. The third stanza makes this disengagement quite specific and makes it in plain, blunt language:

> Wherefore I nyl have neither thank ne blame
> Of al this werk, but prey yow mekely,
> Disblameth me, if any word be lame,
> For as myn auctor seyde, so sey I.

> Ek though I speeke of love unfelyngly,
> No wondre is, for it nothyng of newe is;
> A blynd man kan nat juggen wel in hewis.   II.15–21

The simple *sententia* that ends this stanza draws together completely
the style and meaning of this sequence. In the following two stanzas
the narrator extends his disengagement: he himself is not personally
engaged, we know, and now he suggests in a series of confiding
sententiae that we might not find the behaviour of the lovers fully
convincing. Their language could seem strange:

> Ye knowe ek that in forme of speche is chaunge
> Withinne a thousand yeer, and wordes tho
> That hadden pris, now wonder nyce and straunge
> Us thinketh hem, and yet thei spake hem so,   II.22–5

And a modern lover, he suggests, might well find the actions in-
credible:

> And forthi if it happe in any wyse,
> That here be any lovere in this place
> That herkneth, as the storie wol devise,
> How Troilus com to his lady grace,
> And thenketh, 'so nold I nat love purchace,'
> Or wondreth on his speche or his doynge,
> I noot;   II.29–35

These remarks do, of course, protect the poem against some
sorts of literal-minded criticism, but the major effect of this caution—
a type of *dubitatio*—is to enlarge the distance between the narrator
and his topic: he claims little immediacy for any of it. He explains
the issue directly in the sixth stanza:

> For every wight which that to Rome went,
> Halt nat o path, nor alwey o manere;
> Ek in som lond were al the game shent,
> If that they ferde in love as men don here,
> As thus, in opyn doyng, or in chere,
> In visityng, in forme, or seyde hire sawes;
> Forthi men seyn, ecch contree hath his lawes.   II.36–42

These stanzas indicate both an attitude towards the material of the
story and a developed personality in the narrator. In the prohemium
to Book I the narrator made merely conventional gestures about

himself; the emphasis there was on lovers, their stormy lives and their need for charity. Only the neutrality of the style there implied the narrator's detached position. Here, in a prohemium much more firmly devoted to the narrator's persona, he states overtly his aloof personality in the matter of his words and in their style. The last stanza is extremely blunt and to the point:

> Ek scarsly ben ther in this place thre
> That have in love seid lik, and don, in al;
> For to thi purpos this may liken the,
> And the right nought, yit al is seid, or schal;
> Ek some men grave in tree, som in ston wal,
> As it bitit; but syn I have bigonne,
> Myn auctor shal I folwen, if I konne.   II.43–9

This is lower in style than the opening stanza; it is basically monosyllabic throughout and, especially in lines 44, 45 and 46–7, very compressed: after these lines the brief clause 'As it bitit' has an even more clipped effect than if it stood alone. There is a striking *similitudo* in line 47, but its force is blunt and simple, that of a proverbial simile, not that of the lofty metaphor of the opening stanza: it is tersely expressed and its basic elements, 'tree' and 'ston wal,' are down to earth in character. Throughout the prohemium, then, we find this movement from a high to a humble style, as the narrator states his position and shows his dissatisfaction with the ornate rhetoric that was used in the first stanza to describe Troilus's torment, and which is typically spoken by Troilus throughout the poem.

In the book which is to follow, Troilus's high passionate style is to be seen in conflict with Pandarus's lower style, as Muscatine has demonstrated. Looking at it in a restricted way, this prohemium questions Troilus's style, which against Pandarus's might have appeared truly noble and fine to the medieval audience. But speaking in larger terms we can go farther. Here the verse helps to create the mood of the book, to establish the poem at a distance from Troilus's passionate reactions. The theme of its action will be the reduction of Troilus's nobility to a concern with physical issues: Troilus does not recognise the dislocation between his lofty style and the mundane concerns which come to obsess him and which end in mundane disasters, but the narrator's chosen tone does suit a cool study of Troilus's predicament. Here we see sharply defined the 'distance' that M. W. Bloomfield discusses in his article (see note 38). There is in this way an appropriateness in the narrator's chosen tone which determines the outlook of the whole poem. At the end of the poem the narrator will again speak for the whole book, but in a different style entirely. But before we come to this we find the narrator, in the prohemium to Book III, speaking in a loftier way and again his words have specific purposes in the light of the whole poem.

The third prohemium displays no internal change of style, as did the second, and all seven stanzas move in a fairly elevated way in terms of diction, structure and ornament. The first stanza sets the tone:

> O blisful light, of which the bemes clere
> Adorneth al the thriddle heven faire!
> O sonnes lief, O Joves doughter deere,
> Plesance of love, O goodly debonaire,
> In gentil hertes ay redy to repaire!
> O veray cause of heele and of gladnesse,
> Iheryed be thy myght and thi goodnesse!   III.1–7

The narrator appeals to Venus in the form of *apostrophe* and he addresses her in many guises—it is the rich device of *interpretatio* and some of the terms—'lief' and 'Plesance' are *pronominatio*. There is a good deal of metaphor involved, and the lack of connective words (*dissolutio*) gives an intensifying repetitive effect. The linguistic keystone of the stanza is the main verb in the last line, but this only completes the praise of Venus which has already been given in vocative form. The rhetorical ornament is thus basic to the sense and structure of the stanza. The language is reasonably elevated— 'Adorneth', and, perhaps, 'Plesance' and 'debonaire' give a certain fineness to the stanza,[40] and although the act of praising in the last line is stated straightforwardly enough the line is not quite plain. It is well balanced, with a rather simple *compar* in 'thy myght and thi goodenesse' and 'Iheryed' is a word of some elevation, though of Old English stock.[41]

As a whole the style here is rich, dominated by the figure of *interpretatio*, often used in formal *apostrophe*. The high style is appropriate to the topic, for the stanza celebrates the power of love: it is an idealised love, a love which finds a place in heaven, and the poetry of the stanza creates an impression of the loftiness of the ideal.

The second stanza also glorifies love, and continues at the same level of stylistic richness, but there is a shift of topic and an appropriate change of tone. The stanza opens with *compar*, the poised, balanced language that ended the first stanza:

> In hevene and helle, in erthe and salte see,
> Is felt thi myght, if that I wel descerne;   III.8–9

But this balance is quite overset in the next line; here we have a vigorous multiplication of stresses, the figure that the rhetoricians call *articulus*:

> As man, bird, best, fissh, herbe, and grene tree
> Thee fele in tymes with vapour eterne.   III.10–11

It is a daring and in my judgment an entirely successful attempt to catch in verse the surging vigour of the created world; here the narrator honours love as it actually appears on earth, not as it is in ideal terms. Elsewhere Chaucer has used conventional lists to convey this impression, as we have seen in *The Parlement of Foules*. Here, with the boldness characteristic of the poet who dominates his medium, he crams the line with strong monosyllables, bursting through the familiar metric pattern of the Chaucerian line just as earthly life bursts out under the benign influence of Venus and her 'vapour eterne'. The procreative spirit is suggested with startling success. This fine effect is pressed home in the next line when God himself is associated with this great driving force; we are told in a firm one-line statement:

> God loveth, and to love wol nought werne;   III.12

The meaning of these lines is now made clearer in two lines of *conclusio*, which are more muted in their style and which bring this dramatic stanza to a decelerating close:

> And in this world no lyves creature
> Withouten love is worth, or may endure.   III.13–4

In these two stanzas, then, we have seen a use of ornament and variation which immediately places the passage on the higher levels of style. It would be quite wrong to think that for the style to be 'high' it can only use the more obviously intricate figures like the *interpretatio* of the first stanza. That is a formal, almost incantatory figure which admirably suits an apostrophe to an idealised concept like Love, but the powerful *articulus* of the second stanza is just as 'high' and as well suited to its topic. The difference of effect is important, but it is a difference between varieties of high style, not between levels of style.

Both of these stanzas, and those which follow, are translated fairly directly from Boccaccio (see Root's note for details), but it seems to me that this in no way alters our judgment of them. In the

first stanza the poise and balance of Chaucer's English fully create
the notion of loftiness and in the second he makes us sense the vigour
of earthly love very strongly (more strongly than Boccaccio does, in
fact). We have no feeling that these stanzas are derivative as we read
them and if we, with our modern predispositions, find the earthly
second stanza more immediate than the lofty first stanza, then that
may be our loss. The medieval poet offers two stanzas, replete with
poetic richnesses of different sorts, in praise of love.

The rest of this prohemium cannot, perhaps, excite us as much as
this opening, but it remains complex; the fifth stanza is a typical
example:

> Ye holden regne and hous in unitee;
> Ye sothfast cause of frendshipe ben also;
> Ye knowe al thilke covered qualitee
> Of thynges, which that folk on wondren so,
> Whan they kan nought construe how it may jo,
> She loveth hym, or whi he loveth here,
> As whi this fissh, and naught that, comth to were.

III.29–35

Here the diction is not uniformly high; 'unitee' and 'qualitee' give
the rhyming an aureate air, yet the opposing rhyme is simply 'also'
and 'so'. But the third rhyme is the very rare word 'jo' and 'construe'
in the same line has elevation.[42] In a piece of fairly obtrusive *repetitio* 'Ye' appears three times, continuing the apostrophe begun in
stanza one, and the lines it heads have the even balance of *compar*.
The fourth line, 'Of thynges, which that folk on wondren so', breaks
the *repetitio*, but itself has a complex and balanced structure. The
balance of the sixth line is transformed in the last line into a much
slower *conclusio* that is based on a rather colloquial *similitudo*. The
stanza is not really high, but it could not be described as humble by
any means, and indeed the colloquial last line has some of the sharp
contrast which is often praised by the rhetoricians as a momentary
relief of lofty style.

Since this stanza is not totally in the same style as the opening
stanzas, it seems wise to look at the end of this prohemium, which, it
may confidently be assumed, will have some clear relationship with
the rest of the prohemium, either as support or as contrast:

> Ye in my naked herte sentement
> Inhielde, and do me shewe of thy swetnesse.—
> Caliope, thi vois be now present,

For now is nede; sestow nought my destresse,
How I mot telle anonright the gladnesse
Of Troilus, to Venus heryinge?
To which gladnesse, who nede hath, God hym brynge! III.43–9

In the beginning of this stanza we see the continued *apostrophe* that has formed the structure of the whole prohemium; it is couched here in fairly elaborate language and rather more elaborate organisation —both poetic and syntactic, as the use of 'Inhielde' in the second line shows, for it is striking in both ways. Calliope is conjured in fairly plain words and we miss the metaphorical fireworks of the opening stanza, but the variety of the pauses, the nervousness of the line here, never lets the stanza as a whole fall into the plain style which is briefly and contrastively caught in 'For now is nede'. The sixth line, 'Of Troilus, to Venus heryinge?' is perhaps typical of the tense poetry seen in this stanza. The final line uses again that tripartite movement found in stanzas two, three and five here and the prohemium is brought to a slow, falling end.

Although this stanza is not notable for startling rhetorical effects, it is not at all plain in style when we compare it with, say, the end of the second prohemium. The whole invocation here maintains itself at a reasonably elevated level, with local variations, especially in the final lines of the stanzas, but no basic shift in level appears as it did in the prohemium to Book II: the fineness of the opening stanzas is not quite matched by those that follow it, but it is certainly not contradicted by them. What relation might this poetic judgment have to the book it precedes, and to the rest of the work?

It is important to realise that in keeping this prohemium at a reasonably high level throughout, Chaucer, through the person of his narrator, is honouring Venus and is working with great care on a delicate issue. He is not, I suggest, entirely separate from the narrator when he talks of 'my destresse' in the last stanza, and he is not merely filling in time when he celebrates Venus's power. The poem as a whole is to examine and reject the powers and values of Venus, it is to set aside certain mundane values in favour of other, non-terrestrial ones. But Chaucer does not spurn the world, his poem is not a monastic tract. This prohemium sets itself to show firmly how love, personified in Venus, is a genuine force for good and it seems no accident that one of the best lines here directly states the fructifying power of love:

As man, brid, best, fissh, herbe, and grene tre
Thee fele . . .

The point of the poem is not that Troilus loves an earthly woman, but that he loves her to the exclusion of all else, as most modern commentators have agreed. This prohemium takes great care to give Venus as *Natura naturans* an important part in human life; here Chaucer deals with the issue that Malory raises at the beginning of 'The Knight of the Cart' chapter in his 'Tale of Lancelot and Guinevere' and the issue that Spenser explores in the Mutability Cantos. And if we are to assess Chaucer adequately as a poet it is vital to see that it is by the force of his poetry that he asserts the twin nature of Venus and her power, as much as by the simple meaning of the prohemium. This fine prohemium as a whole gives Venus a place in human life, but a place which Troilus, to his sorrow, will assess wrongly. That mistake is foreshadowed in the last line of the prohemium, when the narrator says darkly:

> To which gladnesse, who nede hath, God hym brynge!

This can be read in several ways, but 'who nede hath' must make us wonder how great is Troilus's need, and what other needs he might have. With this last hint the prohemium has done its complex work; it has provided a just celebration of Venus, against which we are to contrast the place that Troilus and Criseyde give to her, revealed in the compelling ironies that are especially prevalent in Book III. It is for this purpose that Chaucer has, in an inspired moment, taken these stanzas from the fallible mouth of Boccaccio's Troilo and given them to the narrator. Here I can see no real sign that the narrator does not speak for, even as, the author. His words state the position of the poem, acting as an implicit commentary on the action to follow; against them we see developing the inordinate love of Troilus, but the contrast remains implicit. The narrator is to pass through a long period of self-effacement before he speaks to us explicitly about Troilus and the moral to be drawn from the poem.

The keynote of the prohemium to Book IV is set by the fact that it opens with a clause which is dependent on the last line of Book III:

> But al to litel, weylaway the whyle,
> Lasteth swich joie,   IV.1–2

The 'swich' stresses the relationship with III.1818–20:[43]

> My thridde bok now ende ich in this wyse,
> And Troilus in lust and in quiete
> Is with Criseyde, his owen herte swete. .

The fourth prohemium is short, and it most resembles the first one;

it states briefly what is to follow and how this affects the narrator's feelings:

> From Troilus she gan hire brighte face
> Awey to writhe, and tok of hym non heede,
> But caste hym clene out of his lady grace,
> And on hire whiel she sette up Diomede;
> For which right now myn herte gynneth blede,
> And now my penne, allas! with which I write,
> Quaketh for drede of that I moste endite.   IV.8–14

The diction of the stanza is simple, the syntax straightforward. By now the narrator has become established as a persona, it would seem, for the only point which is stressed here is how sad he feels at the events:

> Allas! that they sholde evere cause fynde
> To speke hire harm, and if they on hire lye,
> Iwis, hemself sholde han the vilanye.   IV.19–21

The fourth and last stanza invokes the Furies and Mars; there is no elaboration in the language that summons them, and the stanza has a rather weak ending:

> O ye Herynes, Nyghtes doughtren thre,
> That endeles compleignen evere in pyne,
> Megera, Alete, and ek Thesiphone;
> Thow cruel Mars ek, fader to Quyryne,
> This ilke ferthe book me helpeth fyne,
> So that the losse of lyf and love yfeere
> Of Troilus be fully shewed heere.   IV.22–8

I doubt if this ending is meant to have bathos about it, but it is certainly far from a grand conclusion; this presumably stems from the basic unobtrusiveness of the whole prohemium: it almost vanishes in the progress of the narrative, just as the narrator himself has little part to play in the progress of the fourth book. There is no large point to establish here as there was in each of the first three prohemia, and we are merely reminded of the presence outside the framework of a narrator capable of feeling about, and commenting on the action. The dominance of the narrative over its formal framework reaches a logical conclusion in Book V, which is quite without a prohemium.[44] Its opening stanza makes something like an invocation to the Fates, but it is in fact a part of the narrative:

> Aprochen gan the fatal destyne
> That Joves hath in disposicioun,
> And to yow, angry Parcas, sustren thre,
> Committeth, to don execucioun;
> For which Criseyde moste out of the town,
> And Troilus shal dwellen forth in pyne
> Til Lachesis his thred no lenger twyne.　V.1–7

There is, then, a sense of fitness and balance when we come to the long sequence of direct comment by the narrator at the end of Book V: this is not merely appropriate because the poem is ending, but it is necessary because there is a structural need for the narrator to speak outside the frame in this book as he has in each other one.

The action of Book V as a whole is separated from the ending of the poem by the *envoi* which comes surprisingly early at lines 1786–99. Then, as a preliminary to the narrator's speech rather than as a conclusion to the action, Chaucer recounts the death of Troilus and his ascent to a heaven of a sort. The reason for Troilus's favoured end has exercised most critics of the poem; the theological mechanics of the plot are not the topic of this study, but it seems relevant here to recall the stress placed in the first prohemium on the 'bidding prayer'. This asked the audience of lovers to pray for Troilus and those in his case 'That love hem brynge in heven to solas' (I.31). Troilus's ascent may be the act of a baffling sort of grace, but it is not inconsistent in the poem; we have heard before about such grace coming from a love greater than Troilus's earth-bound variety, and this prolepsis of the end of the poem seems to me the reason why so much emphasis is placed on this issue in the first prohemium.

Troilus's ascent is recounted in the urbane, swift-moving style that is typical of most of the action of the poem:

> And in hymself he lough right at the wo
> Of hem that wepten for his deth so faste;
> And dampned al oure werk that foloweth so
> The blynde lust, the which that may nat laste,
> And sholden al oure herte on heven caste.
> And forth he wente, shortly for to telle,
> Ther as Mercurye sorted hym to dwelle.　V.1821–7

It is a direct sort of poetry, moving with speed and confidence— with such confidence at one point that the syntax shifts sharply, but the effect is not at all harsh; the fluency of the poetry enables us to assume easily a subject like 'we' for 'sholden' in line 1825.[45] As the narrator begins to comment on this situation and upon the whole poem as it is now being expounded, his style changes sharply. It becomes more elaborate, using *repetitio* and *compar* to make a formal *exclamatio*:

> Swich fyn hath, lo, this Troilus for love!
> Swich fyn hath al his grete worthynesse!
> Swich fyn hath his estat real above,
> Swich fyn his lust, swich fyn hath his noblesse!
> Swych fyn hat false worldes brotelnesse!
> And thus bigan his lovyng of Criseyde,
> As I have told, and in this wise he deyde.   V.1828–34

The last two lines are less formal, but they do not act as bathos; the power of the stanza remains and it may well be that their comparative simplicity allows the total effect to avoid a note of exaggeration. Overall, the stanza is formal and rather stiff, and this suits well its rather stiff message: in it the narrator rejects the value of Troilus's life, as he chose to lead it. Indeed, things which have seemed fine in the poem—his 'grete worthynesse' and his 'noblesse' are here placed on the same level as 'false worldes brotelnesse'. It is a strong, even a stern stanza, setting out the negative side of the poem's judgment.

The following stanza is quite different; its task is to outline a more positive judgment, to describe a fuller, more enduring way of life. The style changes into something much more fluent and vital:

> O yonge, fresshe folkes, he or she,
> In which that love up groweth with youre age,
> Repeyreth hom fro worldly vanyte,
> And of youre herte up casteth the visage
> To thilke God that after his ymage
> Yow made, and thynketh al nys but a faire
> This world, that passeth soone as floures faire.   V.1835–41

The diction here is fairly simple, though there is some richness in the rhymes 'vanyte', 'visage' and 'ymage'; there is inventiveness in the rather charming metaphor of the heart's 'visage' and lyricism in the simile of the world as a fair. The poetry supports this effect of natural charm, for the lines are extremely fluid in their movement: the first line pauses at 'folkes' and then runs on to 'age' in a line and a half in which nothing makes us pause, neither heavy stress nor hard consonants (although two plosives fall together in 'up groweth', the *p* is unexploded). 'Repeyreth' begins the third line with a stress greater than any in the previous line; the fourth line, like the second, is light-stressed in its first half. So even lines three and four, which are more nearly end-stopped than the rest of the stanza, are extremely varied in movement. The remaining lines flow into each other smoothly until the stanza closes with the firm stressing, alliteration and *rime riche* of 'floures faire'. The familiar double simile in the last two lines does not seem trite here, as it does in other poems: rather it is a simple and fitting resolution to the stanza, for the delicately shifting verse finally comes to rest in the repeated 'faire'. The *rime riche*, perhaps because of this, avoids its innate danger of predictability, and suggests rather the ambiguity of the word 'faire'—a point close to the centre of the poem's meaning.

But while the stanza flows beautifully, nothing about it seems lofty or formally noble in style; it presents the peaceful beauty of the life that the narrator here advocates. Talbot Donaldson has characterised the stanza as having 'sweetness of tone',[46] and alone, perhaps, it would strike us as being nothing more than mellifluous—but following the stiff previous stanza it is something of a release in style, as it is a release in meaning.

What is said about this stanza applies generally to the opening of the next, which specifies further the positive judgment of the poem:

> And loveth hym, the which that right for love
> Upon a crois, oure soules for to beye,
> First starf, and roos, and sit in hevene above; V.1842-4

The first two lines flow as the previous stanza did: there is a change in the third line, though, as the narrator states in a familiar form of words the majesty and authority of Christ—'First starf, and roos, and sit in hevene above'. The slowing effect of this seems final, and this finality becomes comprehensible in the next lines where we see that this tripartite line, a pattern commonly used by Chaucer for a *rallentando*, is the end, temporarily, of the narrator's positive words. In the next lines he turns back to the negative, to the topic of falseness:

> For he nyl falsen no wight, dar I seye,
> That wol his herte al holly on hym leye.
> And syn he best to love is, and most meke,
> What nedeth feynede loves for to seke? V.1845-8

This rather curious change of direction comes from Chaucer's decision to have a double structure in this ending. The last six stanzas of the poem do, to a considerable extent, stand as two groups of three stanzas, and the stylistic variation in each trio is similar. Having turned back now to the negative side, Chaucer makes another formal rejection of the values embodied in the action of the poem, and so begins the second trio. It is hard to see why Chaucer chose this double pattern. It may have been so that his closing prayer could be truly celebratory rather than argumentative; the end of the first trio is a *contrarium*, a negative proof (seen as a figure of speech it is called this; if it were regarded structurally it would be called *oppositio*, one of the devices of *amplificatio*[47]), while the second trio ends with forceful positiveness. These remarks are, however, analysis and not explanation, and all that can be said really about the structure of this final sequence is that the writer has decided on this pattern and that the power of his verse makes the pattern authoritative.

The formality that began the first trio of stanzas now returns:

> Lo here, of payens corsed olde rites,
> Lo here, what alle hire goddes may availle;
> Lo here, thise wrecched worldes appetites;
> Lo here, the fyn and guerdoun for travaille
> Of Jove, Appollo, of Mars, of swich rascaille!
> Lo here, the forme of olde clerkis speche
> In poetrie, if ye hire bokes seche!   V.1849–55

As in the earlier instance, the body of the stanza is stiffly repetitive and the two less highly wrought lines sum up the whole issue discussed in the stanza. The repetitive list is one line longer here than before, but the variation of the penultimate line is again present; this feature gives greater finality to the last of the repetitive lines.

The rejection stanza is not, this time, followed immediately by flowing verse, though that is to come. Whereas before the verse flowed for a stanza and a half and was then slower for a half-stanza, here the pattern is reversed. We have now a rather quiet and business-like four lines, elevated by a little high diction, as a final *envoi* is given:

> O moral Gower, this book I directe
> To the and to the, philosophical Strode,
> To vouchen sauf, ther nede is, to correcte,
> Of youre benignites and zeles goode.   V.1856–9

The fact that each *envoi* comes before the end of the poem might suggest that Chaucer prized highly the real end: it is certainly well introduced, for after this momentary breather in the moral discussion that is taking place, the poet (and in this closing sequence poet and narrator seem quite indistinguishable) carefully leads his penultimate stanza up to a point of high expectation:

> And to that sothefast Crist, that starf on rode,
> With al myn herte of mercy evere I preye,
> And to the Lord right thus I speke and seye: V.1860–2

A lesser poet would not have had the courage to bring us forward on our seats like this—how, he might have wondered, can the poem be ended without disappointment? Fortunately, Chaucer can fulfil his poetic promises. The last stanza is perhaps the most beautifully measured that even he ever wrote. It is in two sentences. The first is:

> Thow oon, and two, and thre, eterne on lyve,
> That regnest ay in thre, and two, and oon,
> Uncircumscript, and al maist circumscrive,
> Us from visible and invisible foon
> Defende;

The four complete lines have an excellent balance, but not the sort of balance which stops the poetry and gives it a final note. The first two lines have a similar chime, yet it is not a simple parallelism, for one line reverses the movement of the other: the first ascends and the second descends: the two lines together form a *commutatio*. The next two lines are perfectly balanced within themselves, but, again, stiffness is avoided: it is not the heavy, even artificial balance of pure *commutatio* in one line where two elements in the first half-line are reversed in the second. The sound of these two lines is supple and simply poised: there is *contentio* here and *compar* but the balance is not weighty enough to make us stop. Nor can we stop here syntactically, for we have not yet had a verb: with a brilliant *coup de théâtre*, the sharp imperative verb which works against the balance of the first four lines is the prayer which man sends to God—'Defende'. The balances of the first four lines express the peace and rest to be found in God, things not expressed before in the poem, and this divine balance is opposed by man's urgent single prayer. Man's voice is not in this balance, but seeks a relation with it, cries out toward it. It is a triumph of poetic modulation, and the meaning of the stanza is inseparable from the forceful *brevitas* of that one word 'Defende'.

After this Chaucer allows the poem to come at last to a peaceful close, explaining just what he implies in the passionate 'Defende':

> . . . and to thy mercy, everichon,
> So make us, Jesus, for thi mercy digne,
> For love of mayde and moder thyn benigne. V.1867–9

It is perhaps appropriate that the last line of a poem so concerned with sexuality should finally speak of the 'mayde and moder', that the very last word of a poem so full of self-seeking characters should be 'benigne', a word that denotes a movement away from the self. It is in this quality that man may indeed hope to rhyme with God and be 'digne' of his mercy.

In these final stanzas the narrator speaks out at last with an unqualified high style: he has finally found a topic which deserves the poetic richness that we have seen he can utter but which, as the second prohemium implies, is squandered on mundane topics. Alone of the characters in the poem the narrator reserves his true enthusiasm, embodied in his noble eloquence, for the unchangeable. So the narrator at last speaks directly on the issues of the poem, and his style is throughout elevated, though it can vary to suit the nature of what he is saying. In each of his five formal appearances, the four prohemia and this final speech, the narrator has prompted in the reader an attitude towards the poem at the relevant stage. The five formal appearances do not link up into a coherent characterisation of the narrator; rather, they are carefully organised commentaries on the material of the books to which they belong, and on the poem as far as it has gone at the time. And as I have tried to show here, in each of them Chaucer's sense of style (and the meaning that style can bear) is a vital part of their overall success.

NOTES

1. See Chapter V, pp. 132–61.
2. 'Chaucer's Puns', *PMLA*, LXXI (1956), 225–46, see p. 232.
3. Kökeritz's article is 'Rhetorical Word-Play in Chaucer', *PMLA*, LXIX (1954), 937–52.
4. '*Petrus id est Christus*: Word Play in Piers Plowman, the B-Text', *ELH*, XVII (1950), 163–90.
5. There is no precise rhetorician's terms for the 'sinking' effect which seems fully relevant here; *extenuatio* seems the closest. In *A Handbook to Sixteenth Century Rhetoric* (London, 1968), Lee Sonnino translates Quintilian's description of it as 'Meagreness and inadequacy of expression'. Scaliger's remark under the general heading of *eclipsis* also seems relevant: 'We may detract from the value of something by substituting a worse name for the name of something known already to be bad, or by using a lesser style to phrase a particular proposition.' See Sonnino, p. 95.
6. See R. A. Pratt, 'Chaucer and *Le Roman de Troyle et de Criseida*', *SP*, LIII (1956), 509–39, see p. 513.
7. P. 948.
8. This is probably why Kökeritz does not comment on the jingles here: his concern is with proper word-play and with *rime riche* as an extension of it.

H

9. 'Calchas in the Early Versions of the Troilus Story', *Tulane Studies in English*, IV (1954), 5–20, see p. 16.
10. 'The People in Chaucer's Troilus', *PMLA*, LVI (1941), 85–104, see p. 102.
11. See pp. vii and 142.
12. See above, p. xvii–xviii.
13. See 'The Wife of Bath's Prologue and Tale', 1–6.
14. Chaucer gives names to Antigone, Flexippe and Tharbe in this scene, to the off-stage figures Poliphete, Horaste (if he exists) and Argyve, Criseyde's mother. The owl is Escaphilo, V.319. It is tempting to see a similarity with Malory here: he also habitually names people and places which go unspecified in the sources.
15. P. 949.
16. Antigone's Song of Love', *MLN*, XXV (1910), 158.
17. Sister M. Charlotte Borthwick, 'Antigone's Song as "Mirour" in Chaucer's *Troilus and Criseyde*', *MLQ*, XXII (1961), 227–35.
18. P. 230.
19. See 'The Franklin's Prologue and Tale', 1016–18 and p. 196 below.
20. 'Chaucer's Dealings with a Stanza of *Il Filostrato* and the Epilogue of Troilus and Criseyde', *MAE*, XXXIII (1964), 36–46.
21. The fullest discussion of animal metaphors in the poem is by Sanford B. Meech in his voluminous study *Design in Chaucer's Troilus* (Syracuse, 1953), see Chap. III, Section 6, 'The Brute Creation', pp. 320–32.
22. P. 230.
23. See the two well-known essays by Kaske and Donaldson in *Critical Approaches to Medieval Literature*, ed. Dorothy Bethurum (New York, 1960); also see Kaske's review article on Robertson's book, 'Chaucer and Medieval Allegory', *ELH*, XXX (1963), 175–92, and Paul Piehler's comments in *The Visionary Landscape: A Study in Medieval Allegory* (London, 1971), pp. 79–80.
24. Oxford, 1970.
25. 'The Function of the Proverbial Monitory Elements in Chaucer's Troilus and Criseyde', *Tulane Studies in English*, II (1950), 5–48.
26. P. 79; Muscatine concurs with this view, p. 163.
27. P. 114.
28. P. 102.
29. P. 71.
30. 'Diomede: The Traditional Development of a Character', *Essays and Studies in English and Comparative Literature, University of Michigan Publications, Language and Literature*, VIII (Ann Arbor, 1932), pp. 1–25; I quote from p. 24.
31. P. 10.
32. P. 94.
33. 'A Defense of Chaucer's Diomede', *Classical Folia*, XVI (1962), 110–23, see pp. 121 and 123.
34. A. C. Baugh's bibliography gives a number of references to studies of the narrator. Robert Jordan's article 'The Narrator in Chaucer's *Troilus*', *ELH*, XXV (1958), 237–57 is the most important of these. Interesting discussions not mentioned by Baugh are Chapters 6 and 7 in R. O. Payne's *The Key of Remembrance* (New Haven, 1963) which discuss the narrator *passim*; Chapters I and III in Ida Gordon's book; and 'Criseyde and her Narrator', Chapter 5 in Donaldson's *Speaking of Chaucer*. There are also some perceptive remarks about the narrator in Donaldson's 'The Ending of Troilus', printed as Chapter 6 in the same book.
35. Donaldson, pp. 72, 96 and 97–9; Payne, pp. 211–16.
36. In *Essays on Middle English Literature*, Chap. V, 'Troilus and Criseyde'; I quote from p. 131.
37. Root suggests the prohemia to Books II, III and IV may be late work, see p. xii; this may lend support to the view that they are of considerable importance.
38. This prohemium is not often mentioned; Meech and Gordon both pass over it. Jordan makes some reference, p. 239, and M. W. Bloomfield has a longer comment

in 'Distance and Predestination in *Troilus and Criseyde*', *PMLA*, LXXII (1957), 14-26, see p. 20.

39. P. 949.
40. Chaucer is the first to use 'adorn' in English and only uses it here; he is also the first to use 'plesance' and, in its absolute form as here, 'debonaire', though he does use both words quite frequently.
41. Chaucer uses the word ten times in the past participial form (six of them in this poem), and as it always appears in the context of a prayer, the word seems to have an elevated connotation.
42. Trevisa and Langland use 'construe', probably before Chaucer did, but he only uses it three times; 'jo' is even rarer: it appears only here in his work and is an etymological puzzle—cf. Robinson's note on it.
43. Root observes, p. xiii, that some scribes, presumably misled by this bold link, wrongly attached the prohemium of Book IV to the end of Book III.
44. I cannot agree with Root that the opening stanza constitutes a prohemium, cf. his note 5, p. xiii.
45. Donaldson comments shrewdly on this, p. 97.
46. Pp. 97-9.
47. For a discussion of *amplificatio* see pp. 168-72 below.

3. *The Knight's Tale*

The meaning of 'The Knight's Tale' has been the main concern of its critics. Since R. K. Root suggested that it did not have very much meaning at all most writers have argued that he was wrong, demonstrating just how they think the tale is meaningful.[1] A critical orthodoxy has been established, principally through three articles published within a short period by W. H. French, William Frost and Charles Muscatine:[2] they showed to the satisfaction of most readers that the tale is a carefully ordered discussion of human affairs in a superhuman context. They argued that its plot moves according to expectation because Palamon and Arcite are not identical, though they are very similar, and that Theseus is both an embodiment of earthly authority and an interpreter of the ways of Divine Providence.

The structure of the tale has been discussed in terms of its meaning (particularly by Muscatine) but not in terms of itself, and this seems an area where much more could be said, particularly in the light of recent studies in Chaucerian structure. The characterisation of the poem has been thoroughly explored; in fact argument about the meaning of the tale has concentrated on the characters because most critics agree that they are not full characterisations, but are more correctly seen as schematic representations of certain characteristics, and so can be taken as fairly overt channels of meaning—John Halverson says that 'All the characters are, of course, essentially flat; no attempt has been made to achieve psychological dimension'.[3]

And Elizabeth Salter goes further:[4]

Chaucer shows himself far more interested in predicaments than personalities. His lovers, Palamon and Arcite, are distinguishable mainly for their allegiance to differing gods, and the consequences of this—not for their sharply differing characters.

These views of the tale and these methods of approaching it have been common to most recent critics; in addition to those mentioned already, Paul G. Ruggiers, A. C. Spearing and Rodney Delasanta have made notable contributions to the discussion along these lines.[5] The situation is not as settled as this summary might imply, for each critic modifies or supplies some element in the critique—like Spearing's radical treatment of Theseus' last speech[6]—and there are writers like A. H. Marckwardt who are frankly opposed to the main drift of criticism.[7] But in that such views may be seen as deviations, they confirm the existence of a collective thesis.

In these discussions the style of the poem has not been totally overlooked. Muscatine has spoken about the impact of some of the high style passages in the poem—'Formal, rhetorical structure, and a function comparatively unrelated to the practical necessities of the dramatic situation are the rule.'

And he judges the result of this:[8]

The pace of the story is deliberately slow and majestic. Random references to generous periods of time make it chronologically slow. Though Chaucer omits a great deal of the tale originally told by Boccaccio in the *Teseida*, he frequently resorts to the rhetorical device of *occupatio* to summarize in detail events or descriptions in such a way as to shorten the story without lessening its weight and impressiveness. Further, there is an extraordinary amount of rhetorical *descriptio* in the poem, all of which slows the narrative.

This general assessment of the impact of the high style is supported by Salter; she sees much of the formal poetry as '. . . language which stresses the heightened conventions, the almost ritualistic nature of the life led by man in an elevated and aristocratic society.'

But she goes on to see the 'variety of the styles the Knight's Tale contains', assesses in more detail than Muscatine the grand style and its effects and also notes that:[9]

At the other extreme, the drop into harsh realism of language is not carelessly made, but represents one of the basic themes of the poem—the darkness and suffering which exist at the very centre of this radiant chivalric world.

D. V. Harrington's article on 'Rhetoric and Meaning in the *Knight's Tale*' concurs with Muscatine and Salter, but his analysis is hardly a subtle or searching one:[10]

One may fairly conclude from study of the rhetorical devices used to enrich the tournament passage, as well as from recognition of the elaborately developed suspense leading to the combat, that the poet was particularly interested in emphasising this scene.

In his edition of the tale, Spearing offers a short analysis of the effects of oral performance on the style of the tale,[11] but more importantly for this study he makes a number of detailed comments on the style and stylistic effect of passages in his notes, and I will be referring to these at times. Trevor Whittock writes in the Cambridge tradition represented by Spearing and Salter, and has a number of comments on the poem's style, though few of them are as precise as those of his predecessors; other critics who occasionally advert to the style are Speirs, Donaldson, Ian Robinson and R. S. Haller—their comments will be mentioned when they are relevant to the discussion.[12] The imagery of the poem has been discussed by Christopher Dean and by Spearing, and some comment on its word-play has been made by Thomas A. Van and Edward E. Foster, in addition to the remarks by Baum and Kökeritz in their more widely ranging articles.[13]

Few of these discussions have come to grips with the poem in detail. Muscatine was searching for the general effect of the poem's style; of the other writers only Salter and Spearing have offered detailed analysis of any passages, and they were restricted by the nature of their books to brief excursions into this field. I believe, however, that a fairly sustained study of the style of the poem can provide interesting information about Chaucer's character and quality as a poet and about the meaning of the tale as a whole, though the material that is offered here does not controvert the main drift of criticism over recent years—in fact it provides a good deal of support for the French–Frost–Muscatine consensus.

It has not been easy to organise these comments into a coherent whole; the tale does not have a simple, unitarian structure and so any criticism which is itself shaped into a modern, unified argument runs the risk of misrepresenting the poem it discusses. In this study, as in many others on medieval literature, I feel that the medieval type of literary criticism, notes arranged *seriatim*, as in a *Commentary on the Sentences* or a *Summa*, may be the only proper way of handling a text which itself appears to be organised in this serial way, the way characterised by Muscatine, Jordan and others as 'Gothic structure'. But while we are familiar enough with this serial method in the notes to an edition, it would surely be perverse to offer a critical study in such a form now. Consequently I have organised these comments into four areas—Palamon and Arcite; Theseus; the narrator; and the major set-pieces of the poem. There is inevitably some overlapping and some cross-reference to be made, but these are the four areas into which modern criticism of the poem mainly falls, and in the sections themselves I hope it is shown that Chaucer goes about his poetry in these four areas with rather different aims and successes. I do not suggest that the four areas are separate, but that, for the purpose of close study, they are separable, and that when they have been studied we should make the synthesis of styles and of thoughts that, by its interlocking nature, the poem as a whole insists is necessary.

Palamon and Arcite

The opening narrative of Thesus's adventures ends with a simple statement:

> Whan that this worthy duc, this Theseus,
> Hath Creon slayn, and wonne Thebes thus,
> Stille in that feeld he took al nyght his reste,
> And dide with al the contree as hym leste.   1001–4

This is matter-of-fact, straightforward in movement and order; the passage that follows is more complex in order and in language:

> To ransake in the taas of bodyes dede,
> Hem for to strepe of harneys and of wede,
> The pilours diden bisynesse and cure
> After the bataille and disconfiture.   1005–8

The reason for this elevation in style seems to come immediately, for these 'pilours' discover the two heroes of the poem:

> And so bifel that in the taas they founde,
> Thurgh-girt with many a grevous blody wounde,
> Two yonge knyghtes, liggynge by and by,
> Bothe in oon armes, wroght ful richely,
> Of whiche two Arcita highte that oon,
> And that oother knyght highte Palamon.   1009–14

This short passage is not only a little more ornate than what has preceded it, it is ornate in a specific way. Muscatine and Spearing have noted the element of order in the fact that the two heroes lie side by side,[14] but the style itself expresses order and parallelism; the phrase 'by and by' in 1011 is followed by an evenly divided line, and then the heroes' names are given in a couplet with a clear sense of *commutatio*, the second line reversing the order of the first. The style is expressing the equality of the two figures, and this is pursued in the next two lines:

> Nat fully quyke, ne fully dede they were,
> But by hir cote-armures and by hir gere
> The heraudes knewe hem ...   1015–17

The motif of balance, to be so common in a poem where speech balances speech and action weighs against action in the lives of the two heroes, is introduced in the phrases and lines when we first encounter the two lovers-to-be. The end of this opening passage reasserts the motif:

> And in a tour, in angwissh and in wo,
> This Palamon and his felawe Arcite
> For everemoore; ther may no gold hem quite.   1030–2

The last line is not balanced, but this does not mean the motif is forgotten—as soon as the poem moves on, balance is obvious:

> This passeth yeer by yeer and day by day,   1033

There follows the passage which introduces Emily and the topic of love to the poem; as a formal opening to what will be an important scene for the lovers and the poem the young woman and the young season are presented together in a fairly elaborate *descriptio*:

> Till it fil ones, in a morwe of May,
> That Emelye, that fairer was to sene
> Than is the lylie upon his stalke grene,
> And fressher than the May with floures newe—
> For with the rose colour stroof hire hewe,
> I noot which was the fyner of hem two—
> Er it were day, as was hire wone to do,
> She was arisen and al redy dight;
> For May wole have no slogardie a-nyght.   1034–42

The terms of comparison are familiar—the lily and the rose—and so are the epithets as well—'fairer' and 'fressher'. The syntax is extended, for the subject falls in 1035 and its verb in 1041, and this separation calls for a repetition of the subject in 'She'. A little piece of *dubitatio* is inserted, honouring Emily more and making the sentence a little more complex, and the sequence ends with a fine *sententia*. In shape it is a well-modelled passage, but in spite of what some critics have said I cannot feel it is a success;[15] it seems one of those passages fitly described by the word 'conventional' at its limpest. There is little vigour here; the verb to be dominates, and we see epithets being predicated of Emily, rather than her personality creating itself—only the line 'For with the rose colour stroof hir hewe' rises above this slack level, and its vigorous verb is the cause.

As the passage moves on the *descriptio* is extended:

> Yclothed was she fressh, for to devyse:
> Hir yelow heer was broyded in a tresse
> Bihynde hir bak, a yerde long, I gesse.
> And in the gardyn, at the sonne upriste,
> She walketh up and doun, and as hire liste
> She gadereth floures, party white and rede,
> To make a subtil gerland for hire hede;
> And as an aungel hevenysshly she soong.   1048–55

There is more activity in the verbs here, but still the passage seems to limp. The fault now is that many lines are divided and end with a phrase whose main purpose seems to be to drag in the rhyme: only the second line and the last two lines could be exculpated from this charge, and even here 'broyded in a tresse' and 'as an angel' have a certain predictability. It is clear enough that the passage is meant to be the spring opening of an important sequence, that it is meant to give a formal and elevated opening to the scene which shows the birth of love in the poem. But the scene is not up to Chaucer's best efforts in the same vein. It would be unwise, though tempting, to suggest that this is part of the putative early poem 'Palamon and Arcite', but it is inevitable to feel some dissatisfaction with the passage, especially as we need not go as far as the opening of the General Prologue to find a much better example of the same topos—later in this poem, when Arcite in turn walks out on a May morning the thing is done superbly, as we shall see.

Unsatisfactory though it may be, the function of the passage is clear enough; it is to assert the youthful beauty of Emily and the spirit of love and freedom, so different from the harsh imprisonment of the two knights. The harshness is better done, as the narrator turns to:

> The grete tour, that was so thikke and stroong,
> Which of the castel was the chief dongeoun,   1056–7

Spearing remarks aptly on the effect of the consonants here,[16] and in this tower we find the knights. As soon as they are mentioned the motif of balance recurs:

> Bright was the sonne and cleer that morwenynge,
> And Palamoun, this woful prisoner,
> As was his wone, by leve of his gayler,
> Was risen and romed in a chambre an heigh,
> In which he al the noble citee seigh,
> And eek the gardyn, ful of braunches grene,
> Ther as this fresshe Emelye the shene
> Was in hire walk, and romed up and doun.   1062–9

The passage keeps using phrases and clauses in equipoise; it is not the assertive balance that we find in a passage of *repetitio* and *compar*, but the note is irresistibly present; the evenness of the lovers' world is subliminally implied by the style in which they are presented. The poet uses a good number of divided lines, but here the second half-line tells us something and so avoids the danger of seeming a line-filler, as it became in the description of Emily:

> And so bifel, by aventure or cas,
> That thurgh a wyndow, thikke of many a barre
> Of iren greet and square as any sparre,
> He cast his eye upon Emelya,
> And therwithal he bleynte and cride, 'A!'
> As though he stongen were unto the herte.   1074–9

The enjambement in the second line avoids a series of short phrases and leads into a sequence of evenly balanced whole lines; thus the poetry is supple in its effect, not repeating a single pattern of organisation for too long, but creating an impression of order throughout. As the poem continues, the actions of the lovers and the overt balance of their speeches and emotions will show more clearly how similar they are, but even at this early stage Chaucer begins to sketch in a slight difference, cutting acrosss their equivalence.

Palamon's sudden cry of love brings a concerned reaction from Arcite; his first words are clipped:

> And with that cry Arcite anon up sterte,
> And seyde, 'Cosyn myn, what eyleth thee,
> That art so pale and deedly on to see?
> Why cridestow? Who hath thee doon offence?   1080–3

The rest of his speech is thoughtful and compassionate, but it is not fluent:

> For Goddes love, taak al in pacience
> Oure prisoun, for it may noon oother be.
> Fortune hath yeven us this adversitee.
> Som wikke aspect or disposicioun
> Of Saturne, by som constellacioun,
> Hath yeven us this, although we hadde it sworn;
> So stood the hevene whan that we were born.
> We most endure it; this is the short and playn.   1084–91

The determinist nature of Arcite's reaction has been well analysed by the critics, but attention has not been paid to the stylistic implications of his last words. There is here a clear tendency towards the 'short and playn'; it is not a crude and simple speech, as we might expect from the Miller or the Reeve (though they can surprise us), but it has a brisk, unadorned quality about it, filled with pauses and firm, brief utterances. Palamon's answer to him is not so brisk:

> This Palamon answerde and seyde agayn:
> 'Cosyn, for sothe, of this opinioun
> Thow hast a veyn ymaginacioun.
> This prison caused me nat for to crye,
> But I was hurt right now thurghout myn ye
> Into myn herte, that wol my bane be.   1092–7

The difference in style is not a radical one; Palamon's speech does have fewer pauses and short phrases, it is true, but it is only as he goes on to elaborate his feelings that the contrast grows marked:

> And therwithal on knees doun he fil,
> And seyde: 'Venus, if it be thy wil
> Yow in this gardyn thus to transfigure
> Bifore me, sorweful, wrecched creature,
> Out of this prisoun help that we may scapen.
> And if so be my destynee be shapen
> By eterne word to dyen in prisoun,
> Of oure lynage have som compassioun,
> That is so lowe ybroght by tirannye.'   1103–11

Palamon's syntax here is much more extended than Arcite's was, for it flows evenly in long sentences and is highly subordinated. The diction is fairly elevated—'transfigure' is only used here and in *Boece* by Chaucer, 'tirranye' is first used by Chaucer, though he uses it fifteen times; the words 'compassioun', 'destynee' and 'lynage' all first appear in the fourteenth century from French and may have some ornate quality about them.

When Arcite in turn speaks of his suddenly discovered love the contrast between the cousins is maintained. He says:

'The fresshe beautee sleeth me sodeynly
Of hire that rometh in the yonder place,
And but I have hir mercy and hir grace,
That I may seen hire atte leeste weye,
I nam but deed; ther nis namoore to sey.'   1118–22

There is nothing clownish about this reaction; for four lines it is a noble and even speech, but in the last line the crispness of the earlier speech is reasserted in 'I nam but deed' and the last words make quite explicit Arcite's economic habit of speech. The style of the two lovers is in accord with their perceptions: Palamon sees an occasion to ask Venus to 'transfigure Bifore me', while Arcite sees a woman 'that rometh in the yonder place'. This distinction between them is to be developed at length and with great importance for the poem, and here, when it first appears, the poet modulates his style to make the distinction the more convincing.

The lovers each make one more speech in this scene, and in these the poet continues this pattern. They speak the same language, as it were, but a difference of idiolect is plain. Palamon speaks with some anger, but with great fluency:

This Palamon gan knytte his browes tweye.
'It nere,' quod he, 'to thee no great honour
For to be fals, ne for to be traitour
To me, that am thy cosyn and thy brother
Ysworn ful depe, and ech of us til oother,
That nevere, for to dyen in the peyne,
Til that the deeth departe shal us tweyne,
Neither of us in love to hyndre oother,
Ne in noon oother cas, my leeve brother;
But that thou sholdest trewely forthren me
In every cas, as I shal forthren thee,—
This was thyn ooth, and myn also, certeyn;
I woot right wel, thou darst it nat withseyn.   1128–40

Robinson places a semi-colon at the end of line 1136, but the speech is really one long and complex discussion of their oath. The syntax is elaborate and at several points threatens to lose its way, but does not do so. Equally noticeable is the interweaving of sound in the passage; the rhymes seem like those of an elaborate stanza form. The rhyme 'brother'/'oother' is repeated, 'peyne'/'tweyne' chimes with 'certeyn'/withseyn'; in 1137–8 the word 'forthren' is repeated, just a syllable away from the rhyme word, and this links strikingly with the 'brother'/'oother' rhymes. This aural word-play brings into high prominence the crucial word 'ooth' which falls at the end of the long interlocking sequence. In part this stresses that the 'ooth' of *amicitia* is beginning to be broken, but it also asserts Palamon's power as a speaker of passionate and elaborate poetry. The rest is not so ornate, though in 1147–48 there is a repetition of the 'brother'/ 'forthre' assonance; the principal effect is made in the early part of the speech.[17]

Against this fluency, Arcite's words seem a little brusque:

> 'Thow shalt,' quod he, 'be rather fals than I;
> And thou art fals, I telle thee outrely,
> For paramour I loved hire first er thow.
> What wiltow seyen? Thow woost nat yet now
> Wheither she been a womman or goddesse!   1153–7

The syntax units are much shorter, and the pithy question and the monosyllabic force of 1156 make a striking contrast with Palamon's words. Arcite's speech, like Palamon's, relaxes in style after striking such a contrastive note at first; he does not continue in this dramatically crisp vein, but still the rest of his speech moves in sequences of only one or two lines, includes the colloquial 'by my pan' in line 1165 and the down-to-earth simile of hounds fighting for a bone. The plainer style of Arcite is thus kept in the audience's mind throughout the speech and, as in his two previous speeches, he ends with a crisply final note:

> And soothly, leeve brother, this is al.
> Heere in this prisoun moote we endure,
> And everich of us take his aventure.'   1184–6

The narrator has spent some time on this important scene, and is keen to hurry on—'But to th' effect' he says in line 1189. The scene and the implications of the lovers' speeches have been much discussed by the critics, for here the characters of the cousins already seem divergent, in spite of the equality that is also present. The careful modulating of the poetry is an important part of the powerful effect of the scene; it implicitly creates the differing personalities of the lovers, and so plays a most important part in establishing the meaning of the poem.

After Perotheus's visit parts the lovers the poet continues this characterisation in the laments they speak. Arcite's passion is forcefully described:

> How greet a sorwe suffreth now Arcite!
> The deeth he feeleth thurgh his herte smyte;
> He wepeth, wayleth, crieth pitously;
> To sleen himself he waiteth prively.　1219–22

The verbs press his grief upon the audience, especially in the *articulus* of line 1221, and when he speaks his passion is dramatically demonstrated:

> He seyde, 'Allas that day that I was born!
> Now is my prisoun worse than biforn;
> Now is me shape eternally to dwelle
> Noght in purgatorie, but in helle.
> Allas, that evere knewe I Perotheus!　1223–7

The *apostrophe* is expressed through *repetitio* and *compar*. It is not an extended example of this elaborate figure, however, and the bulk of the speech is relatively simple, though its diction is quite elevated and the length of syntax is greater than Arcite has used before:

> But I, that am exiled and bareyne
> Of alle grace, and in so gret dispeir,
> That ther nys erthe, water, fir ne eir,
> Ne creature that of hem maked is,
> That may me helpe or doon confort in this,
> Wel oughte I sterve in wanhope and distresse.　1244–9

Consequently, Arcite's passion is, after his first words, restrained and never rises above the level of the passage that follows this wretched statement:

> Farewel my lif, my lust, and my gladnesse!
> Allas, why pleynen folk so in commune
> On purveiaunce of God, or of Fortune,
> That yeveth hem ful ofte in many a gyse
> Wel bettre than they kan hemself devyse?　1250–4

In this passage, as in the beginning of the speech, the opportunity for an extended passage of rhetorical figures is avoided by the poet; Arcite begins with elaboration, but moves quickly into closely argued stoicism. As before, he uses some plain similes:

> We faren as he that dronke is as a mous.
> A dronke man woot wel he hath an hous,
> But he noot which the righte wey is thider,
> And to a dronke man the wey is slider. 1261–4

And once more he ends with a briskly final statement:

> Syn that I may nat seen you, Emelye,
> I nam but deed; ther nys no remedye.' 1273–4

This second use by Arcite of the unvarnished statement 'I nam but deed' reasserts the directness of his character, and the speech is an interesting mixture of noble feelings and plain utterances. Arcite shows moments of elevation, but soon moves back to earth again.

Palamon's grief is at an equal pitch:

> Upon that oother syde Palamon,
> Whan that he wiste Arcite was agon,
> Swich sorwe he maketh that the grete tour
> Resouneth of his youlyng and clamour.
> The pure fettres on his shynes grete
> Weren of his bittre, salte teeres wete. 1275–80

The picture is very similar to that given of Arcite, but looking back it is interesting to see that the syntax here is more extended than in the preface to Arcite's lament, and this passage does not have the driving power given there by the packed verbs. The rather melodramatic figure of the moistened fetters helps to give Palamon's introduction a more ornate tone, but against this, when he begins to speak he seems less elaborate than did Arcite:

> 'Allas,' quod he, 'Arcita, cosyn myn,
> Of all oure strif, God woot, the fruyt is thyn. 1281–82

The syntax of Palamon's opening statement is, after these lines, more extended than was Arcite's opening, but it is less rhetorical and it is simple in movement, mostly co-ordinate in construction:

> Thou mayst, syn thou hast wisdom and manhede,
> Assemblen alle the folk of oure kynrede,
> And make a werre so sharp on this citee,
> That by som aventure or some tretee
> Thow mayst have hire to lady and to wyf
> For whom that I moste nedes lese my lyf. 1285–90

Palamon's speech so far seems, in general, at a rather lower level than Arcite's, and this would appear to contradict the argument being put forward here, but these moderate remarks are not all Palamon says; they are, rather, the preface to his real 'youlyng', for now his passions rise:

> Therwith the fyr of jalousie up sterte
> Withinne his brest and hente him by the herte
> So woodly that he lyk was to biholde
> The boxtree or the asshen dede and colde.   1299–1302

This swift moving sequence builds up through a *significatio* on 'woodly' to a double simile with a classical flavour, and then Palamon's passion flows out in a fine lament:

> Thanne seyde he, 'O crueel goddes that governe
> This world with byndyng of youre word eterne,
> And writen in the table of atthamaunt
> Youre parlement and youre eterne graunt,
> What is mankynde moore unto you holde
> Than is the sheep that rouketh in the folde?   1303–8

The *apostrophe* moves swiftly and easily, and the diction is fairly elevated—'atthamaunt' is only used four times by Chaucer, here and in *The Romaunt of the Rose*, 'eterne' is first used by Chaucer, though he uses it fairly often (mostly here and in *Boece*, however) and the more common Romance words 'governe', 'graunt' and 'parlement' support this rise in style. The next line dramatises man's misery with quick monosyllabic stresses, and then Palamon continues with a fine sense of balance:

> For slayn is man right as another beest,
> And dwelleth eek in prisoun and arreest,
> And hath siknesse and greet adversitee,
> And ofte times giltelees, pardee.   1309–12

The pause at 'pardee' breaks the *compar* of the passage, but this is not the end of the higher style; indeed it now reaches its climax as Palamon questions the divine order in very ornate language:

> What governance is in this prescience
> That giltelees tormenteth innocence?
> And yet encresseth this al my penaunce,
> That man is bounden to his observaunce,
> For Goddes sake, to letten of his wille,
> Ther as a beest may al his lust fulfille.   1313–18

The language simplifies towards the end of this passage; it is a change

of diction, not a change in passion and stylistic control, for the next
lines state with slow monosyllables the misery he feels:

> And whan a beest is deed he hath no peyne;
> But man after his deeth moot wepe and pleyne,
> Though in this world he have care and wo.
> Withouten doute it may stonden so.   1319–22

The eloquence that Palamon displays here is quite above anything
Arcite has commanded. But as happened in several previous speeches,
the effect is made by the earlier part of the speech, and it ends in a
less spectacular way. If the last lines alone were taken, either of the
lovers could have spoken them:

> But I moot been in prisoun thurgh Saturne,
> And eek thurgh Juno, jalous and eek wood,
> That hath destroyed wel ny al the blood
> Of Thebes with his waste walles wyde;
> And Venus sleeth me on that oother syde
> For jalousie and fere of hym Arcite.'   1328–33

This is fluent enough, and it does not have the finality that characterises the ends of Arcite's speeches, but it is nothing like what has
gone before. Clearly, the concern of the poet is not to erect consistently elevated speeches for Palamon, nor consistently brisk ones
for Arcite. But in general the effect is that Palamon is more elevated
than his rival, and the elevation points towards a greater nobility of
character; he controls a greater eloquence just as he sees further
than Arcite in terms of love and of the heavens. Equal as the lovers
are in birth and opportunity, there is a difference. In the first part
of the poem, now ending, the poet has taken some care to distinguish between the lovers in their attitudes and in their speech. It is
only a difference in one aspect, of course: the *demande d'amour* which
ends this part draws attention to their similarity. But already a
distinction has been made that is to direct the whole poem, and the
distinction is made in the texture of the poetry as well as in other,
more widely discussed ways.

As the second part of the poem begins we hear a good deal about
Arcite and his condition; there is no lack of interest in him as a
character, but he is described in fairly simple verse and the narrator
introduces a note of haste:

> Whan that Arcite to Thebes comen was,
> Ful ofte a day he swelte and seyde 'Allas!'
> For seen his lady shal he nevere mo.

I

> And shortly to concluden al his wo,
> So muche sorwe hadde nevere creature
> That is, or shal, whil that the world may dure.   1355–60

The narrator's briskness seems meant more to create an ambience of crispness about Arcite than to imply a lack of interest, for the lover's state is elaborated at some length. The nature of the elaboration itself helps to enlarge the personality of Arcite; the verse is vigorous, densely packed:

> His slep, his mete, his drynke, is hym biraft,
> That lene he wex and drye as is a shaft;
> His eyen holwe, and grisly to biholde,
> His hewe falow and pale as asshen colde,
> And solitarie he was and evere allone,
> And waillynge al the nyght, makynge his mone: 1361–6

The absence of connectives in the first four lines may be given the rhetorical name *dissolutio*, and its impact is clear enough; it works with the co-ordinate syntax and the massing of information to maintain a vigorous tone, even when the lover is languishing. Arcite's brisk personality is thus reinforced by the nature of the description and as soon as he returns to action a remarkable series of active lines, mostly beginning with 'And', further assert his nature:

> And with that word he caughte a greet mirour,
> And saugh that chaunged was al his colour,
> And saugh his visage al in another kynde.
> And right anon it ran hym in his mynde,
> That, sith his face was so disfigured
> Of maladye the which he hadde endured,
> He myghte wel, if that he bar hym lowe,
> Lyve in Atthenes everemoore unknowe.
> And seen his lady wel ny day by day.
> And right anon he chaunged his aray,
> And cladde hym as a povre laborer,
> And al allone, save oonly a squier
> That knewe his privetee and al his cas,
> Which was disgised povrely as he was,
> To Atthenes is he goon the nexte way.
> And to the court he went upon a day,
> And at the gate he profreth his servyse
> To drugge and drawe, what so men wol devyse.   1399–416

This long quotation illustrates excellently how co-ordinate syntax and forceful verbs characterise Arcite. There is a repetitive pattern, but it is not like the stiff *repetitio* that we find, for example, at the end of *Troilus and Criseyde* (see p. 91) and elsewhere in 'The Knight's Tale', for enjambement tends to break up the regular movement of the passage (lines 1403–4 and 1410–11) and almost every new line asserts a new action. The effect implies a forceful, active personality. The passage which follows is not quite so striking, but it still moves with great speed, a new action in nearly every line leading Arcite to his final position of trust:

> And eek men broghte him out of his contree,
> From yeer to yeer, full pryvely his rente;
> But honestly and slyly he it spente,
> That no man wondred how that he it hadde.
> And thre yeer in this wise his lif he ladde,
> And bar hym so, in pees and eek in werre,
> Ther was no man that Theseus hath derre.   1442–8

The narrator now turns to Arcite's rival and his situation:

> In derknesse and horrible and strong prisoun
> Thise seven yeer hath seten Palamoun
> Forpyned, what for wo and for distresse.
> Who feeleth double soor and hevynesse
> But Palamon, that love destreyneth so
> That wood out of his wit he goth for wo?
> And eek thereto he is a prisoner
> Perpetuelly, noght oonly for a yer.
>   Who koude ryme in Englyssh proprely
> His martirdom? for sothe it am nat I;
> Therfore I passe as lightly as I may.   1451–61

The opening sentence is more complex in structure than was the opening sentence about Arcite (lines 1355–7, above) and a lot of enjambement makes the movement subtle. The prominent device of *interrogatio* is used to describe Palamon's woe, where a massing of detail was the means of characterising Arcite in distress. Here, as when describing Arcite, the narrator moves on quickly, but where he previously just said 'shortly to concluden al his wo' here the moving on is presented with *interrogatio* and *dubitatio*. The difference between the two passages maintains the tonal distinction between the lovers. And when Palamon acts the distinction is maintained; we have seen Arcite's bustling action, but it takes a long time to relate a single action by Palamon:

> It fel that in the seventhe yer, of May
> The thridde nyght, (as olde bookes seyn,
> That al this storie tellen moore pleyn)
> Were it by aventure or destynee—
> As, whan a thyng is shapen, it shal be—
> That soone after the mydnyght Palamoun,
> By helpyng of a freend, brak his prisoun
> And fleeth the citee fast as he may go   1462–9

The recounting of Palamon's escape finds time for a precise date, for a parenthesis about the sources and for a short speculation on the shaping forces behind the action. Palamon does act, but the extended syntax of the paragraph and the additional material it contains tend to take away any note of urgency, whereas Arcite's actions were nothing if not urgent. More action follows this opening, and it is fairly simply and quickly recounted; as we have now often seen, the tone of the passage is created in its beginning and then the poetry moves on in a less remarkable way, but even then it is not as driving as was the account of Arcite's actions—Palamon's thoughts and motives are given in a more ample way:

> For, shortly, this was his opinion,
> That in that grove he wolde hym hyde al day,
> And in the nyght thanne wolde he take his way
> To Thebes-ward, his freendes for to preye
> On Theseus to helpe hym to werreye;
> And shortly, outher he wolde lese his lif,
> Or wynnen Emelye unto his wyf.
> This is th' effect and his entente pleyn.   1480–7

There is some strikingly monosyllabic writing here, especially in lines 1481–2, and the sequence ends briskly; this should remind us of the delicate nature of the distinction between the two lovers, for they are equals in almost every particular. The one difference is vital, of course, and the style has insisted on it at the beginning of this description of Palamon. The fact that the end of this sequence is very much in the style associated with Arcite is interesting and is not, I suggest, an accident nor a contradiction to the thesis being offered here. The long sequence that follows shows the lovers at their most similar; in the encounter in the grove they are both impassioned and noble, and there is very little between them in terms of meaning or of style. The function performed by the style in this long passage is to assert their nobility; afterwards the poem will return, and crucially, to their difference.

The elevation of the following scene is well indicated by its beginning. Arcite rises to do his observance to May, and the season is invoked with a brief but magnificent formal opening:

> The bisy larke, messager of day,
> Salueth in hir song the morwe gray,
> And firy Phebus riseth up so bright
> That al the orient laugheth of the light,
> And with his stremes dryeth in the greves
> The silver dropes hangynge on the leves.   1491–6

This passage is in many ways superior to the earlier spring scene, when Emily made her appearance; the imagination is more powerful in that here we have forceful metaphor—'messager', 'Salueth', 'laugheth'—where before only familiar epithets were used. Here there is epithet, but it is functional; Phebus is 'firy', but his fire is seen in action, drying the richly described dew. And where before qualities were merely predicated with the verb to be, here active verbs show us qualities in motion and creation. The rhetorical figures of *descriptio*, *translatio* and *interpretatio* are in the passage, and the audience would recognise its elevation partly from identifying the figures, but whatever our poetic tradition the passage is powerful and leads us to look forward to a passage of some beauty—and perhaps of some 'firy' passion as well.[18]

The note of elaboration and vitality is immediately supported by the fine picture of Arcite:

> Remembrynge on the poynt of his desir,
> He on a courser, startlynge as the fir,
> Is riden into the feeldes hym to pleye,   1501–3

Arcite makes garlands and sings; his actions are fully those that the audience would expect from a lover (the narrator's view of lovers, expressed at this point, is of great interest, and is discussed below, p. 139). Finally Arcite sits 'withouten any moore'—perhaps a touch of the brisk lover of previous scenes—and makes his lament:

> 'Allas', quod he, 'that day that I was bore!
> How longe, Juno, thurgh thy crueltee,
> Woltow werreyen Thebes the citee?
>   Allas, ybroght is to confusioun
> The blood roial of Cadme and Amphioun, —
> Of Cadmus, which that was the firste man
> That Thebes bulte, or first the toun bigan
> And of the citee first was crouned kyng.   1542–9

The speech is quite complex; *exclamatio* and *interrogatio* are here, and there is an extended elaboration and amplification that have not been part of Arcite before. We should read this as a sign of his nobility, of his passion and of the over-riding elevation of the scene.[19] It is not, by any means, the most elaborate piece of rhetoric in the poem, but the note of elevation is maintained:

> Allas, thou felle Mars! allas, Juno!
> Thus hath youre ire oure lynage al fordo,
> Save oonly me and wrecched Palamoun,
> That Theseus martireth in prisoun.
> And over al this, to sleen me outrely,
> Love hath his firy dart so brennyngly
> Ystiked thurgh my trewe, careful herte,
> That shapen was my deeth erst than my sherte.
> Ye sleen me with youre eyen, Emelye!
> Ye been the cause wherfore that I dye.   1559–68

Palamon overhears, and the elevated tension of the scene is well sustained as the poet says in a dramatic metaphor that he:

> . . . thoughte that thurgh his herte
> He felte a coold swerd sodeynliche glyde,   1574–5

Palamon addresses Arcite in a passionate but not very elaborate speech; it moves quickly, and is filled with emotion, but it is less rhetorical than the formal lament Arcite has just given:

> He stirte hym up out of the buskes thikke,
> And seide: 'Arcite, false traytour wikke,
> Now artow hent, that lovest my lady so,
> For whom that I have al this peyne and wo,
> And art my blood, and to my conseil sworn,
> As I ful ofte have told thee heerbiforn,
> And hast byjaped heere duc Theseus,
> And falsly chaunged hast thy name thus!
> I wol be deed, or elles thou shalt dye.   1579–87

Palamon here speaks with the vigour and speed that has often characterised Arcite, but although Arcite has just spoken with some elaboration himself, this does not mean that they have exchanged characters here, or that Palamon is meant to seem brusquer than Arcite for once. Arcite's previous speech was a formal soliloquy, not a piece of angry dialogue, and the equality of the lovers in this scene is stressed when Arcite's reply to Palamon adopts the style that he used:

. . . 'By God that sit above,
Nere it that thou art sik and wood for love,
And eek that thow no wepne hast in this place,
Thou sholdest nevere out of this grove pace,
That thou ne sholdest dyen of myn hond.
For I defye the seurete and the bond
Which that thou seist that I have maad to thee. 1599–1605

There is perhaps a less fluent note in the last two lines here, that may
be stressed in the next two:

What, verray fool, thynk wel that love is free,
And I wol love hire maugree al thy myght! 1606–7

And the end of Arcite's speech is certainly monosyllabic and straightforwardly stoic:

And if so be that thou my lady wynne,
And sle me in this wode ther I am inne,
Thow mayst wel have thy lady as for me.' 1617–19

But any difference in character between the two lovers here is only
slight and can only be detected minimally in their style; their
equality is forcefully stated in the description of their encounter on
the following morning:

Ther nas no good day, ne no saluyng,
But streight, withouten word or rehersyng,
Everich of hem heelp for to armen oother
As freendly as he were his owene brother;
And after that, with sharpe speres stronge
They foynen ech at oother wonder longe.
Thou myghtest wene that this Palamon
In his fightyng were a wood leon,
And as a crueel tigre was Arcite;
As wilde bores gonne they to smyte,
That frothen whit as foom for ire wood.
Up to the ancle foghte they in hir blood. 1649–60

The passage moves evenly, line by line, with a good deal of parallelism in the phrasing that is brought to a head in the equal similes of
the lovers and the even process of the last three lines. The parallelism
is invoked again in a vivid sentence as Theseus sees them:

Under the sonne he looketh, and anon
He was war of Arcite and Palamon,
That foughten breme, as it were bores two. 1697–9

There is one more relevant speech in this scene, and Palamon makes it; this gives each lover two speeches in the sequence, and this second speech by Palamon structurally balances the first one by Arcite, though it comes a day later. Palamon's speech is not a soliloquy, but it is extremely formal, a noble reply to Theseus. The two highly formal speeches are almost the same length—Arcite's is thirty lines long and Palamon's twenty-seven lines. Both are similar in style as were the lovers' intervening angry speeches to each other. Palamon's speech is not an *apostrophe* and does not use the figures that Arcite employed, but its level of elevation is much the same. His plea is that they are both guilty, and the speech is very notable for its sense of balance:

> This Palamon answerde hastily,
> And seyde, 'Sire, what nedeth wordes mo?
> We have the deeth disserved bothe two.
> Two woful wrecches been we, two caytyves,
> That been encombred of oure owene lyves;   1714–18

He makes extensive use of *repetitio* and *compar*:

> Ne yif us neither mercy ne refuge,
> But sle me first, for seinte charitee!
> But sle my felawe eek as wel as me;
> Or sle him first, for though thow knowest it lite,
> This is thy mortal foo, this is Arcite,   1720–4

The entire speech is dominated by these figures of balance, embellished in line 1736 with a delicate *commutatio*:

> I make pleynly my confessioun
> That I am thilke woful Palamoun
> That hath thy prisoun broken wikkedly.
> I am thy mortal foo, and it am I
> That loveth so hoote Emelye the brighte
> That I wol dye present in hir sighte.   1733–8

The nature and length of this speech asserts the equivalent function of the two lovers, just as in its own style and sense it urges this parallelism. Theseus accepts Palamon's argument, and the last we hear of the lovers in this part of the poem uses Palamon's chosen figures to assert that equality:

> Who looketh lightly now but Palamoun?
> Who spryngeth up for joye but Arcite?   1870–71

The second part of the poem leaves the lovers like this, sentenced to establish in battle which of them is the better man. The rest of the poem will set out the complex processes by which this is decided, and also will show how fine are the means of the decision. This part of the poem has established stylistically their noble equivalence, but it began with a subtle reminder that there is a difference between them, and at their next appearance that difference will be more clearly expounded; the crucial tension between their equal nobility and their fatal difference is consequently based on a thorough establishment of the nature of the lovers, both in the poetry which they themselves speak and in the poetry which describes them.

The description of the three temples built into the stadium and the detailed accounts of Lygurge and Emetreus all have considerable stylistic interest and relevance for a study of the two lovers, their attitudes and nature, but as the relation is not a direct one, these passages will be discussed below, among other set-pieces in the poem. The two lovers are briefly mentioned when they return to Athens with their troops, but this is merely a preface to the elaborate account of the two kings who lead the opposing battles.

The narrator moves aside to discuss Lygurge and Emetreus, and the lovers only reappear in the story with any extended presence when Palamon goes to pray. His prayer is elaborately prefaced:

> The Sonday nyght, er day bigan to sprynge,
> Whan Palamon the larke herde synge,
> (Although it nere nat day by houres two,
> Yet song the larke) and Palamon right tho
> With hooly herte and with a heigh corage,
> He roos to wenden on his pilgrymage
> Unto the blisful Citherea benigne,—
> I mene Venus, honurable and digne.   2209–16

As before, in lines 1451–61, a description of Palamon moving to action finds time for elaboration: we find a parenthetical comment, a circuitous statement of the time and rhetorical figures—the narrator breaks in with *praecisio* to give a *definitio* in the last line. It is only after this ornate and slow-moving introduction that Palamon acts:

> And in hir houre he walketh forth a pas
> Unto the lystes ther hire temple was,
> And doun he kneleth, and with humble cheere
> And herte soor, he seyde as ye shal heere: 2217–20

From this elaborate preface, and remembering how Palamon has previously been characterised we would expect something ornate, and there is no disappointment:

> 'Faireste of faire, O lady myn, Venus,
> Doughter to Jove, and spouse of Vulcanus,
> Thow gladere of the mount of Citheron,
> For thilke love thow haddest to Adoon,
> Have pitee of my bittre teeris smerte,
> And taak myn humble preyere at thyn herte.   2221-6

The *apostrophe* opens with three lines of *exclamatio*, using *pronominatio* and *interpretatio*; these are highly wrought devices that are to be associated with the highest levels of passion and style—the opening of Book III of *Troilus and Criseyde* reads rather like this passage; there too the verb is delayed and epithet is multiplied as in 'bittre teeris smerte'. The opening reasserts Palamon's passion and his noble mastery of the high style, but once again the opening tone is not maintained. Palamon offers an extended example of *dubitatio*, the modesty topos:

> Alas! I ne have no langage to telle
> Th' effectes ne the tormentz of myn helle;
> Myn herte may myn harmes nat biwreye;
> I am so confus that I kan noght seye
> But, 'Mercy, lady bright, that knowest weele
> My thought, and seest what harmes that I feele!'   2227-32

After this, as if in accordance with its sentiment, the style is much simplified; the speech is still fluent and measured—in fact much of it seems to move in three, or perhaps six, line stanzas—ending with two firm and direct couplets:

> Thy temple wol I worshipe everemo,
> And on thyn auter, where I ride or go,
> I wol doon sacrifice and fires beete.
> And if ye wol nat so, my lady sweete,
> Thanne preye I thee, tomorwe with a spere
> That Arcita me thurgh the herte bere.
> Thanne rekke I noght, whan I have lost my lyf,
> Though that Arcita wynne hire to his wyf.
> This is th'effect and end of my preyere:
> Yif me my love, thow blisful lady deere.'   2251-60

This part of the speech could easily have been spoken—in terms of style—by Arcite, especially in view of its brisk end. But the opening of the speech has maintained the characteristic note of Palamon.[20] Arcite's speech will equally show certain of the characteristics previously identified with him, but there is an interval before he speaks. Venus's rather enigmatic reaction to Palamon's prayer is followed by Emily's prayer; this begins with an invocation very much like Palamon's, and is notable also for fluency, though not for any ornate figures (lines 2314–21 are especially easy in movement). Some discussion of this speech is made below, with relevance to the narrator's treatment of it, p. 142.

When Arcite appears, the short preface to his prayer is simpler than the one preceding Palamon's prayer. Even Emily's introduction had some ornateness ('Up roos the sonne, and up roos Emelye', 2273), but the time of Arcite's prayer is given briskly, there are no parentheses, and the narrator makes no delay:

> The nexte houre of Mars folwynge this,
> Arcite unto the temple walked is
> Of fierse Mars, to doon his sacrifise,
> With alle the rytes of his payen wyse.
> With pitous herte and heigh devocioun
> Right thus to Mars he seyde his orisoun: 2367–72

Arcite is by no means ignoble, as we have seen; his nobility just takes a different direction from Palamon's, and so it is quite fitting that his prayer should open with an invocation, but one a little less ornate than Palamon's:

> 'O stronge god, that in the regnes colde
> Of Trace honoured art and lord yholde,
> And hast in every regne and every lond
> Of armes al the brydel in thyn hond
> And hem fortunest as thee lyst devyse,
> Accepte of me my pitous sacrifise.   2373–8

It is *apostrophe* and the verb is delayed as long as Palamon's, but after the opening *exclamatio* here we find none of the epithets of *interpretatio* and the amplification of the god's name is not made by *pronominatio* but by a co-ordinate series of relative clauses (Muscatine is wrong to say that all three invocations use *pronominatio*[21]). The prayer is quite complex in construction and uses some vigorous *articulus* and crisp *compar:*

> For thilke peyne and thilke hoote fir
> In which thow whilom brendest for desir,
> Whan that thow usedest the beautee
> Of faire, yonge, fresshe, Venus free,
> And haddest hire in armes at thy wille—
> Although the ones on a tyme mysfille,
> Whan Vulcanus hadde caught thee in his las,
> And found thee liggynge by his wyf, allas!—
> For thilke sorwe that was in thyn herte,
> Have routhe as wel upon my peynes smerte.   2383–92

Though it is without the even measure of Palamon's speech, this too is fluent, as at its close:

> And everemo, unto that day I dye,
> Eterne fir I wol bifore thee fynde.
> And eek to this avow I wol me bynde:
> My beerd, myn heer, that hongeth long adoun,
> That nevere yet ne felte offensioun
> Of rasour nor of shere, I wol thee yive,
> And ben thy trewe servant whil I lyve.
> Now, lord, have routhe upon my sorwes soore;
> Yif me victorie, I aske thee namoore.'   2412–20

The end is a little brusquer than Palamon's, but the conclusion to this passage makes more strongly the distinction between the lovers. Where Palamon merely 'dide' his 'sacrifise' and 'observaunces' we see Arcite in quick action:

> And Arcita anon his hand up haf,
> And moore encens into the fyr he caste,
> With othere rytes mo;   2428–30

And the god reacts in a simple and clear-cut way:

> . . . and atte laste
> The statue of Mars bigan his hauberk rynge;
> And with that soun he herde a murmurynge
> Ful lowe and dym, and seyde thus, 'Victorie!'   2430–3

It is very different from the unclear reaction of Venus (2265–9) where complex syntax was needed to explain Palamon's arrival at a state of contentment.

    There is, then, a distinction in style at the beginning and end of the prayers, and in the reaction of the divinities, but these contrasts are not major. The two different gods, and the crucial difference in the prayers carry the weight of the characterisation here, but Chaucer does maintain a delicate reminiscence of the lovers' differing styles that were carefully set out in the first part, while insisting at the same time upon Arcite's nobility.

This prayer scene has made the difference between the lovers overt, and because of their differing allegiances and prayers the story now moves steadily against Arcite—as Saturn's intervening speech makes quite clear. The equality of the lovers in all but this respect is restated in the formal epic similes of the battle scene:

> Ther nas no tygre in the vale of Galgopheye,
> Whan that hir whelp is stole whan it is lite,
> So crueel on the hunte as is Arcite
> For jelous herte upon this Palamon.
> Ne in Belmarye ther nys so fel leon,
> That hunted is, or for his hunger wood,
> Ne of his praye desireth so the blood,
> As Palamon to sleen his foo Arcite.   2626–33

The meticulous balance of the similes recalls the careful equivalence of style that in the very beginning asserted poetically how equal the two men were; their difference has now been absorbed in the progress of the story, has been made overt in the temple scenes and so is not now dealt with in the style. Indeed, in a sense it has been forgotten, for as the story moves on Arcite becomes a tragic hero destroyed by his 'fortunate flaw', and in accordance with this elevated emotional position, his last speech—after the prayers it is the only time either lover speaks—strikes a level of passionate rhetoric that he has not before commanded, higher, I think, than even Palamon has attained:

> Allas, the wo! allas, the peynes stronge,
> That I for yow have suffred, and so longe!
> Allas, the deeth! allas, myn Emelye!
> Allas, departynge of oure compaignye!
> Allas, myn hertes queene! allas, my wyf!
> Myn hertes lady, endere of my lyf!
> What is this world? What asketh men to have?
> Now with his love, now in his colde grave
> Allone, withouten any compaignye.
> Fare wel, my sweete foo, myn Emelye!   2771–80

It is both a successful, convincing setting out of noble passion and a grandly rhetorical climax to the careful modulation of the poetry spoken by and used about the two lovers. The *repetitio* and *compar* that are so often used in the poem are obvious, but we also find Arcite using oxymoron to express his sense of loss and waste in 2776, 2780 and, implicitly, in 2773. Metaphor and *interpretatio* find a place in his addressing of Emily in various passionate ways; the speech modulates easily from elevated lament to a finely rhetorical stoic questioning of the world. The high point of the speech, showing how Chaucer moulds together formal cadences and almost colloquial patterns of speech, is in the two great lines 2778-9; the placing of the word 'Allone' itself proclaims the masterful confidence of the great poet.[22]

Palamon does not have a passionate and rhetorical answer, though, as I will later discuss, the poem itself does provide one. This is proper, for as many critics have said, the characters are not predominantly people, 'organic' personalities, but are channels for ideas and for representing attitudes. And to go further, the style of the poem, as seen in these two characters, does not stand out itself, in its own right; the poem is not merely a vehicle for grand rhetorical speeches, aureation and poetic fireworks, for if it were only this Palamon would tear a passion to tatters over Arcite's bier. Rather, the style of the poem is the servant of its total meaning, and it is through Theseus and the court—or world—at large that the poem expresses grief for Arcite. Palamon has had fine speeches when he represented the lover's urge to love, but this was his function and it is done. Arcite did not have such fine speeches, for he represented a quality less verbal and less beautiful, but now that he is the channel for a sense of tragedy, his tongue in turn is set free. To study the style of the poetry used by and used about these two characters is not only to see that the general critical view of the lovers is sound, but it is also to see the power of Chaucer's poetic ability and the tact with which it is employed in the service of his art at large.

Theseus

At the opening of the poem Theseus's achievements are generally described and, then he is seen returning to Athens; this beginning, as will be discussed below, p. 136, is rather straightforward in style and one notable feature is the absence of enjambement—the only line that approaches being run-on is 897-98. But as soon as Theseus speaks, this changes:

'What folk been ye, that at myn homcomynge
Perturben so my feste with criynge?'
Quod Theseus. 'Have ye so greet envye
Of myn honour, that thus compleyne and crye?'   905–8

The same motif is present as the lady speaks:

She seyde: 'Lord, to whom Fortune hath yiven
Victorie, . . .   915–16

Although it does appear again, this is not a major stylistic device; Chaucer does not give to Theseus a particular prosodic characteristic as he does to characters elsewhere; rather the enjambement here is part of the steady elevation of style that takes place throughout this sequence. The lady's speech is a poised and stylish one, as Spearing has shown in his note on it,[23] and this demonstrates both her noble feelings and also the sort of discourse appropriate towards Theseus. He is a lord and his lordly status is being established; the slight complexity of enjambement first suggests this, and it will be asserted in many ways through the poem. But Theseus is not only a noble duke; he is also a man of action and this is also shown within the tale. The opening account of his activities was brisk and after the lady's speech a swift passage of co-ordinate narrative, a verb of action in nearly every line, demonstrates his vigorous personality:

And in his armes he hem alle up hente,
And hem conforteth in ful good entente,
And swoor his ooth, as he was trewe knyght,
He wolde doon so ferforthly his myght
Upon the tiraunt Creon hem to wreke,
That al the peple of Grece sholde speke
How Creon was of Theseus yserved
As he that hadde his deeth ful wel deserved.   957–64

These two characteristics, nobility and martial vigour, are well summed up and brought together in the emblem-like *descriptio* of Theseus' banner:

The rede statue of Mars, with spere and targe,
So shyneth in his white baner large,
That al the feeldes glyteren up and doun;
And by his baner born is his penoun
Of gold ful riche, in which ther was ybete
The Mynotaur, which that he slough in Crete.
Thus rit this duc, thus rit this conquerour,   975–81

We have already seen Theseus in action and heard of his exploits; by this formal *descriptio* the poem asserts that to deal properly with Theseus elevated language is needed, and the figures of rhetoric must be employed to match the poem to the man. Muscatine remarks that Chaucer here is 'at his very best as a poet' but gives no further analysis, and Frost is satisfied with observing that the passage is typical of Chaucer's 'rich, allusive and concrete' style.[24] Compared with later passages in this poem it is not very ornate or extended, and it does not use figures much—there is some *conduplicatio* in 981, and the brightness of the banner is conveyed by something of a *superlatio* in 977. The diction is not strikingly ornate, though it is chivalric: 'penoun' is only used here by Chaucer, and Barbour is the only writer recorded using it before him, but the other words here with chivalric connotations—'baner', 'large', 'targe'—are quite common in Chaucer and other writers of the fourteenth century. The ornate effect of the passage depends on its use of richly visual epithets, giving the scene strong colour and the force of an emblem which expounds the noble nature of Theseus to the reader. The fact that it is a martial nature is implicit in the iconography, and this is acted out as the narrator moves from this static description into active poetry:

> But shortly for to speken of this thyng,
> With Creon, which that was of Thebes kyng,
> He faught, and slough hym manly as a knyght
> In pleyn bataille, and putte the folk to flyght;
> And by assaut he wan the citee after,
> And rente adoun bothe wall and sparre and rafter;   985–90

The aggressive, monosyllabic verbs set the tone of the passage: 'faught', 'slough', 'putte', 'wan' and 'rente'.

Forcefulness and nobility will be the two characteristics of Theseus that the poem will most reveal, and this early scene establishes them clearly enough. As the sequence draws to its close the first important point in the plot-development occurs; the bodies of the cousins, lovers-to-be, are discovered. Theseus's treatment of them is recounted interestingly:

> Out of the taas the pilours han hem torn,
> And han hem caried softe unto the tente
> Of Theseus; and he ful soone hem sente
> To Atthenes, to dwellen in prisoun
> Perpetuelly,—he nolde no raunsoun.   1020–4

As before, enjambement is employed in a rather obtrusive way to make the poetry more complex, a little more elevated when Theseus engages in his royal function of disposing of the lives of those about him. And acting together with the slightly elaborate note created in this way is the vigorous, crisp ending of the passage, which implies Theseus's firmness and decisive power. In the scenes that follow we will see the poet showing both the active, decisive character of the duke and his noble, formal aspect as the ordainer of the life about him.

Theseus is involved in a brisk scene with Perotheus that ends with Arcite's release, but the next important sequence involving the duke is when he goes hunting and encounters the lovers. The scene begins with a lively, springing account of the duke's active nature:

> This mene I now by myghty Theseus,
> That for to hunten is so desirus,
> And namely at the grete hert in May,
> That in his bed ther daweth hym no day
> That he nys clad, and redy for to ryde
> With hunte and horn and houndes hym bisyde.   1673–8

The excitement conveyed, the vigorous rhythms and the alliteration, especially of the last line, are rather reminiscent of the great hunting scenes in *Sir Gawain and the Green Knight*, and when he sees the lovers Theseus acts with the authority and decisiveness of a Bercilak:

> This duc his courser with his spores smoot,
> And at a stert he was bitwix hem two,
> And pulled out a swerd, and cride, 'Hoo!   1704–6

After Palamon's formal speech admitting the lovers' mutual guilt Theseus is brusque in decision:

> This worthy duc answerde anon agayn,
> And seyde, 'This is a short conclusioun.
> Youre owene mouth, by youre confessioun,
> Hath damnped yow, and I wol it recorde;
> It nedeth noght to pyne yow with the corde.
> Ye shal be deed, by myghty Mars the rede!'   1742–7

The women plead for mercy, and this touches Theseus' noble nature—'For pitee renneth soone in gentil herte,' (1761)—and there follows a careful and interesting paragraph in which the poet explores the steps by which Theseus moves from quick sentence to merciful reconsideration:

K

> And though he first for ire quook and sterte,
> He hath considered shortly, in a clause,
> The trespas of hem bothe, and eek the cause,
> And although that his ire hir gilt accused,
> Yet in his resoun he hem bothe excused,
> As thus: he thoghte wel that every man
> Wol helpe hymself in love, if that he kan,
> And eek delivere hymself out of prisoun.   1762–9

The interest of the speech is not really in its stylistic character, though it is fluent and very carefully organised; rather its importance is as a development of Theseus's true nobility, even as a short essay on lordship. The speech asserts the need for reason and discretion, as well as for decisiveness in a lord; it thus extends the requirements of lordship beyond the more common chivalric virtues, just as the description of the knight in the General Prologue stressed his rarer virtues of humility and courtesy to all estates. Theseus reasons:

> . . .' Fy
> Upon a lord that wol have no mercy,
> But been a leon, bothe in word and dede,
> To hem that been in repentaunce and drede,
> As wel as to a proud despitous man
> That wol mayntene that he first began.   1773–8

Theseus is not only lordly in person and in battle: we see that he is also the owner of a noble intellect. This is to be most important at the end of the poem, of course, when Theseus speaks as inter-locutor between man and heaven, and this fuller sense of his nobility is now confirmed poetically. When Theseus speaks aloud, he speaks for the first time in a truly elevated style, in a formal, royal speech displaying a number of overt rhetorical figures as well as showing a quick and compassionate mind:

> Lo heere this Arcite and this Palamoun,
> That quitly weren out of my prisoun,
> And myghte han lyved in Thebes roially,
> And witen I am hir mortal enemy,
> And that hir deth lith in my myght also;
> And yet hath love, maugree hir eyen two,
> Broght hem hyder bothe for to dye.
> Now looketh, is nat that an heigh folye?
> Who may been a fool, but if he love?
> Bihoold, for Goddes sake that sit above,
> Se how they blede! be they noght wel arrayed?   1791–1801

Exclamatio, interrogatio and *repetitio* gather here to lift the style, but this is not merely a speech in praise of the ennobling power of love; the percipient Theseus also sees the ironies and they are stated in a blunter figure:

> But this is yet the beste game of all,
> That she for whom they han this jolitee
> Kan hem therfore as muche thank as me.
> She woot namore of al this hoote fare,
> By God, than woot a cokkow or an hare!   1806–10

The dual note, of noble fluency and clear-sighted common sense, is maintained as Theseus begins the second part of his speech:

> 'To speke of roial lynage and richesse,
> Though that she were a queene or a princesse,
> Ech of you bothe is worthy, doutelees,   ·
> To wedden whan tyme is, but nathelees
> I speke as for my suster Emelye,
> For whom ye have this strif and jalousye.   1829–34

This sentence is extended and quite complex in construction, though it is without figures, and immediately afterwards the tone simplifies further, into a brisk statement of fact:

> Ye woot yourself she may nat wedden two
> Atones, though ye fighten everemo.
> That oon of you, al be hym looth or lief,
> He moot go pipen in an yvy leef;   1835–8

This mixture of styles is used to suggest and to underline the complex significance that Theseus has. He is a noble lord, and there is enough elevation about the poetry when he appears in person and when he speaks to connote this, but he is also a man of forceful action and of clear sight. In turn the poetry that characterises him adopts varying tones to represent these sides of his personality. These various notes are heard again when he appears later in the poem.

After the short syntax of the busy, noisy introduction to part four (discussed below, p. 155), there is a striking extension of syntax which leads up to the most notable assertion of Theseus's importance in the poem:

> The grete Theseus, that of his sleep awaked
> With mynstralcie and noyse that was maked,
> Heeld yet the chambre of his paleys riche,

> Til that the Thebane knyghtes, bothe yliche
> Honured, were into the paleys fet.
> Duc Theseus was at a wyndow set,
> Arrayed right as he were a god in trone.   2523–9

The noise of the preparation for the tournament wakes Theseus, and this smooth flowing passage seems quiet by comparison with what has gone before. The slow and impressive last line states overtly Theseus's importance and, by its weight, slows down the passage; the following lines stress this *rallentando*:

> An heraud on a scaffold made a 'Oo!'
> Til al the noyse of peple was ydo,
> And whan he saugh the peple of noyse al stille,
> Tho shewed he the myghty dukes wille.   2533–6

The poetry creates the dignified manner that is appropriate to Theseus's rank, and then his formal speech is read by the herald; this in itself is enough to denote its official character, but the style of the 'speech' is itself judicial, as was the duke's speech to the lovers in the grove. It opens with some elaborate diction and continues in all the formal stiffness of *repetitio* and *compar*:

> 'The lord hath of his heigh discrecioun
> Considered that it were destruccioun
> To gentil blood to fighten in the gyse
> Of mortal bataille now in this emprise.
> Wherfore, to shapen that they shal nat dye,
> He wol his firste purpos modifye.
> No man therfore, up peyne of los of lyf,
> No maner shot, ne polax, ne short knyf
> Into the lystes sende, or thider brynge;
> Ne short swerd, for to stoke with poynt bitynge,
> No man ne drawe, ne bere it by his syde.
> Ne no man shal unto his felawe ryde
> But o cours, with a sharpe ygrounde spere;   2537–49

The speech moves evenly to its remarkably slow, controlled end:

> God spede you! gooth forth, and ley on faste!
> With long swerd and with maces fighteth your fille.
> Gooth now youre wey, this is the lordes wille.'   2558–60

Especially in contrast with the preceding sequence, this passage forcefully creates in its movement both Theseus's 'heigh discrecioun' and an impression of the irresistible rightness of 'the lordes wille'.

A less obvious but subtly effective piece of stylistic modelling further enforces Theseus's authority at the end of the battle; after Saturn and Venus have held their brief discussion, the account of Arcite's accident is related in lines 2676–99. These lines curiously fall into a series of four-line sentences, but the rhyme does not follow the punctuation—the stanzas, as it were, rhyme ABBC. It is a curious effect, one that we will see below in 'The Franklin's Tale' at a moment of high emotion (cf. p. 190). Order and disorder are conveyed at the same time by the device, and as these lines are read there is a lack of resolution in each sentence; we are led on to the next rhyme all the time, and this is well illustrated in the last of these 'stanzas':

> Tho was he korven out of his harneys,
> And in a bed ybrought ful faire and blyve;
> For he was yet in memorie and alyve,
> And alwey criynge after Emelye.   2696–9

In this 'stanza', as in the preceding one, the syntax break in the middle further removes any feeling of resolution, breaking up even the middle rhyme.

In the ambience of Arcite, then, there is no poetic resolution, no rest in the prosody, but note how much there is in the next three lines, where at last the syntax falls with the rhyme:

> Duc Theseus, with al his compaignye,
> Is comen hoom to Atthenes his citee,
> With all blisse and greet solempnitee.   2700–2

The fact that it is as near to a multiple rhyme as Chaucer gets in this poem makes the effect even more forceful. The poetry gives confidence in Theseus, a sense that he is the figure who can resolve discordances. As we have already seen in the cases of Palamon and Arcite, the style implies things that are later to be stated overtly about characters, and so when that overt statement comes it fulfils expectations that have—perhaps subliminally—been aroused in us.

Our confidence in Theseus is to be satisfied in his last and greatest speech. When the Athenian parliament has met at the very end of the poem, silence once more indicates the duke's importance, and again the pause is made in the poetry as well as in explicit statement:

> Whan they were set, and hust was al the place,
> And Theseus abiden hadde a space
> Er any word cam fram his wise brest,

> His eyen sette he ther as was his lest.
> And with a sad visage he siked stille,
> And after that right thus he seyde his wille: 2981–6

The lines move slowly, with their monosyllabic stresses leading steadily to the long last line; the hush of the audience is created and the passage is indeed 'sad' in the medieval sense—'heavy, steady, sober, earnest' to quote Robinson's gloss. The speech that follows is in the same tone, as Theseus seeks to explicate the events of the poem by referring to divine providence. The speech has been much discussed; some critics have seen it as a fully convincing resolution of the poem's themes, while others have been less happy with it. Spearing even suggests that the speech is meant to be unsatisfactory.[25] I cannot agree with this, for, as I hope to show, the speech does deal adequately with the problems raised by the poem as far as a human agency can do so.

The opening part of the speech is very thoughtful; the syntax is not very extended, for Theseus attempts to be clear, rather than elaborate, and even a long sentence does not move with speed:

> That same Prince and that Moevere,' quod he,
> Hath stablissed in this wrecched world adoun
> Certeyne dayes and duracioun
> To al that is engendred in this place,
> Over the whiche day they may nat pace,
> Al mowe they yet tho dayes wel abregge.   2994–9

The syntax is not elevated by having many subordinated clauses in loose conjunction or apposition as we have sometimes seen (cf. 2221–6) nor by presenting a series of coordinate clauses (cf. 2771–80). Rather it is the complex sentence of the grammarians, working around one main clause, elaborated where necessary for clarity and precision. Some of the diction is elaborate, but here again precision is the purpose, not elevation:

> For nature hath nat taken his bigynnyng
> Of no partie or cantel of a thyng,
> But of a thyng that parfit is and stable,
> Descendynge so til it be corrumpable.
> And therfore, of his wise purveiaunce,
> He hath so wel biset his ordinaunce,
> That speces of thynges and progressiouns
> Shullen enduren by successiouns,
> And nat eterne, withouten any lye.   3007–15

The words that appear ornate here are not courtly or chivalric in their ambience; rather they are Boethian. Apart from their appearance in this poem 'purveiaunce', 'ordinaunce', 'progressioun' and 'successioun' appear almost exclusively in *Boece*; 'speces' is used here, three times in *Boece* and eighteen times in 'The Parson's Tale', so it too has a learned context. The word 'cantel' only appears here in Chaucer but its context elsewhere does not seem courtly, and the word 'corrumpable' is first used by Chaucer and used twice, but he uses the 'corrump-' stem eight other times. The language, like the thought, is intellectual and functional rather than demonstrative and affective. Muscatine calls this passage 'scholastic'[26] but as most of the ideas and many of the words come from Boethius it seems an anachronistic term.

This part of the speech, then, represents that wise insight that Theseus has previously demonstrated being raised to a level unprecedented in the poem. But in the last line of the quoted passage the phrase 'withouten any lye' strikes a simpler note and this is no accident; as so often happens in Chaucer the end of a passage contains the tone of the next. In the following line a change of method is foreshadowed:

> This maystow understonde and seen at ye.   3016

In the language of medieval disputation this means that the speaker is to proceed by exemplary argument; the theoretical discussion is completed and now will be illustrated. The style of the illustration is, fittingly, plain and lucid:

> Loo the ook, that hath so long a norisshynge
> From tyme that it first bigynneth to sprynge,
> And hath so long a lif, as we may see,
> Yet at the laste wasted is the tree.   3017–20

Even the syntax changes from a careful argument to an asyntactic demonstration; the last line of this passage is linked by *anacoluthon* to the rest, and the first three lines have a wavering syntax.

That the style becomes simple when the poem gives simple demonstration seems straightforward enough and little remarkable, but as Theseus continues a more subtle note seems to come through. A certain ornateness enters his style, though it is not in conflict with simplicity; he adopts briefly *repetitio* and *compar*:

> Of man and womman seen we wel also
> That nedes, in oon of this termes two,
> This is to seyn, in youthe or elles age,

> He moot be deed, the kyng as shal a page;
> Som in his bed, som in the depe see,
> Som in the large feeld as men may see;
> There helpeth noght, al goth that ilke weye.   3027–33

The topic is the omnipresence of death and the style recalls earlier passages where death was discussed; the driving repetitions of the description of Mars's temple and of Saturn's self-revelation are here recalled, and perhaps the death of Arcite as well. It seems that the style of the speech is reinforcing its overall attempt to embrace and explain the disturbing features of the story. The first part of the speech, meticulous and learned, reflected in a muted fashion the style of the elaborate and painful complaints made by Palamon and Arcite, and this later part works into its fabric the mode in which the other jarring material was presented. The magnificent rhetoric of Arcite's funeral drew together the threads of nobility in the poem and now Theseus seeks to give an answer to the disturbing questions about human life that the poem has not flinched from raising. One of the triumphs of the poem is that through the magnificent temple-descriptions in particular Chaucer extends his scope beyond that of a story of love-rivalry, and makes the love-plot a vehicle for discussing more widely human wishes, frustrations and disasters. And in this final speech not only the problems of the lovers are being considered—the miseries of all mankind are included. The stylistic variety of the speech is something like a poetic reminiscence of the poem's most disturbing passages. This is not done at great length, but I believe the changing nature of the speech serves this larger subtle purpose as well as following the more simple development of its argument from theory to practical demonstration. If this is so, then the speech is the more satisfying as an end to the poem, in that it provides a conceptual and a stylistic resolution to the conflicting ideas and styles of the poem.

The resolution in the speech is not, though, a total explanation of the poem, for Theseus does not lay out the cosmos for our understanding, but I believe this is not the intent of the speech. After all, its theme is our human limitations and it would be inconsistent for the human Theseus then to speak with superhuman wisdom. Theseus is not superior to the action, as is the Duke in *Measure for Measure*. Rather, his speech sets out the view that, faced with these problems and with these mysterious events, all that man can do (and Theseus includes himself) is to react as wisely as he can. The steps by which we should make this pragmatic reaction are carefully laid out in a passage of straightforward co-ordination, the syntax making plain the plodding nature of man's attempt to cope with his puzzling world:

> Thanne is it wysdom, as it thynketh me,
> To maken vertu of necessitee,
> And take it weel that we may nat eschue,
> And namely that to us alle is due.
> And whoso gruccheth ought, he dooth folye,
> And rebel is to hym that al may gye.
> And certeinly a man hath most honour
> To dyen in his excellence and flour,
> Whan he is siker of his goode name; 3041–9

Theseus throughout the poem has not been a 'rethor', though he is capable of formal speeches as a duke. His understanding of the cosmos is not given at great length, and it is self-confessedly limited and human; the inconsistency between the theme of the speech and the notion that Palamon and Emily have 'O parfit joye, lastynge evermo' (3072) may imply this limitation on Theseus's part. But the speech seems to me to deal adequately with the problems of the poem as far as the middle ages would expect a man to deal with them. Delasanta states this well:

> . . . we need go no further than Theseus' faire-cheyne-of-love speech to be reminded that for the medieval mind the discernible order of a hierarchical universe was preferrable to the implicit nihilism that lurked even in stoical dependencies upon Fortune.

In this way the speech satisfies the expectation we have formed of Theseus; it is shown at length that he is, as he has always seemed to be, a wise leader. Confirmed in this role, he finally speaks in elaborate and formal syntax to Emily:

> 'Suster,' quod he, 'this is my fulle assent,
> With al th'avys heere of my parlement,
> That gentil Palamon, youre owene knyght,
> That serveth yow with wille herte, and myght,
> And ever hath doon syn ye first hym knewe,
> That ye shul of youre grace upon hym rewe,
> And taken hym for housbonde and for lord. 3075–81

The last we see of Theseus is as a true lord, one who gives wise orders and is loyally and gladly obeyed. The concern of the poet in characterising him has been to convince us that this really is his nature; throughout the poem he acts and speaks like a lord who has power but knows how to use it, and the careful modulation of the poetry has played a considerable part in making Theseus a figure of wise authority in the poem.

The Narrator

As the Knight begins to speak, he uses the style that has dominated the General Prologue, lucid without ever being assertively rhetorical in high or in low style. It moves quickly and tells us a good deal:

> Whilom, as olde stories tellen us,
> Ther was a duc that highte Theseus;
> Of Atthenes he was lord and governour,
> And in his tyme swich a conquerour,
> That gretter was ther noon under the sonne.   859–63

Some names that are associated with lofty legend are used in this introduction—'Scithia', 'Ypolita' are notable ones—and occasionally words like 'governour' and 'conquerour' are used, which are in themselves fairly ornate, but these details are used here as terms inevitable in describing this particular duke—they do not add up to an ornate passage. It is as brisk an introduction to a famous lord and warrior as we could conceive, and I have no idea why Whittock calls it a 'somewhat grand opening'; I would concur with Harrington's judgment of the passage as having a 'general, flat manner.'[28]

The implicit suggestion is that the narrator is not directly concerned with Theseus as hero, and this impression is confirmed when, very shortly, we encounter the first of the many *occupationes* in the poem:

> And thus with victorie and with melodye
> Lete I this noble duc to Atthenes ryde,
> And al his hoost in armes hym bisyde.
>   And certes, if it nere to long to heere,
> I wolde have toold yow fully the manere
> How wonnen was the reigne of Femenye
> By Theseus and by his chivalrye;   872–8

Occupatio is, of course, one of the common figures of style and must be regarded as having some elevation. But this particular example has no other elevated elements; the language is simple, there is no sign of the formal *repetitio* which will adorn the great *occupatio* towards the end of the poem. The device here does not alter the tone of this opening, but rather confirms it as with some haste the narrator avoids recounting events of an obviously heroic nature. The impression that we receive of the narrator is that of a business-like and relatively simple man, conscious of the size of the task ahead. This impression is immediately made overt in a figure whose simplicity conforms to what has gone before:

> But al that thyng I moot as now forbere.
> I have, God woot, a large feeld to ere,
> And wayke been the oxen in my plough.
> The remenant of the tale is long ynough.   885–8

The passage is a short *dubitatio* and it uses a metaphor of some force, but these recognisable figures do not conflict with the narrator's persona. The metaphor is a mundane one and the *dubitatio* does not therefore seem arch, as many tend to do. It furthers our picture of the narrator—practical and perhaps more humble than his abilities deserve, and this is quite in accord with the picture of the knight in the General Prologue. The passage creates that distance between the narrator and his story that is common in sophisticated medieval story—*Troilus and Criseyde*, Malory's Arthuriad and *Sir Gawain and the Green Knight* all show this feature.

This personality is asserted as the narrator indicates his control over the tale, making a series of clipped statements whose tone and meaning support his brisk persona. One follows immediately:

> Lat every felawe telle his tale aboute,
> And lat se now who shal the soper wynne;
> And ther I lefte, I wol ageyn bigynne.   890–2

As we have seen, the style of the narrative is sensitive to the nobility of its characters; the description of Theseus's banner and the higher style which introduces the lovers are examples of this, but the narrator disassociates himself from these loftier moments. After describing the banner he says 'But shortly for to speken of this thyng' (985) and after relating how the cousins landed in prison he says of Theseus:

> And ther he lyveth in joye and in honour
> Terme of his lyf; what nedeth wordes mo?   1028–9

Throughout the ensuing narrative we are reminded of the presence and personality of the narrator by a series of clipped comments,

which cut off flowing passages of the story. Brief illustrations will
show this in action:

> Greet was the strif and long bitwix hem tweye,
> If that I hadde leyser for to seye,
> But to th'effect.   1187–9

> That whan that oon was deed, soothly to telle,
> His felawe wente and soughte hym doun in helle,—
> But of that storie list me nat to write.   1199–201

> Ther nas noon oother remedie ne reed;
> But taketh his leve, and homward he him spedde!
> Lat hym be war! his nekke lith to wedde.   1216–18

> I noot which hath the wofuller mester.
> For, shortly for to seyn, this Palamoun
> Perpetuelly is dampned to prisoun   1340–2

> Now demeth as yow liste, ye that kan,
> For I wol telle forth as I bigan.   1353–4

> And shortly, turned was al up so doun
> Bothe habit and eek disposicioun
> Of hym, this woful lovere daun Arcite.
> What sholde I al day of his wo endite?   1377–80

> And shortly of this matere for to seyn,
> He fil in office with a chamberleyn   1417–18

> Who koude ryme in Englyssh proprely
> His martirdom? for sothe it am nat I;
> Therfore I passe as lightly as I may.   1459–61

In rhetorical terms some of these short passages are *occupatio*, some
continuatio and some *dubitatio*. These are all devices whereby the
narrator withdraws himself from the surface of his narrative; all of
them are clipped in their phrasing and this compounds the impression that the narrator is in a sense alienated from his elaborate
tale and the high passions that inform it. Throughout these sequences
this persona is quite consistent, though only intermittently brought
before our eyes.

    In a longer passage which follows, the narrator's persona is en-
larged and his attitude to the lofty feelings of the lovers is made
clearer. After the high point of the richly described dawn scene, the
narrator steps forward with a sententious comment on the action:

> But sooth is seyd, go sithen many yeres,
> That 'feeld hath eyen, and the wode hath eres.'
> It is ful fair a man to bere hym evene,
> For al day meeteth men at unset stevene. 1521–4

As if emboldened by this sage incursion into the story, the narrator offers his plain man's views on love:

> Whan that Arcite hadde romed al his fille,
> And songen al the roundel lustily,
> Into a studie he fil sodeynly,
> As doon thise loveres in hir queynte geres,
> Now in the crope, now doun in the breres,
> Now up, now doun, as boket in a welle.
> Right as the Friday, soothly for to telle,
> Now it shyneth, now it reyneth faste,
> Right so kan geery Venus overcaste
> The hertes of hir folk; right as hir day
> Is gereful, right so chaungeth she array.
> Selde is the Friday al the wowke ylike. 1528–39

The comment makes effective use of *repetitio* and *compar* in a limited compass, but it is still down-to-earth in tone, as its mundane similes insist. It is very like some of the comments by the narrator of *Troilus and Criseyde*, though its sententious repetition may make it sound more like the Franklin speaking, or an aside in 'The Nun's Priest's Tale'. The last line itself is reminiscent of the pithy single lines the narrator has employed before, and as a whole the passage is a climax to the characterisation of the narrator in the opening stages of the poem. But it is not only a culmination in this sense, it also seems to be the end of a stage in the revelation of the narrator, for from this point on he appears to adopt a new function in the poem. For a considerable period he does not seem to be alienated from the poem, but rather concurs wholeheartedly with the passions and ideals of the characters.

There is now an absence of those little comments which indicated the narrator's wish to hurry on and to avoid an over-expansive treatment of any topic, but this is negative evidence. Within a hundred lines of this sententious comment on love's vagaries the narrator speaks of love in a rather different way:

> O Cupide, out of alle charitee!
> O regne, that wolt no felawe have with thee!
> Full sooth is seyd that love ne lordshipe
> Wol noght, his thankes, have no felaweshipe. 1623–6

The narrator's view of love is not that of a lover—plainly he can see the dictatorial side of the God of Love, and Spearing suggests that he punningly implies that love is *cupiditas*.[29] If the *significatio* is there (and I am inclined to agree that it is, though some might feel it belongs to the poet, not the narrator) it works with the *exclamatio* to indicate a heightening of the style. R. S. Haller argues that the style is discordantly low—a view I cannot share, as 'charitee' is no mundane word, at this time.[30] This rather elevated opening seems in key with a change in the narrator's attitude: there is admiration as well as insight into love's harshness, and as the passage continues it seems that the narrator is no longer quite alienated from the lovers and their concerns. The level of his narrative is raised quite sharply as he offers an elaborate epic simile about the lovers:

> This Arcite and this Palamon ben met.
> Tho chaungen gan the colour in hir face,
> Right as the hunters in the regne of Trace,
> That stondeth at the gappe with a spere,
> Whan hunted is the leon or the bere,
> And hereth hym come russhyng in the greves,
> And breketh bothe bowes and the leves,
> And thynketh, 'Heere cometh my mortal enemy!
> Withoute faille, he moot be deed, or I;
> For outher I moot sleen hym at the gappe,
> Or he moot sleen me, if that me myshappe,'—
> So ferden they in chaungyng of hir hewe,
> As fer as everich of hem oother knewe.   1636–48

It is a swift and powerful piece of poetry, stylishly developing an epic simile with vigorous verbs, and the speaker of it seems fully engaged with the feelings of those he is describing.[31] This is a new attitude for the narrator and the finer style signals his adoption of the lovers' passionate attitude. It may, of course, be a partial explanation of this that the knight seems sympathetic towards them now they are fighting men, not merely sighing lovers.

Immediately afterwards he comments on the action with no sense of alienation and no mundane tone:

> The destinee, ministre general,
> That executeth in the world over al
> The purveiaunce that God hath seyn biforn,
> So strong it is that, though the world had sworn
> The contrarie of a thyng by ye or nay.

> Yet somtyme it shal fallen on a day
> That falleth nat eft withinne a thousand yeer.
> For certeinly, oure appetites heer,
> Be it of werre, or pees, or hate, or love,
> Al is this reuled by the sighte above.   1663-72

Here the narrator speaks in a manner that in diction and in theme
foreshadows Theseus's final speech. Where before the narrator stood
aside from the passion and loftiness of the story, here he is fully involved in it: the passage as a whole shows this, but the single word
'oure' in line 1670 confirms it.

This new position for the narrator is seen again at the end of this
second part of the poem where he joins in enthusiastically with the
tone of the whole section, and gives no trace of the mechanical
continuatio or *occupatio* that occurred at the end of part one and at the
end of most major sequences previously:

> Who looketh lightly now but Palamoun?
> Who spryngeth up for joye but Arcite?
> Who kouthe telle, or who kouthe it endite,
> The joye that is maked in the place
> Whan Theseus hath doon so fair a grace?
> But doun on knees wente every maner wight,
> And thonked hym with al hir herte and myght,
> And namely the Thebans often sithe.
> And thus with good hope and with herte blithe
> They taken hir leve, and homward gonne they ride
> To Thebes, with his olde walles wyde.   1870-80

Interrogatio and *repetitio* give the passage elevation of style, and the
balance throughout it supports the equivalence of the lovers, so often
stated in the poem.

In the following part of the poem the narrator remains an engaged observer; he is literally so when, in the description of the
temples of Mars and Diana he says 'I saugh' rather than the less
personal 'maystow se' used of Venus's temple. (The change after the
first description perhaps indicates the growing involvement of the
narrator in the poem; I would not press this as an explanation of
the odd difference, but it certainly is an effect of it.) The narrator's
enthusiasm is plain enough when he says:

> For if ther fille tomorwe swich a cas
> Ye knowen wel that every lusty knyght
> That loveth paramours and hath his myght,

> Were it in Engelond or elleswhere,
> They wolde, hir thankes, wilnen to be there,—
> To fighte for a lady, *benedicitee!*
> It were a lusty sighte for to see. 2110–16

The effect of this change in the narrator's style and his attitude to his story is to make more forceful the passions and ethics demonstrated in the poem; beginning coolly, the narrator's interest and enthusiasm is aroused in the way that the author hopes the audience's feelings will be aroused. It seems to me that this is successfully achieved, though the narrator's enthusiasm is only a small part of the rising tempo through the second and third parts of the poem; the major speeches of the second part and the great set-pieces of the third part are the main instruments that bring this about.

So far the narrator has first given some sense of speed to the otherwise slow-moving poem, and has then helped to create the rising emotional pitch of the middle section. As the author moves on he still uses the narrator for these two functions, but we cannot trace a development in the persona through a change from one mode to the other; rather the narrator functions intermittently in these two roles. This underlines the fact that, as has been argued above, Chaucer is not creating convincing and rounded characters so much as using his figures to express ideas and emotions at various points, and when this is effected there is no drive for overall consistency.

Thus, during the two passages involving Diana and Emily we find a number of the narrative cut-offs that were used in the early disposition of the narrative; after detailing some of the pictures in Diana's temple the narrator says:

> Ther saugh I many another wonder storie,
> The which me list nat drawen to memorie. 2073–4

In the two other temple descriptions he is not nearly so dismissive when moving from the pictures to the figure of the divinity (cf. 1953–4 and 2039–40). The end of the temple description is, as has been mentioned above, rather bathetic and when Emily herself appears in the temple her prayer is ended with a familiar brusqueness:

> And hoom she goth anon the nexte weye.
> This is th' effect; ther is namoore to seye. 2365–6

The narrator here is the means by which the poet imparts speed to two passages that are necessary for the balance of his structure, but which are of restricted interest otherwise.

Towards the end of the poem the narrator's detached tone performs a last function for the author. The often discussed remarks after Arcite's death change the tone of the poem, presaging a move from a tragic threnody on Arcite to a cooler assessment of man's affairs. In the general movement from the tone of Arcite's dying speech to Theseus's philosophic summing-up the narrator's two comments are important; they introduce the cooler tone that Theseus will use after the elaborate funeral:

> His spirit chaunged hous and wente ther,
> As I cam nevere, I kan nat tellen wher.
> Therfore I stynte, I nam no divinistre;
> Of soules fynde I nat in this registre,
> Ne me ne list thilke opinions to telle
> Of hem, though that they writen wher they dwelle.
> Arcite is coold, ther Mars his soule gye!
> Now wol I speken forth of Emelye. 2809–16

This changes the tone unmistakably, and when he speaks of Emily it is in the same manner:

> For in swich cas wommen have swich sorwe,
> Whan that hir housbondes ben from hem ago,
> That for the moore part they sorewen so,
> Or ellis fallen in swich maladye,
> That at the laste certeinly they dye. 2822–6

The last two lines of these two passages strike a particularly matter of fact note.

The presence of this dry tone does not mean that the narrator cannot, in the last stages of the poem, show enthusiasm as well. Indeed, he can be elaborate and honour the nobility of the poem's world while ostensibly seeking speed, as we see in his use of *occupatio* at this stage. In the earlier part of the poem it was a frank device for abbreviating from Boccaccio, for moving quickly through material that was not needed—a sort of epic footnote. After the descriptions of Lygurge and Emetreus an *occupatio* is again used, but it is much more ornate than before.[32] It is a part of the general sense of *amplificatio* hereabouts:

> The mynstralcye, the service at the feeste
> The grete yiftes to the meeste and leeste,
> The riche array of Theseus paleys,
> Ne who sat first ne last upon the deys,

L

> What ladyes fairest been of best daunsynge,
> Or which of hem kan dauncen best and synge,
> Ne who moost felyngly speketh of love;
> What haukes sitten on the perche above,
> What houndes liggen on the floor adoun,—
> Of al this make I now no mencioun,
> But all th'effect, that thynketh me the beste.   2197–207

Here the narrator serves the ornate tone of the context in an *occupatio* which would have become more famous were it not surpassed by the later one—for which this could well be a study. *Repetitio*, *compar*, balance are all here to give the passage elegance and formality, and its effects are expanded in the refusal to describe Arcite's funeral rites.

There is not a great deal to say about this famous passage, for it has been well discussed.[33] It is an immensely long co-ordinate passage, brilliant and *sui generis*. It opens with a strongly classical list of trees (and surely Frost is wrong to think that this is ironic merely because they 'are listed with no more ceremony of adjective than it is now customary to give the names in a telephone directory'[34]) and continues with a thirty-eight line negative description that is formally repetitive and supple in its movement:

> Ne hou the goddes ronnen up and doun,
> Disherited of hire habitacioun,
> In which they woneden in reste and pees,
> Nymphes, fawnes and amadrides;
> Ne hou the beestes and the briddes alle
> Fledden for fere, whan the wode was falle;
> Ne how the ground agast was of the light,
> That was nat wont to seen the sonne bright;
> Ne how the fyr was couched first with stree,
> And thanne with drye stikkes cloven a thre,
> And thanne with grene wode and spicerye,
> And thanne with clooth of gold and with perrye,
> And gerlandes, hangynge with ful many a flour;   2925–37

The passage is both Chaucer's most striking statement of his powers as an ornate poet and also the demonstration of earthly honour; its stylistic power shows the author's skill with words, but we also see here his power to work that skill into his poem at large. This passage is a part of the argument of the poem which, as Theseus sums up, is a poem about worldly affairs; this sequence more than any other asserts that human life can encompass honour and beauty as well as all its miseries and dismays. The sequence is a part of the poem's full argument, as well as being an admirable set-piece.

The variety of the narrator's tone and function is well shown by the fact that the great *occupatio* is followed by another one, or—to put it differently—is continued in a very changed style. After the elaboration comes a passage simple in tone and style which recalls the opening of the poem, and which brings the tone of the poem down for its thoughtful ending:

> I wol nat tellen eek how that they goon
> Hoom til Atthenes, whan the pley is doon;
> But shortly to the point thanne wol I wende,
> And maken of my longe tale an ende.   2963–6

The narrator has completed his last engagement with the passion and the pity of the tale, and with the poem he now moves to a cool, detached close:

> Thus endeth Palamon and Emelye;
> And God save al this faire compaignye! Amen.   3107–8

Like Palamon and Arcite and like Theseus, the narrator is in this way not an organic personality, but the tool of the author. He does not make consistent and regular appearances like the narrators of Fielding or Thackerary; he appears sometimes and each time he may well not link up with his previous appearances. The functions that he serves are usually clear enough, though: at times he is a device to give a sense of speed and at other times he is used to intensify the emotion: the two functions can almost coincide, as in the great *occupatio*, with that disregard for a modern sense of consistency which disturbs many readers of Chaucer. The varying style of the narrator is an excellent key to his varying function, and, if we start by following the modulation of the poetry that presents him, it is not hard to perceive the ways in which this elusive, even contradictory personality affects the development and meaning of the whole poem.

Set-Pieces

I have tried to show how the poet modulates his style for meaningful purposes when dealing with his major characters and how when the narrator is clearly before us in the tale a similar process goes on. But there are large sections of the tale where the major characters are not speaking or being described and where the narrator is not plainly in sight; among these sections there are several very striking sequences of poetry, where a study of the style and its modulation can tell us a good deal about the poem and the poet. To call these 'set-pieces' is to use a partly misleading title, because I shall argue here (as has already been argued about the long *occupatio*) that these passages are more than prosodic firework displays, that in them the meaning of the poem is powerfully advanced; but it is a convenient title—more so than 'Miscellaneous Passages' for example—since most readers of the poem will know the passages referred to; in any case it is not an entirely false title since admiration of the poem does in part depend upon one's admiration for it as performance, and in this context these passages are pre-eminent.

The first of these sequences is at the beginning of part three of the poem, as the poet starts to describe the 'lystes' that Theseus builds for the coming tournament. At first we have a general description of the stadium:

> The circuit a myle was aboute,
> Walled of stoon, and dyched al withoute.
> Round was the shap, in manere of compas,
> Ful of degrees, the heighte of sixty pas,
> That whan a man was set on o degree,
> He letted nat his felawe for to see,
> Estward ther stood a gate of marbul whit,
> Westward right swich another in the opposit.   1887–94

It is a fairly dense list of details, slow-moving and forceful in its effect; it shows very clearly the 'balanced pentameter' that Ian Robinson identifies frequently in Chaucer,[35] and the last two lines seem especially poised and slow. As often happens when Chaucer gives his poetry a strong movement the opening syllable in the line is frequently a stressed one. The main note in this sequence is of detail, density and force: it is a note which will be sustained. Not all is to be vigour and force, though; there is a promise of beauty here in the flowing syntax and light movement of this passage:

> And northward, in a touret on the wal,
> Of alabastre whit and and reed coral,
> An oratorie, riche for to see,
> In worshipe of Dyane of chastitee,
> Hath Theseus doon wroght in noble wyse.   1909–13

This first temple to be described is that of Venus; the style is formal, patterned. It is not as simply vigorous as the opening of this sequence, for the dense description is formally laid out in *compar:*

> First in the temple of Venus maystow se
> Wrought on the wal, ful pitous to biholde,
> The broken slepes, and the sikes colde,
> The sacred teeris, and the waymentynge,
> The firy strokes of the desirynge
> That loves servantz in this lyf enduren;
> The othes that hir covenantz assuren;
> Plesaunce and Hope, Desir, Foolhardynesse,
> Beautee and Youthe, Bauderie, Richesse,
> Charmes and Force, Lesynges, Flaterye,
> Despense, Bisynesse, and Jalousye,
> That wered of yelewe gooldes a gerland,
> And a cokkow sittynge on hir hand;   1918–30

The lines are regular, setting in even balance the conflicting aspects of love. The syntax of the whole description is extended, though little of it is as notably rhetorical as this. The description of the goddess is vivid but not highly wrought; like the earlier *descriptio* of Theseus's banner it depends on clustering epithets and a visual imagination more than on any stylistic motifs:

> The statue of Venus, glorious for to se,
> Was naked, fletynge in the large see,
> And fro the navele doun al covered was
> With wawes grene, and brighte as any glas.
> A citole in hir right hand hadde she,
> And on hir heed, ful semely for to se,
> A rose gerland, fressh and wel smellynge;
> Above her heed hir dowves flikerynge.   1955–62

The entire description of the temple conveys an impression of formalism; it is a little languid, for its sentences are long and repetitive without the heavy stressing or the fast movement that give vigour of one sort or another:

> Nat was foryeten the porter, Ydelnesse,
> Ne Narcisus the faire of yore agon,
> Ne yet the folye of kyng Salomon,
> Ne yet the grete strengthe of Ercules—
> Th' enchauntementz of Medea and Circes—
> Ne of Turnus, with the hardy fiers corage,
> The riche Cresus, kaytyf in servage.   1940–6

Only the last line of this passage has any crispness; it is noticeable that the construction is parenthetic, each name having a phrase in apposition or a line of explanation. The style as a whole is very like that found before to be characteristic of Palamon, easy, elegant and not too hurried.

It is not surprising, then, to find that the temple of Mars is described in a style which is a concentrated and dramatic version of the brisk manner found before to be typical of Arcite. The opening is startling and brilliant:

> First on the wal was peynted a forest,
> In which ther dwelleth neither man ne best,
> With knotty, knarry, bareyne trees olde,
> Of stubbes sharpe and hidouse to biholde,
> In which ther ran a rumbel in a swough,
> As though a storm sholde bresten every bough. 1975–80

The qualities of this passage and the one that follows it describing the doorway to the temple have often been discussed, and it is not necessary to enlarge here upon the power and effect of the poetry.[36] Where Venus was introduced with iconographic characteristics in formal order, Mars is introduced with noise, violence and an atmosphere of threat. Once we are within the temple we find characteristics and attributes of things martial, and as in Venus's temple they are listed formally, though the lines are less regular:

> Ther saugh I first the derk ymaginyng
> Of Felonye, and al the compassyng;
> The crueel Ire, reed as any gleede;
> The pykepurs, and eek the pale Drede;
> The smylere with the knyf under the cloke;
> The shepne brennynge with the blake smoke;
> The tresoun of the mordrynge in the bedde;
> The open werre, with woundes al bibledde;
> Contek, with blody knyf and sharp manace.
> Al ful of chirkyng was that sory place. 1995–2004

In the opening lines of the passage there is a tendency towards the four-stressed line and the alliteration which develops in lines 1998–2000 confirms this movement towards the driving, martial tone of alliterative poetry. The structure of the passage is deliberately simple, forcing home its harsh images one after another. The contrast between this passage and the opening of the description of Venus's temple, where a series of lines also started with 'The' is very pronounced, and shows how different poetic strategies can make two passages different in effect, although both are technically *repetitio*.

The greater vigour of this sequence, compared with that devoted to Venus, is not only in the sound of the language and the pungency of the imagination; it is very noticeable that whereas Venus's personifications were all given together, those belonging to Mars are mixed up with realistic figures, as the passage quoted above shows. Both divinities have personified figures, but Venus's were listed in a static form, without any further description or action, and those belonging to Mars are seen in action or are given vigorous epithets:

> Amyddes of the temple sat Meschaunce,
> With disconfort and sory contenaunce.
> Yet saugh I Woodnesse, laughynge in his rage,
> Armed Compleint, Outhees, and fiers Outrage;   2009-12

As is clear from these quotations, the syntax of the Mars passage is abrupt, largely restricted to one-line sentences; even the formal emblem of the divinity which ends the description is more broken up syntactically than was that of Venus:

> The statue of Mars upon a carte stood
> Armed, and looked grym as he were wood;
> And over his heed ther shynen two figures
> Of sterres, that been cleped in scriptures,
> That oon Puella, that oother Rubeus—
> This god of armes was arrayed thus.
> A wolf ther stood biforn hym at his feet
> With eyen rede, and of a man he eet;   2041-8

The passage has none of the fluency that Venus's *effictio* had; the two enjambements and the parenthesis seem to stop it moving forward, since none of them is followed by a long syntactic unit—a series of pauses is the only effect here. The impact of the passage is indicated by its brief and threatening end in the last couplet.

The poetry of the whole Mars passage, then, enforces the violent and threatening persona of the god. It is quite like the Venus description in structure—the illustrations are described and then the figure of the divinity depicted, but the Mars passage is a good deal longer and a good deal more striking, and this seems to be because it fires the poet's imagination; simply as a set-piece it is magnificent. But it does work in the poem; just as Venus's temple was depicted in Palamon's characteristic style, so this passage suggests—and exaggerates—Arcite's tendencies of brusqueness: this is to reverse the business, of course, for it is really the two lovers who take on the aspects of the divinities (or planets) they follow, but the poem leads us the other way about, thus making these two descriptions not only intrinsically impressive, but also making them an explanation and resolution of the differing styles the lovers have used. Apart from this importance, critics have taken the description of Mars's temple as being central to the thematic argument of the poem, feeling that it states incontrovertibly the harsh elements of human life. In that it does this, it is the poetic brilliance of the passage, ordering and communicating the author's poweful imagination, that is at the heart of the effect.

I do not here discuss the description of the temple of Diana as it hardly seems to be a set-piece; it is rather short and as we have seen above the narrator hurries it along. Chaucer seems here to have been caught by his plan to keep the poem balanced, and it may be that the fact that the Diana passage comes third here and second in the prayers may show some indecision—perhaps he could not finally decide where to tuck these pieces away where they would do least harm. But it is relevant to say something here about Saturn's speech. This follows Arcite's prayer to Mars, and is strongly reminiscent of the description of Mars's temple:

> Myn is the drenchyng in the see so wan;
> Myn is the prison in the derke cote;
> Myn is the stranglyng and hangyng by the throte,
> The murmure and the cherles rebellyng,
> The groynynge and the pryvee empoysonyng;
> I do vengeance and pleyn correccioun,
> Whil I dwelle in the signe of the leoun.
> Myn is the ruyne of the hye halles,
> The fallynge of the toures and of the walles
> Upon the mynour or the carpenter.
> I slow Sampsoun, shakynge the piler;
> And myne be the maladyes colde,
> The derke tresons, and the castes olde;
> My lookyng is the fader of pestilence.　2456–69

It is not easy to distinguish between the sorts of disasters that Mars and Saturn traditionally supervise, for although Mars is basically concerned with bloodshed, other disasters of an accidental sort come under his sway. Saturn's disasters tend to avoid bloodshed and to show malice. In a similar way it is hard to divide the two passages stylistically. To a large extent this speech sounds like cancelled lines from the Mars passage, brushed up with the first person and frugally used. Although the disasters traditionally belong to Saturn the speech, by its nature, fails to assert an independent personality for him. It is of course true that characterisation is not a constant feature of the poem, yet Chaucer has so carefully and successfully created a poetic characterisation for Mars and Venus and has carefully set Diana aside in a position of lesser importance that this forceful speech, sounding so like Mars's own style, must seem something of a failure. Indeed the whole sequence here between Saturn and Venus suggests a plot which is creaking rather loudly, and this speech, gripping enough in itself, does not seem to integrate with the poem as a whole as successfully as do other striking passages in the poem.

Another set-piece worth closer attention than has been paid it is the passage containing the *effictiones* of Lygurge and Emetreus. As the two lovers return to Athens with their supporters the narrator speaks in a measured but fairly unexcited way:

> And sikerly ther trowed many a man
> That nevere, sithen that the world bigan,
> As for to speke of knyghthod of hir hond,
> As fer as God hath maked see or lond,
> Nas of so fewe so noble a compaignye.   2101–5

As he continues he grows more exited at the spectacle and the tournament to come, as we have seen:

> To fighte for a lady, *benedicitee!*
> It were a lusty sighte for to see.   2115–16

And the style of the passage grows finer to match this increase in excitement:

> Som wol ben armed in a haubergeoun,
> And in a brestplate and a light gypoun;
> And some wol have a paire plates large;
> And som wol have a Pruce sheeld or a targe;
> Som wol ben armed on his legges weel,
> And have an ax, and som a mace of steel—
> Ther is no newe gyse that it nas old.   2119–25

This passage of detailed observation, implying a sharp professional eye, is cut off in the last line and is not resolved with a rhyme; it is a lead in to a larger passage, the formal and elaborate *effictio* of Lygurge:

> Blak was his berd, and manly was his face;
> The cercles of his eyen in his heed,
> They gloweden bitwixen yelow and reed,
> And like a grifphon looked he aboute.
> With kempe heeris on his browes stoute;
> His lymes grete, his brawnes harde and stronge,
> His shuldres brode, his armes rounde and longe;   2130–6

This extensive and elaborate description is followed by an account of his clothes and ornaments, emphasising the colour and animal vigour of the man:

> In stede of cote-armure over his harnays,
> With nayles yelewe and brighte as any gold,
> He hadde a beres skyn, col-blak for old.
> His longe heer was kembd bihynde his bak;
> As any ravenes fethere it shoon for blak;   2140–4

The description of Emetreus which follows is equivalent in length, diction and detailed density. It provides different colours and different animals to characterise him, but the effect is plainly to shape two equivalent figures of splendid force:

> His crispe heer lyk rynges was yronne,
> And that was yelow, and glytered as the sonne.
> His nose was heigh, his eyen bright citryn,
> His lyppes rounde, his colour was sangwyn;
> A fewe frakenes in his face yspreynd,
> Bitwixen yelow and somdel blak ymeynd;
> And as a leon he his lookyng caste.   2165–70

Muscatine has commented well on the general function and nature of the two passages; he mentions them as one of the ways in which Chaucer 'produced a poem much more symmetrical than its source' and says of the two princes:[37]

Their varicolored magnificence, like Theseus' banner, makes the whole field glitter up and down—black, white, yellow, red, green, and gold. Their personal attributes—the trumpet voice of Emetrius, the great brawn of Lygurge, their looks, like lion and griffin—give both a martial quality that we are to attribute to the whole company. About the chariot of Lygurge run great, white, muzzled hunting dogs, big as bullocks. Emetrius' pet animals are a white eagle, lions, and leopards. The fact that these animals are tame only makes the comparison with their masters the more impressive. And practically every other detail is a superlative, the quality of which contributes to martial or royal magnificence.

This is true, but it is worth adding that the stylistic treatment of the two passages helps to create this effect. The syntax in the two is very similar; it is generally co-ordinate and falls quickly into a list of attributes. The syntax of Lygurge's description is a little more extended, taken overall, than is Emetreus's and this may be a small reminiscence of the early distinction made syntactically between Palamon and Arcite, but if this is so it is a subtle point indeed. The style is basically the dense manner that has been used in various ways to describe the temples and will be used in the tournament scene; here as in both those cases many of the lines seem to have the four-stress movement which seems a Chaucerian habit when a martial note is appropriate.

The diction of the two passages is also worth noting; some of the most elaborate language in the poem is used, and the elaboration is evenly divided between the two descriptions. There are a number of words here that only appear once or twice in Chaucer, and some that he is first to use, as far as the dictionaries tell us. From Lygurge's description 'grifphon', 'wrethe', 'alauntz', 'mosel' and 'kempe' only appear once in Chaucer and the last three appear to be being used for the first time in the language. The words 'dyamauntz' and 'tourettes' only appear in one other Chaucerian poem, *The Romaunt of the Rose*, itself a work enriched with elaborate diction. This pre-valence of rare words makes the passage one of the most ornate, in this sense, in the poem, and it is very striking to see that Emetreus's description provides very similar results. There, 'citryn', 'frakenes' and 'deduyt' appear only once in Chaucer and the first two words here find their first use in English; 'dyapred' also appears once in *The Romaunt of the Rose* and 'trapped' only appears twice, both times in 'The Knight's Tale'. Both descriptions, then, are elevated with rare diction; most of it is French, but it is interesting to note two words of Norse origin appearing here first—'kempe' and 'frakenes'. Perhaps Norse words seem appropriate about great warriors—and perhaps Chaucer knew more Norse words that we might suspect; certainly these usages suggest that he might have been able to understand *Sir Gawain and the Green Knight* quite easily. In general, then, I would not disagree with Muscatine's assessment of these passages, but I would want to assert the importance of their stylistic character, both in making them rich poetically and in making them balanced. Without these primary powers, the passages could never have made their effect so well.

Finally, I wish to look at an extended sequence that starts at the beginning of part four, where a series of stylistic variations make the poem interesting in its surface movement and also imply a good deal about the personalities and the meaning of the tale as a whole. This part opens busily and quickly drops into a dense poetry where the stresses fall firmly—and the lines may have from three to six of them:

> And to the paleys rood ther many a route
> Of lordes upon steedes and palfreys.
> Ther maystow seen devisynge of harneys
> So unkouth and so riche, and wroght so weel
> Of goldsmythrye, of browdynge, and of steel;
> The sheeldes brighte, testeres, and trappures,
> Gold-hewen helmes, hauberkes, cote-armures;
> Lordes in parementz on hir courseres,
> Knyghtes of retenue, and eek squieres
> Nailynge the speres, and helmes bokelynge;
> Giggynge of sheeldes, with layneres lacynge
> (There as nede is they weren no thyng ydel);   2494–505

The movement of the passage is vigorous and uneven, but after the particularly long line 2500, the movement settles down into a steady four-stress beat and in the last of these lines, 2504, the two final stresses alliterate. Just as happened in the passage discussed above, the alliterative measure seems to be forcing its way into the lines, insisting that it is the proper style for this sort of narrative. It is a small foreshadowing of what is to come later; as so often we have seen, Chaucer's finest effects are not sprung as a surprise, but have been led up to with care, so that they come as a release of expectation, a resolution of the minor discordancies in the narrative leading up to them. The passage remains boldly stressed, aggressive, and alliteration hovers about:

> Yemen on foote, and communes many oon
> With shorte staves, thikke as they may goon;
> Pypes, trompes, nakers, clariounes,
> That in the bataille blowen blody sounes;   2509–12

The success of this bustling scene has been commented on; Salter says it[38]

> . . . accumulates vocabulary of strong visual and aural appeal to convey a scene of material splendour. . . . But it is crowded, not

chaotic. The narrator passes rapidly and logically from one object, activity and person to another, even observing social rank, as he moves from 'lordes in parementz' down to 'yemen on foote and communes many oon'.

Spearing has felt that its success arises because 'an atmosphere of breathless haste is conveyed by the running on of the sense from line to line and from one couplet to another', but as he finds only two enjambements in a passage of at least thirty lines (i.e. 2502–3 and 2506–7) this seems unconvincing.[39] The effect is surely made by the steady succession of end-stopped lines, falling firmly after each other just as the strong stresses fall in succession and just as new details keep pouring into the passage; the enjambements (and only the second of them has no pause at all at the line's end) merely vary this pattern momentarily.

As we have seen this noisy scene is made to fall quiet when Theseus appears (cf. p. 130 above), but even before its end it is resolved into something more orderly, without losing its forceful compactness:

> Somme seyden thus, somme seyde 'it shal be so';
> Somme helden with hym with the blake berd,
> Somme with the balled, somme with the thikke herd;
> Somme seyde he looked grymme, and he wolde fighte;
> 'He hath a sparth of twenty pound of wighte.' 2516–20

It is a delightful vignette of a stadium crowd, but it also calms the passage down and makes more fluent the narrator's withdrawal from the scene. It is with ease that he turns to Theseus in a quieter vein, more suitable for a great duke:

> Thus was the halle ful of divynynge,
> Long after that the sonne gan to sprynge. 2521–2

After Theseus's lofty speech has been read, the narrative moves with a fairly straightforward way up to the tournament. The balance of the style is notable as the contestants enter, for a six-line 'stanza' brings them in:

> And westward, thurgh the gates under Marte,
> Arcite, and eek the hondred of his parte,
> With baner reed is entred right anon;
> And in that selve moment Palamon
> Is under Venus, estward in the place,
> With baner whyt, and hardy chiere and face. 2581–6

A measure of Chaucer's skill is in the ease with which the poetry here makes us accept completely the overt statement in the next line:

> In al the world, to seken up and doun,
> So evene, withouten variacioun,
> Ther nere swiche compaignyes tweye; 2587–9

The scene in which these 'compaignyes' finally meet to resolve their apparent equality has often been described and praised; much has been made of its alliterative lines, especially by Spearing,[40] but I would want to insist that, as before at the beginning of this long sequence, the alliteration only asserts itself towards the end of the passage. True, the opening of the tournament gives a taste of it:

> 'Do now youre devoir, yonge knyghtes proude!' 2598

But the opening part of the fight is in heavily stressed lines with little sign of alliteration:

> Now ryngen trompes loud and clarioun.
> Ther is namoore to seyne, but west and est
> In goon the speres ful sadly in arrest;
> In gooth the sharpe spore into the syde. 2600–3

The heavy stresses establish themselves first as the mode of the passage, and only towards the end are they joined by alliteration to satisfy our expectations of a fully martial style:

> Out goon the swerdes as the silver bright;
> The helmes they tohewen and toshrede;
> Out brest the blood with stierne stremes rede;
> With myghty maces the bones they tobreste. 2608–11

As with so many of Chaucer's stylistic effects, modulation is the method; the style changes slowly and takes on a certain aspect. It is not alliterative poetry, it just sounds rather like it. Chaucer could no doubt have written a thumping piece in the metre of the alliterative *Morte Arthure* had he chosen to, but here as elsewhere suggestion is the purpose of his stylistic modulation. Just as he made Palamon and Arcite sound a little different from each other without radical alterations in style, so here he gives a fine sounding battle without adopting fully the alliterative style. Some of the lines have four stresses, but most have the more usual five, and only line 2605 could come from an alliterative poem; even in *Piers Plowman* the others would seem odd. The result of this is that the effect is subtle and that it is easily quietened: the skill with which the alliteration fades out on the unobtrusive letter 'h' typifies Chaucer's concern with letting the poem flow on:

> He foyneth on his feet with his tronchoun,
> And he hym hurtleth with his hors adoun;
> He thurgh the body is hurt and sithen take,
> Maugree his heed and broght unto the stake:
> As forward was, right ther he moste abyde. 2615–19

This battle dies away and we hear of Palamon's capture and Arcite's death; reference has been made above to the skill with which Theseus's authority is asserted at the point. Arcite makes his last speech and dies, and in passing we might note how the ugly death scene is made the more striking as the active verbs tend to fall at the beginning of the lines, a device seen before in the poem, cf. p. 140.

In the ensuing sorrow it is Egeus who begins the upturn of the poem towards its end; Theseus will initiate the funeral and speak the poem's conclusion but even such a powerful figure needs help and reassurance at times (an interesting point, against those critics who see Theseus as having divine aspects; here, as in his last speech, he is very human). Egeus' poised experience is expressed in a style of perfect balance:

> No man myghte gladen Theseus,
> Savynge his olde fader Egeus,
> That knew this worldes transmutacioun,
> As he hadde seyn it chaunge bothe up and doun,
> Joye after wo, and wo after gladnesse,
> And shewed hem ensamples and liknesse.
>   'Right as ther dyed nevere man,' quod he,
> 'That he ne lyvede in erthe in some degree,
> Right so ther lyvede never man,' he seyde,
> 'In al this world, that som tyme he ne deyde.
> This world nys but a thurghfare ful of wo,
> And we been pilgrymes, passynge to and fro.
> Deeth is an ende of every worldly soore.' 2837–49

As William Frost remarks, Egeus 'has been taken by some critics for a dotard',[41] but this is to see the shadow of Polonius looming over him. His speech is certainly very simple, but its sentiment is developed in Theseus's final speech, and its equipoise is a fully Boethian one. What Egeus does not say is that man may win honour in the world, and this idea is now worked out in action, as Theseus prepares a grand worldly spectacle to honour the worldly glory of Arcite. As he moves towards this the syntax lengthens stating both the decision to have a funeral service and also the level at which it will be conducted:

> And at the last he took conclusioun
> That ther as first Arcite and Palamoun
> Hadden for love the bataille hem bitwene,
> That in that selve grove, swoote and grene,
> Ther as he hadde his amorouse desires,
> His compleynte, and for love his hoote fires,
> He wolde make a fyr in which the office
> Funeral he myghte al accomplice.   2857–64

The sentence works skilfully up to its conclusion, where Theseus's 'conclusioun' is given in the main verb 'wolde make' and where the elaborate diction of the run-on last couplet prepares us for something fine to come. But it could not possibly prepare us for the magnificent sequence that we do find.

First we have a full *descriptio* of Arcite's bier, including a line that Shakespeare was not ashamed to adopt—'He leyde hym, bare the visage, on the bere' (2877)—and then the poet moves on swiftly, with much visual detail through the marshalling of the procession. The mode is that we have seen so often in this poem; densely packed list of details, epithets and emblematic sights, with subordinate and parenthetic amplification to make the scene more elaborate and slower moving:

> Duc Theseus leet forth thre steedes brynge,
> That trapped were in steel al gliterynge,
> And covered with the armes of daun Arcite.
> Upon these steedes, that weren grete and white,
> Ther seten folk, of whiche oon baar his sheeld,
> Another his spere up on his hondes heeld,
> The thridde baar with hym his bowe Turkeys
> (Of brend gold was the caas and eek the harneys);   2889–96

But this confident and familiar pattern is only the beginning, for in this last of the set-pieces in this poem Chaucer sets out to overgo all the others and to amaze his audience with the splendour of the great *occupatio*. This is the climax of the high style in the poem, but as I have argued above it also finds a place in the conceptual strategy of the poem and it is carefully embedded in the ongoing narrative. The poem builds steadily up to the long *occupatio* and then after it the poem is deliberately moved down to a lower pitch, though Theseus's last speech has some subtle effects of style. In this way the last sequence of the poem fully supports the general thesis of this chapter, for I have tried to show how Chaucer's stylistic powers are not only used for public display, but move away from that limited and ultimately sterile process and are rather used as a vital element in his creation of a work of art.

The function of the style in 'The Knight's Tale' cannot be summed up simply, for it is a long poem and the style is various in nature and effect. In some cases the variation of the style serves a purpose no more complex than to keep an extended poem moving with a varied and interesting surface. It is also true that some of the great set-pieces must have had some autonomous force as craftsmanship alone —especially if we are to imagine the poem performed by the author. But the poem's full quality can be seen in the fact that these craft-functions of the style are not all; that while achieving this level of artistry the complex and changing style also often works to sharpen the meaning of the poem and even, at its subtlest, to imply meaning before it is made explicit. I believe 'The Knight's Tale' has been well explicated by its major critics in recent years and hope that what is said here will confirm the view of the poem that generally obtains. I also hope that these remarks will give some explanation in poetic terms why 'The Knights' Tale' remains such a compelling, stimulating and ultimately testing poem.

NOTES

1. *The Poetry of Chaucer* (Boston, 1922), see pp. 169–72 especially.
2. French, 'The Lovers in the *Knight's Tale*', *JEGP*, XLVIII (1949), 320–8; Frost, 'An Interpretation of Chaucer's Knight's Tale', *RES*, XXV (1940), 289–304; Muscatine, 'Form, Texture and Meaning in Chaucer's *Knight's Tale*', *PMLA*, LXV (1950), 911–29: this is reprinted, with some changes, as pp. 175–90 of *Chaucer and the French Tradition* and as I have used this book elsewhere in this study, it is from this that I quote.
3. 'Aspects of Order in the Knight's Tale', *SP*, LVII (1960), 606–21; see p. 621.
4. *The Knight's Tale and the Clerk's Tale*, *Studies in English Literature*, 5 (London, 1962); see p. 10.
5. Ruggiers, *The Art of the Canterbury Tales* (Madison, 1965), pp. 151–66; Spearing, *The Knight's Tale* (Cambridge, 1966), Introduction, pp. 1–79; Delasanta, 'Uncommon Commonplaces in "The Knight's Tale" ', *NM*, LXX (1969), 683–90.
6. Pp. 75–8.
7. *Characterization in Chaucer's Knight's Tale*, *University of Michigan Contributions in Modern Philology*, no. 5 (Ann Arbor, 1947).
8. P. 177, both quotations.
9. Pp. 13, 12 and 13 respectively.
10. *Papers on Language and Literature*, III, Supplement (1967), 71–79; see p. 78.
11. Pp. 43–7.
12. Speirs, pp. 122–6; Donaldson, pp. 48–51; Ian Robinson, *Chaucer's Prosody* (London, 1971), pp. 156–60; Haller, 'The *Knight's Tale* and the Epic Tradition', *CR*, I (1966–7), 67–84.

M

13. Dean, 'Imagery in the *Knight's Tale* and the *Miller's Tale*', *MS*, XXXI (1969), 149–63; Van, 'Second Meanings in Chaucer's *Knight's Tale*', *CR*, III (1968–9), 69–76; for Baum and Kökeritz see notes 2 and 3, p. 95 above; Foster, 'Humor in the *Knight's Tale*', *CR*, III (1968–9), 88–94.
14. Muscatine, p. 179; Spearing, p. 22.
15. Speirs finds the passage 'fresh' and 'real' because of its 'conversational' tone, p. 122; Trevor Whittock, in *A Reading of the Canterbury Tales* (Cambridge, 1968), finds 'freshness and natural vigour', 'beauty and force' and 'simplicity and elegance' in the passage, pp. 60–1; Spearing remarks, more aptly in my view, on the fact that 'Emelye appears less as a person than as a personification', pp. 12 and 40.
16. P. 41.
17. Cf. Spearing, p. 160.
18. Whittock finds 'fertility and joy' and 'a spontaneous benison' here, p. 67; Spearing discusses the scene less exotically but with good sense, p. 167.
19. Spearing gives a short discussion of this speech, p. 169.
20. Spearing sees a change of style in Palamon's prayer; I cannot see at line 2236 a sharp 'descent in this line from the dignified language used earlier in his prayer' (line 1378 in Spearing's numbering); as I have tried to show, the effect seems to me more general than this.
21. P. 180.
22. Muscatine discusses the relation of Arcite's sickness to this speech, p. 187 and Spearing comments briefly, pp. 64 and 185.
23. Pp. 156–7.
24. Muscatine, p. 182; Frost, p. 294.
25. Pp. 75–8.
26. P. 184.
27. P. 689.
28. Whittock, p. 529; Harrington, p. 77.
29. P. 16.
30. P. 79; Patricia Thomson quotes this passage as an example of Chaucer's power to raise the style suddenly, *Sir Thomas Wyatt and His Background* (London, 1964), p. 115.
31. Spearing and J. A. W. Bennett feel that 'breketh' here is ambiguous, apparently having the hunter as subject, but seeming more applicable to the animal itself, see Spearing, p. 170, Bennett, *The Knight's Tale* (London, 1954), p. 126.
32. Spearing comments briefly on the difference between an early and a late *occupatio*, pp. 34–5.
33. Whittock, pp. 73–4; Spearing, pp. 34–6.
34. P. 304.
35. See especially his discussion in pp. 151–75.
36. Speirs, pp. 124–5; Whittock, pp. 63–4; Salter, p. 17; Spearing, pp. 60–1.
37. Pp. 180 and 182 respectively.
38. P. 15.
39. P. 42.
40. Whittock, p. 70; Spearing, p. 43 and *Criticism and Medieval Poetry*, p. 19.
41. P. 299.

4. *The Manciple's Tale and The Franklin's Tale*

As in Chapter 1, here I discuss two poems which have some similarities and a considerable number of differences; once again the purpose is both to offer an account of the two works in terms of their style and to use the one to illustrate the other. These two poems are generically more closely related than those studied in Chapter 1 for they are both part of *The Canterbury Tales*, but this leaves room for dispartity between them. I am not, of course, suggesting that this is yet another Canterbury group! Rather I take these two because they are stylistically interesting, because little has been said about this aspect of them and because they offer a useful contrast in the person of their narrators. 'The Manciple's Tale', I will argue, does have real qualities and certain characteristics that have not been adequately described, but in comparison with 'The Franklin's Tale' it not only lacks poetic subtlety but it is also without the integration with the rest of *The Canterbury Tales* that is the mark of the best of this varied collection of poems.

I. *'The Manciple's Tale'*

Critical reaction to 'The Manciple's Tale' has been similar to that shown to most of Chaucer's less famous works; the more senior critics of the modern period regarded it rather coolly as a slight and unsuccessful work, but more recently, in keeping with the *crescendo* in enthusiasm for Chaucer, some critics have found a variety of reasons to see the tale as a masterpiece. The shift from polite dismissal to near-adulation has been a remarkable one, and neither extreme seems justified by a close study of the poem; here, as in the case of *Anelida and Arcite*, I am drawn to a medial position for there are elements of truth on both sides. In what follows I shall be discussing not merely the style of the poem, but also the nature of the poem and its narrator as they emerge from a study of the style and so it is necessary to make a more ample summary of critical opinion that has generally been appropriate here.

Manly thought this poem 'one of the least known and least interesting of the tales' and felt that it was

> . . . not particularly appropriate to the Manciple or indeed to any of the other pilgrims, and that no effort is made to adapt it to him.[1]

But although it lacked interest for Manly it was useful to his argument, for he asserted that Chaucer 'developed the tale, not imaginatively, but rhetorically'; in support of this he offered statistics, saying the tale contained

> 32 lines of *sententiae*, 36 of *exempla*, 18 of *exclamatio*, 14 of *sermocinatio*, 3 of technical transition, and mechanical additions, clever enough as mere writing, but entirely devoid of life.[2]

As a general critique he said

> If the tale had been written as a school exercise, to illustrate the manner in which rhetorical padding could be introduced into a narrative framework, the process of composition would not have been more mechanical or the result more distressing.[3]

The flaws in Manly's arguments are obvious enough: he does not demonstrate that these figures are 'devoid of life' and he assumes that to name a figure as 'rhetorical' is to define it as without vitality, although the figures he mentions—in particular *sermocinatio*, direct speech and *demonstratio*, vivid description—are common enough in all types of fiction. But to dispute Manly's methods of argument does not necessarily dispose of his conclusions; his judgment that the tale is 'devoid of life' and 'mechanical' is worth considering, if only as the affective reaction of an experienced Chaucerian to this tale, and I shall return to this.

The view that the tale is a sterile rhetorical exercise receives some support from Robinson, who holds that the 'treatment is rhetorically formal, even somewhat pedantic'.[4] Robinson also gives his weight to Manly's judgment that the tale does not typify its teller when he says 'the tale bears no indication of having been written for one of the Canterbury pilgrims.' J. R. Hulbert is in agreement: '. . . the Greek setting, the rather learned rhetorical development, and the moral disquisition are completely incongruous with the dishonest Manciple.'[5]

Robinson's view of this disparity between the tale and the teller leads him to support, with some caution, the view put forward by Gustav Plessow that the tale was an earlier poem re-used for the Manciple.[6] Plessow's edition also analyses some of the rhetorical figures in the tale and so, although he eschews evaluation, his views on the tale's date and its rhetorical features have been taken as evidence by the critics who judge the tale as a failure and see it as an early exercise, not properly assimilated to its new place in *The Canterbury Tales*.

More recent critics have taken a different view, finding various reasons to praise the poem. One modern attempt to demonstrate it as a masterpiece is, because of its method, quite unconvincing. The title of Richard Hazelton's article '*The Manciple's Tale*: Parody and Critique' will itself suggest to experienced Chaucerians what it sets out to do. The thesis is that when Chaucer appears to write badly he is parodying other writers and that any crudity in his work is automatically a sharp thrust at crudity in general. This approach explains everything about the poem with a sweeping confidence:[7]

> The combination of elements and style that gives the *Manciple's Tale* the appearance of a literary patchwork is a carefully designed combination, a pastiche, achieved by the conscious juxtaposition of incongruous matters and styles for the purposes of parody.

This statement is based on several stylistic features of the poem; the *occupatio* in lines 121–2 is found funny, the description of Phebus is said to be comic because 'its extravagance and profusion are the clue to its comic function' and in general, it is argued:[8]

> The style is pompously inflated for comic purposes, with its *exclamationes*, and with its apostrophes aimed in all directions.

But we are not shown that this so-called *occupatio* (it is really just *brevitas*, being without the negatively introduced description of *occupatio*) is more comic than others by Chaucer that are seriously meant, nor that the *exclamationes* are themselves inflated, nor that the *apostrophes* are more various in direction than others in perfectly serious poems. To show that an effect is parodic a critic must make a careful analysis; he must demonstrate the type of thing that is being parodied, the precise verbal links between the two and, most important, he must reveal the exaggerations or infelicities which insist that this version *is* parodic. Chaucer can write parody, as has been shown in the cases of 'Sir Thopas' and 'The Miller's Tale',[9] but in both cases scholarly critics have set out the verbal evidence and there is also a strong contextual suggestion that parody is the mode. In this case the author neither offers verbal detail nor quotes any contextual support (there is none); what is offered as criticism is merely an idiosyncratic reading of a text, looking much like Chaucerian bardolatry. But this is not the only ground on which I would disagree with Hazelton's reading of the poem. I hope to show below that this is not a 'literary patchwork', that it is, rather, a coherent and in certain terms a successful rhetorical structure in which each element has a fit place. Consequently even the beginning of this argument for parody is without foundation.

A different approach has been taken by a group of modern critics, who have argued that the prologue and tale are related and that the tale does dramatise the Manciple's personality. This 'tale-teller relationship' approach seeks to align 'The Manciple's Prologue and Tale' with tales like the Knight's and the Pardoner's, where it is generally agreed that the tale is shaped by the author's idea of the teller's personality and is itself a further revelation of that personality. J. Burke Severs argues that the Manciple's character is revealed sharply at line 307, where 'he suddenly changes the basis of his judgment from morality to expediency.'[10] Severs depends heavily on the Manciple's use of the word 'lemman' to show his 'lewed' character, as described in the General Prologue, and he offers a number of arguments to discount the effect of apparently 'lered' elements in the tale, especially its rhetorical and sententious aspects; I will discuss these arguments below, when looking at the relevant passages.

Morton Donner, in a much shorter article, argues similarly that the idea of discretion presented in the tale is a working out of the Manciple's reactions in the prologue, and says that:[11]

> Fragment IX can no longer be considered a mediocre tale arbitrarily appended to a brilliant prologue, but rather a well-integrated whole, in which the material presented in the Prologue is further developed in the Tale.

These two critiques largely ignore the style of the poem but Earle Birney sets out to give this viewpoint detailed support by showing that the tale is in the Manciple's voice. He identifies a lack of classical background, an ignorance of chivalry (in that archery is highly regarded) and feels that the word 'lemman' and the crow's blunt language also show that the tale:[12]

> . . . has, in fact, all the earmarks of an unsuccessful attempt at a 'gentil' tale by a fundamentally 'lewed' man.

This is a forceful argument, admirable in method and packed with the detail and ingenuity we would expect from its author. The three articles may be taken together, in that they move in the same direction, but Birney's is the only one which tackles the problem that arises because the prologue and the tale seem so different in style and approach. He tries to bring the two closer together, but I do not feel his arguments are very strong; his point about 'lemman' is, as I shall argue below, defeated in the text, and it would surely take a great lack of classical background to turn Phebus into a proper medieval knight. When discussing the nature of the tale and the type of teller implied by it I will try to show why the arguments of these three critics do not successfully bring together the prologue and tale.

Where these critics pursued the 'tale-teller relationship' line, Wayne Shumaker has defended the tale on the equally respectable 'tale-group' principle. He argues that the tale is carefully linked with 'The Parson's Tale' and 'The Retracciouns' and that the thesis of this group is that 'a careful watch ought to be put upon the tongue at all times, and in all circumstances.'[13] (The relevance to 'The Retracciouns' is an attractive part of the thesis.) Shumaker's argument oversimplifies the thesis of 'The Parson's Tale', for that extensive sermon preaches on other topics as well as the need for Christian restraint of the tongue. 'The Manciple's Tale' does clearly treat this topic directly, and Shumaker deals with the prologue by saying that it illustrates the thesis 'by contrast'. But he makes no detailed attempt to show links between the prologue and the tale, and so, ingenious as his argument is, it tends to emphasise the disparity between the two.

The main cause of this disparity is the tale itself; it fits awkwardly after a prologue which is in no way surprising to the reader, for it is one of a number of similar dramatic links in *The Canterbury Tales*. Before looking at the tale it is necessary to establish the nature of the prologue and the sort of expectation it arouses in the reader.

'The Manciple's Prologue' begins by setting out some of the mechanics of the pilgrimage; in a brisk voice the narrator locates this tale towards the end of the trip to Canterbury:

> Woot ye nat where ther stant a litel toun
> Which that ycleped is Bobbe-up-and-doun,
> Under the Blee, in Caunterbury Weye? 1–3

And he goes on to present one of the little dramas typical of these linking passages; as usual the Host is at the centre of it, boisterously drawing attention to the Cook's torpor:

> Ther gan our Hooste for to jape and pleye,
> And seyde, 'Sires, what! Dun is in the myre!
> Is ther no man, for preyere ne for hyre,
> That wole awake oure felawe al bihynde? 4–7

The Host is a shrewd judge of a man's status and the respect due to him, and he speaks with a jocular bluntness to the Cook:

> Hastow had fleen al nyght, or artow dronke?
> Or hastow with som quene al nyght yswonke,
> So that thow mayst nat holden up thyn heed?' 17–19

The crisp verse and the forceful language here, as in several other places, create masterfully the Host's personality and give an index of the social standing of the person he addresses.

Another familiar feature in these links is a conflict between pilgrims that gives rise to a tale, and this now follows. The Manciple chooses to step in and 'excuse' the drunken Cook from his tale, and his words outline something of his personality. He begins by being almost fussily polite:

> 'Wel,' quod the Maunciple, 'if it may don ese
> To thee, sire Cook, and to no wight displese,
> Which that heere rideth in this compaignye,
> And that oure Hoost wole, of his curteisye,
> I wol as now excuse thee of thy tale. 25–9

The tone is similar to that in which the Host has spoken to the Prioress and although the Manciple does address the Cook as 'thee' he also calls him 'sire'; this opening seems credible as the voice of a man who, the General Prologue has told us, makes good profit by a show of humility. But as he goes on the Manciple abandons this polite concessive syntax:

> For, in good feith, thy visage is ful pale,
> Thyne eyen daswen eek, as that me thynketh,
> And, wel I woot, thy breeth ful soure stynketh: 30–2

In contrast to what has come before this is direct, but it is still filled with asides that maintain a cautious note. As the Manciple goes on, however, he grows more confident, perhaps because the Cook seems unable to answer:

> See how he ganeth, lo! this dronken wight,
> As though he wolde swolwe us anonright. 35-6

Against this impotent target the Manciple becomes even bolder:

> Hoold cloos thy mouth, man, by the fader kyn! 37

And he abuses the Cook confidently, now using pauses which emphasise his attack and seeking to involve the other pilgrims on his side:

> Fy, stynkyng swyn! fy, foule moote thee falle!
> A, taketh heede, sires, of this lusty man. 40-1

The speech is developed with great skill by the poet, for it moves swiftly from careful politeness to open castigation as the Cook reveals himself helpless. His total inability is underlined as he loses all control:

> . . . on the Manciple he gan nodde faste
> For lakke of speche, and doun the hors hym caste,
> Where as he lay, til that men hym up took. 47-9

And the narrator, following general opinion as usual, joins in the scorn:

> This was a fair chyvachee of a cook!
> Alas! he nadde holde hym by his ladel! 50-1

The Manciple seems to have won in this little encounter, but now the Host takes part again. At first he concurs with the Manciple's judgment and dismisses the Cook:

> Telle on thy tale; of hym make I no fors. 68

But the Host makes little more 'fors' of the Manciple; he orders him to tell a tale—the Manciple has not offered—and as the Host goes on he takes the Manciple up on his treatment of the Cook:

> But yet, Manciple, in feith thou art to nyce,
> Thus openly repreve hym of his vice. 69-70

And the reasons the Host gives for this statement are aimed shrewdly at the Manciple:

> Another day he wole, peraventure,
> Reclayme thee and brynge thee to lure;
> I meene, he speke wole of smale thynges,
> As for to pynchen at thy rekenynges,
> That were nat honest, if it cam to preef. 71-5

With considerable cunning the Host appears to side with the Manciple, warning him of the trouble the Cook could cause, but the last line is as open a criticism as the Host makes of any pilgrim, and the phrase 'nat honest' sums up the drift of the General Prologue's discussion of the Manciple.

The passage as a whole has quick wit and skilful writing; the nature of the Manciple's self-righteous speech, the comic discomfiture of the Cook and the swift turning of the scene against the Manciple are all effected with vigour and economy. The scene ends finely, as the Manciple hastily back-tracks:

> That that I spak, I seyde it in my bourde.   81

And, as the final irony, the Manciple shows how frail his moral judgments are by quickly offering the Cook 'A draghte of wyn, of a ripe grape' (83). The Cook, who beside the Manciple seems a disarmingly straightforward, even charitable figure, drinks happily 'And thanked him in swich wise as he koude.' (93) The Host, having had his say and having organised the next tale, now smooths things over by imputing the concord to the benefits of wine rather than to the Manciple's shifty character, and invites the Manciple to proceed.

This prologue is typical of the dramatic mode of *The Canterbury Tales* at its best; it is generically similar to the prologues of the Miller, Franklin and Pardoner, to name a few, in that it is amusing and lively, filled with sharp observation and subtle revelation of the characters involved. In it the person who is to tell the next tale is revealed to us to some extent and we look forward to see what sort of tale he will tell and, especially, to see what more we shall discover about his personality and ideas in the progress of his tale. But this time we are to be disappointed; the tale as it unfolds does not tell us more about the Manciple. It has a coherent nature, but nothing about that nature relates to the Manciple as he has so far been shown to us.

A study of 'The Manciple's Tale' shows it to be a restrained but thorough working out of the medieval concept of *amplificatio*. The poem depends on a brief story with a simple moral, but is developed by a series of structural devices into a thoughtful discussion of aspects of human nature. It rarely departs from a middle style, and the most striking thing about it as poetry is the way it steadily builds itself up into a whole. In order to comprehend this structural development it is first necessary to discuss the concept of *amplificatio*.

Geoffrey of Vinsauf is the only rhetorician to develop this topic at any length; indeed, it is omitted from Baldwin's 'Synoptic Index' which purports to epitomise the views of the rhetoricians, probably because Baldwin has such a low opinion of Geoffrey.[14] *Amplificatio* has been misrepresented by most of the commentators on rhetoric; they have regarded it as being a technique of detailed style and as being without meaningful content, rather than as a method of structure devoted to developing simultaneously the body of the poem and its meaning. The account most critics have given makes *amplificatio* seem like the medieval word for the 'padding' that schoolchildren are advised against in their essays. Faral's analysis has probably given rise to much of this; he says that by *amplificatio* 'les anciens entendaient "rehausser (une idée), la faire valoir",' whereas 'les théoriciens du XIIe et du XIIIe siècle entendent par là "développer, allonger (un sujet)".'[15] The distinction is valid, but the medieval writers' concern with the form does not mean they ignore the content: Faral is careful to insert '(un sujet)', though I feel he may not have realised the word's full significance. But later critics ignored this parenthesis and seemed to think the rhetoricians cared nothing for content. Atkins sees Geoffrey's discussion as being intended to expound 'methods of amplifying and abbreviating expression'—as a mere figure of style, that is—and perhaps as a consequence he sees no place in it for a development of meaning; it is just a 'decorative conception.'[16] Baldwin similarly says that 'Geoffrey devotes most of his book to the rhetorical means of dilation', here referring to the figures of style as well, and letting 'dilation' stand as an implied pejorative: even Douglas Kelly, in his re-appraisal of Geoffrey, accepts the traditional view in this issue.[17]

But if Geoffrey is read without bias it is clear that when he discusses *amplificatio* and *abbrevatio* he regards them as methods by which the author can develop the main body of his work. He has previously discussed methods of beginning the work and then says:[18]

> The poem's development now invites you onward. Keeping to our image, direct your steps further along the road's course.

In a recent article Jane Baltzell Kopp has shown that Geoffrey has structure in mind here,[19] but she does not demonstrate the importance to him of meaning throughout this section. It is this which separates his *amplificatio* from 'padding', and it seems important to establish his understanding of *amplificatio* in general and the devices which create it in particular. The metaphor that he uses to describe the process of moving forward in the poem is, characteristically, an illuminating one:[20]

The material to be moulded, like the moulding of wax, is at first
hard to the touch. If intense concentration enkindle native ability,
the material is soon made pliant by the mind's fire, and submits
to the hand in whatever way it requires, malleable to any form.
The hand of the mind controls it, either to amplify or curtail.

The critical premises behind the metaphor may seem inadequate
in the light of modern critical theory: Geoffrey's assumption that
the hard wax, or topic, exists before the treatment of it would
arouse modern nervousness about separating form and content
(though there are several indications elsewhere that Geoffrey
recognises this separation to be an over-simplification).[21] But the
metaphor makes it quite clear that it is the topic of the poem that
the mind works on through *amplificatio* and *abbrevatio*, that they are
ways of shaping the meaning of the poem. To confirm this, Geoffrey's
opening discussion, giving, as it were the contents of his book,
describes the second section, which is usually entitled '*Amplificatio*
and *Abbrevatio*', in this way:[22]

Its second care: with what scales to establish a delicate balance
if meaning is to be given the weight appropriate to it.

An examination of Geoffrey's division of *amplificatio* shows how
he sets out these various ways of elaborating and confirming the
work's *sententia*. *Descriptio* is a familiar enough part of literary
structure, especially when we realise that Geoffrey includes under
this heading the description of scenes of action as well (he would
have applauded the hunting scenes in *Sir Gawain and the Green Knight*
as very fine *descriptiones*, rich and dense); *prosopopoeia* or personification (*conformatio* in Latin terminology) is merely a method of giving
speech to an animal, object or abstraction that would not be expected
in logical terms, to speak; *apostrophe* and *digressio* are (as their
etymologies suggest) devices wherein the narrator turns away from
the ongoing course of the action, but Geoffrey's very full examples
show that these are not merely occasions for interpolated set-pieces:
they are meant to provide an extension of or an elaboration of the
moral of the work (it is because the gap between the moralised
apostrophe and *digressio* and their matrix is too great that they become
comic in 'The Nun's Priest's Tale'); *oppositio* is, in a similar way,
not narrative but it is a confirmation, by negative means, of what
has just been said; *collatio* also expands the work, but it too is based
on an element already in the work: the metaphor or simile enlarges
the nature of an object, person or action in the narrative. It is a

premise of the amplified style that ornateness is, if not bombastic (all the rhetoricians warn against this), a good thing, and accordingly Geoffrey prefers metaphor because it is more complex. The same aesthetic is behind the justification of *interpretatio* and *circuitio*, the first two methods of amplification that Geoffrey discusses; both are ways of creating that sense of a rich fulness that is natural to the amplified style in poetry.

To the modern reader this may sound only like a programme for bombast, but this depends completely on how the poet handles it. Geoffrey is not advising the poet what to say in his poem, merely recommending certain structural methods of varying the surface of his poem and moving onwards with his topic. Many of these are perfectly natural in a poem, and even the more ornate devices, such as *interpretatio* and *collatio*, will seem perfectly acceptable if used with decorum—if, as Geoffrey foreshadows in his introduction, the balance is right between the meaning and the expression. Thus in 'The Knight's Tale' and *Paradise Lost* much amplification is used with great success, whereas in 'The Nun's Priest's Tale' it is made ludicrous. Geoffrey's final remark shows that this sort of structure is basically a way of building something magnificent:[23]

> In this way, plentiful harvest springs from a little seed; great rivers draw their source from a tiny spring; from a slender twig a great tree rises and spreads.

'The Manciple's Tale' certainly only has a 'little seed' of plot, and it is not hard to see how the poet has built up on this with the device of *amplificatio*; this presumably is the 'rather learned rhetorical development' that Hulbert referred to, though he did not spell it out, and when Robinson called the tale 'rhetorically formal' he must have meant this aspect of it as well. It should be noted, however, that though the development of the tale does seem to owe a good deal to Geoffrey's notion of *amplificatio* this does not mean that Chaucer knew Geoffrey's work at first hand. Earlier critics have assumed he did, but J. J. Murphy has shown good reasons why even the direct reference to Geoffrey in 'The Nun's Priest's Tale' need not imply first-hand knowledge,[24] and if, as he shows, Chaucer may have known anthology pieces from Geoffrey's work he may just as well have known his analysis of *amplificatio* from this sort of source, especially since it is much fuller than similar passages in the other rhetoricians,[25] and may have been considered worth excerpting for that reason.

One scholar has written on *amplificatio* in the tale; in his scrupulous edition Plessow noted that several of the devices of *amplificatio* were to be found in it, and he also recognised that Geoffrey saw this as a structural system:[26]

> Klar ausgesprochene Regeln für den Bau des Haupteils einer Dichtung vermissen wir ganz.
>
> So wäre, was an Anweisungen vorhanden ist, nicht allzu aufschlussreich für uns, wenn nicht in den mittelalterlichen Rhetoriken ein Abschnitt ausführliche Hinweise auf Bauglieder enthielte, die in ihrer Gesamtheit das, was uns fehlend dünkt, grossenteils ersetzen. Es sind die Anweisungen für den Gebrauch von Amplifikations- und Abbreviationsmitteln.

But as Plessow was not writing a critical study, in our sense of the word, he did not go on to elucidate the effect of the tale's rhetorical nature. He also failed to distinguish sufficiently between devices of amplification and figures of style which may seem similar (Kopp makes this error too).[27] Under *amplificatio*, devices are discussed solely as structural elements: it is how *collatio occulta*, metaphor fits into its context and how it develops the poem that is of interest here, whereas when Geoffrey discusses metaphor as the 'difficult ornament' *translatio*, to give it its commonest name (Geoffrey calls it *transsumptio*), he gives a painstaking verbal analysis of the mechanics of the metaphor. The different names given to metaphor in the two sections show very clearly how it is differently regarded. In this respect, as in several others, critics have not recognised Geoffrey's clear mind and orderly method.

In what follows I shall given an account of the poem, showing how it develops as a piece of *amplificatio*, and how overall it implies quite a strong personality in its narrator, though not one that bears any resemblance to the Manciple as we know him.

The tale begins simply, without any of the elaborate openings Geoffrey has recommended for a work of real complexity, and it launches straight into a *descriptio* of its leading character:

> Whan Phebus dwelled heere in this erthe adoun,
> As olde bookes maken mencioun,
> He was the mooste lusty bachiler
> In al this world, and eek the best archer.   105–8

The *descriptio* is elaborated and confirmed with a short *oppositio*:

> Certes the kyng of Thebes, Amphioun,
> That with his syngyng walled that citee,
> Koude nevere syngen half so wel as hee.   116–18

The language is not ornate—'mencioun' and 'bachiler' are not new or rare words at this time—and the syntax, while being capable of subordination, is not very complex. It is an unremarkable middle style, and the poem continues methodically as we now read a *descriptio* of Phebus's crow: it is shorter than that given to Phebus, but its structure is very similar. First we are given a statement of the crow's qualities:

> Whit was this crowe as is a snow-whit swan,
> And countrefete the speche of every man
> He koude, whan he sholde telle a tale.   133–5

And then the crow's prowess is asserted further by an *oppositio*:

> Therwith in al this world no nyghtyngale
> Ne koude, by an hondred thousand deel,
> Syngen so wonder myrily and weel.   136–8

The story moves on and the methodical tone given by the structural similarity and even style of these two descriptions is supported by verbal repetition; the previous paragraph began:

> Now hadde this Phebus in his hous a crowe   130

and this one starts:

> Now hadde this Phebus in his hous a wyf   139

This effect of careful, but rather unimaginative development is strengthened by the frequent repetition of 'This Phebus' at the beginning of paragraphs; first used at line 125, it is found in the two lines just quoted and then again, prominent at the beginning of the lines, at lines 156, 196 and 262.

But the development of the poem also has variation; for we do not have a *descriptio* of Phebus's wife; instead, another method of *amplificatio* is employed as the narrator gives a short *digressio* on wives and their proper treatment:

> A good wyf, that is clene of werk and thoght,
> Sholde nat been kept in noon awayt, certayn;
> And trewely, the labour is in vayn
> To kepe a shrewe, for it wol nat bee.
> This hold I for a verray nycetee,
> To spille labour for to kepe wyves:
> Thus writen olde clerkes in hir lyves.   148–54

The style, remains even and unremarkable; it is a direct and informative *sententia*, dilating in a thoughtful way upon an element in the narrative. But there is little more to be said about the passage: although it is the first appearance of the narrator it tells us nothing about him that we can relate directly to the Manciple. This is an admonitory comment, it is true, and we have seen the Manciple rebuking the Cook, but he was offended more by bad breath and social disruption than by the immorality of drinking. Nothing in the Manciple's characterisation has suggested he has a clerkly sagacity. The voice is given no special prosodic character that could tell us about the speaker (unless a neutral tone can be called character). The expectations raised by the subtle drama of the prologue are in no way satisfied here.

The story goes on briefly as we hear of Phebus's attempts to keep his wife happy:

> This worthy Phebus dooth al that he kan
> To plesen hire . . .   156–7

But the narrator again interrupts:

> But God it woot, ther may no man embrace
> As to destreyne a thyng which that nature
> Hath natureelly set in a creature.   160–2

The comment is sententious and its language has some polysyllabic character, though none of the words is uncommon; this note of restrained learning is developed as this brief *digressio* leads into a series of 'ensaumples', to use the narrator's accurate description of them (line 187). The *exemplum* is more a device of preaching than of classical poetry but it is clearly similar to what Geoffrey calls *collatio aperta*, a 'comparison which is made openly'.[28] Geoffrey seems here to be speaking about epic simile, but the *exempla* in 'The Manciple's Tale' function in a similar way. By introducing extensive analogies they fill out the material, they expound more fully what has just been said and they are, in their own right, of interest. I quote the second of the three:

> Lat take a cat, and fostre hym wel with milk
> And tendre flessh, and make his couche of silk
> And lat hym seen a mous go by the wal,
> Anon he weyveth milk and flessh and al,
> And every deyntee that is in that hous,
> Swich appetit hath he to ete a mous.   175–80

Simply as an *exemplum*, it is excellent; the domestic scene is presented in straightforward, largely monosyllabic language. The phrasing is very crisp: the opening 'Lat take a cat' and the closing 'ete a mous' in particular convey well the speedy, instinctive reaction which is the point of the *exemplum*. The selection of words like 'couche' and 'weyveth', unusual and filled with implication about the cat's dignity, gives sharpness to the little scene and overall there is that shrewd observation and easy lucidity that is one of Chaucer's hallmarks.

Fine as it is in itself, the passage does not sound like the work of the Manciple; it shows a capable and self-aware narrator (he knows they are 'ensaumples'), and it is ended with a crisp *conclusio*:

> Lo, heere hath lust his dominacioun,
> And appetit fleemeth discrecioun.   181–2

The words 'dominacioun' and 'discrecioun' are first used by Chaucer, but are quite common in his work; the speaker does not seem to be straining for an effect of rare diction, but rather seems to give his stylish *conclusio* with learned economy and a practiced sense of balance. It seems far from the Manciple, whose only utterance of any length showed a marked lack of temper and control.

As the narrator moves on he continues to be self-aware and rather subtle; he makes one of those complicated apologies of which Chaucer was so fond:

> Alle thise ensamples speke I by thise men
> That been untrewe, and nothyng by wommen.
> For men han evere a likerous appetit
> On lower thyng to parfourne hir delit
> Than on hire wyves, be they never so faire,
> Ne never so trewe, ne so debonaire.   187–92

This cannot, of course, be taken at face value; it quite contradicts the drift of the three *exempla*, following as they do the discussion of the wife and the 'nature' of this 'creature'. The irony is fairly transparent, just as it is at the end of 'The Clerk's Tale' in a similar passage, but the voice is too subtle to sound like the Manciple; he might be capable of such duplicity, but there was little verbal skill in either his attack on the Cook or his apology for the attack. Rather this passage takes its place as another elaboration of meaning in a tale of developing breadth and complexity, whose narrator is proving to be learned and also fairly generous with his learning.

N

A little more action follows, telling how Phebus is deceived and this quickly leads to another diversion:

> And so bifel, whan Phebus was absent,
> His wyf anon hath for hir lemman sent.
> Hir lemman? Certes, this is a knavyssh speche!
> Foryeveth it me, and that I yow biseche.   203–6

There follows a lengthy *digressio* explaining why the word has been used, and asserting that it is only a social distinction between a 'lady' and a 'lemman'. This in turn leads to a comparison with the distinction between a 'tiraunt' and a common criminal. The digressionary explanation is thus itself elaborated with an analogy; it is a dual piece of *amplificatio*, with a strong air of pedantry, but the speaker assures us that he is a plain man:

> I am a boystous man, right thus seye I,
> Ther nys no difference, trewely,
> Bitwixe a wyf that is of heigh degree,
> If of hir body dishonest she bee,
> And a povre wenche, oother than this—
> If it so be they werke bothe amys—
> But that the gentile, in estaat above,
> She shal be cleped his lady, as in love;
> And for that other is a povre womman,
> She shal be cleped his wenche or his lemman.   211–20

With great skill this passage creates the impression of a rather sententious man giving his views fully and with a desire to be properly understood: it is carefully argued, with several parentheses to clarify further issues that already seem fairly clear. The language is still rather straightforward, however; the speaker is not weaving an elaborate spell, just plodding along with all the things he wants to tell us. He moves steadily through his thoughts on tyrants and criminals and ends with the reassurance, typical of the embryonic bore, that he is really a brisk fellow:

> But, for I am a man noght textueel,
> I wol noght telle of textes nevere a deel:
> I wol go to my tale, as I bigan.   235–7

There are some ideas here that Chaucer uses elsewhere—the style is not unlike that of the Franklin in his more sententious mood, and the 'lady/wench' idea is similar to that used at the end of Alisoun's description in 'The Miller's Tale', but the passage does not suffer by comparison with others. A real character comes across in these lines, a narrator who strikes a pose of straightforwardness in order to develop his pedantry less objectionably. And yet, in a sense, there is some plainness about him: his wisdom is not really 'textueel', he does not quote from learned works. This note, almost suggesting the sententious wisdom of a self-taught, man is in keeping with the methodical, rather unstylish nature of the tale's development so far. Is this personality consistent with the Manciple as we know him, however? Birney feels these lines fit well with the Manciple's simplicity, and Severs also exploits the General Prologue's description of him as 'lewed.' There is a shadowy link, it is true; the speaker of this passage offers his modest pedantry under the guise of being 'boystous', just as the Manciple tricks his learned masters by seeming 'lewed' and the word 'lemman' is the way of introducing this *digressio*. But the possible link is not clarified and no suggestion is made of the major characteristic of the Manciple; the speaking voice is without any of the cunning, shiftiness and aggression that are audible in the prologue to the tale. The speaker of this *digressio* is clearly striking an attitude, but it is not the same as that struck by the Manciple previously.

A little more action follows as the crow begins to warn Phebus, and then the crow speaks with a fineness that reminds us how excellently he was said to sing. Direct speech by an animal is *prosopopoeia*, of course, another of the methods of amplification:

> 'By God!' quod he, 'I synge nat amys.
> 'Phebus,' quod he, 'for al thy worthynesse,
> For al thy beautee and thy gentilesse,
> For al thy song and al thy mynstralcye,
> For al thy waityng, blered is thyn ye
> With oon of litel reputacioun,
> Noght worth to thee, as in comparisoun,
> The montance of a gnat, so moot I thryve!
> For on thy bed thy wyf I saugh hym swyve.' 248–56

Birney has made much of the crude word 'swyve' here, but it is hard to see in this evidence of the narrator's 'lewed' nature when the rest of the speech is so fluent and so excellently balanced. The effect of 'swyve' is rather to make a highly dramatic contrast with the preceding eight lines, to stress the ugliness of the word and the decisive nature of the moment when the crow tells Phebus this. The narrator is clearly aware of the drama of the moment and the way in which it is stressed, when he goes on to say 'What wol ye moore?' (257). He asks this in the confidence that he has led us skilfully up to the crisis of the story.

The crow has previously been described as a fine singer, and his speech is fittingly fluent. He develops a lengthy sentence with *repetitio* and *compar* and then cuts it off. Similarly his speech has a number of finely polysyllabic words which are then opposed sharply by the blunt 'swyve'. But the polysyllables are not truly ornate: 'mystralcye', 'comparisoun' and 'montance' are all relatively common in the fourteenth century and Chaucer; 'reputacioun' is perhaps a little rarer, being first recorded in Wyclif and Chaucer, and Chaucer only uses it six times—three of them, oddly enough, in this tale. The crow's speech is, then, a skilled performance at, perhaps, the upper limit of the middle style. The speech does not sound inconsistent with the crisply effective language we have seen so far in the tale, though nothing about it points to the Manciple as the narrator. In the following lines the narrator continues to show his dexterity as a story-teller:

> His bowe he bente, and sette therinne a flo,
> And in his ire his wyf thanne hath he slayn.
> This is th'effect, ther is namoore to sayn: 264–6

This dreadful consequence is related with monosyllabic force, and the narrator again shows that he is well aware of the drama of this passage; it is an interesting example of the effect created when *abbrevatio* is suddenly used to structure a poem that has so far developed with *amplificatio*. The contrast is great and the shock effect excellent.

As Phebus now speaks, a similarly high level of control is revealed in the poem, for, as decorum would demand, in this impassioned situation he speaks in a truly high style. The speech is *apostrophe*, another of the elements of *amplificatio*:

> 'Traitour,' quod he, 'with tonge of scorpioun,
> Thou hast me broght to my confusioun;
> Allas, that I was wroght! why nere I deed?
> O deere wyf! O gemme of lustiheed?   271–4

Exclamatio and *ratiocinatio* are found here (*exclamatio* is the figure of style in which a person is addressed, *apostrophe* being the structural name for passionate address) and also the difficult ornaments *translatio* ('tonge of scorpioun') and *pronominatio* ('gemme of lusti-heed'). There is a little elaboration in the diction: the romance words 'Traitour' and 'confusion' seem common enough at this time and in Chaucer; 'scorpioun' is by no means a new word, though as Chaucer only uses it eight times, three of them in an astrological context, it may have some rarity. The word 'gemme' is clearly ornate despite its presence in Old English; Chaucer uses it four times and each time it is, as here, in a highly-wrought *apostrophe*.[29]

As Phebus goes on the *exclamatio* develops:

> O rakel hand, to doon so foule amys!
> O trouble wit, o ire recchelees,
> That unavysed smyteth gilteles!
> O wantrust, ful of fals suspecion,
> Where was thy wit and thy discrecion?
> O every man, be war of rakelnesse! 278–83

It is passionate and excellently shaped, moving from 'rakel hand' through a polysyllabic lament to 'rakelnesse'. In this passage 'rakel', 'rakelnesse', 'trouble', and 'unavysed' all seem to be rare words, elevating the diction to match the impassioned multiple *exclamatio*. The speech rises into the high style, or as high as Chaucer ever goes, and in this it stands out from the rest of the tale. It might, also, seem inconsistent from a narrator more noted for crispness than grand passion and who does indeed seem 'not textueel'. However, it is quite common for Chaucer to exercise licence in this way—the Reeve, the Knight and the Summoner all show an eloquence not fully explained by their characters and the Franklin, as I shall discuss below, is another good example. But this does not mean that this makes the Manciple any more credible as the speaker of this tale: less so, if anything, as this speech seems even more beyond him than what we have had before. In each of the other cases there is at least some clear characterisation of the tellers as their tale proceeds and the reader is therefore better able to suspend his disbelief at the unusual skills displayed. Here no such help is offered, no bridge is made between the Manciple and the tale. If the Manciple had been plainly present before, we would probably have accepted this fine speech as Chaucer's artistic licence; as it is, this licence enables the speech to fit easily enough beside the rest of the tale, methodical and lower-toned as it is: the teller does not seem worryingly inconsistent as a result. But he does not seem any more like the Manciple because of that.

However, in terms of the tale itself, Phebus's noble passion is well created, bringing to a fine climax the amplifications of the story; when Phebus acts against the crow this too is well told in brusque co-ordinate action:

> And to the crow he stirte, and that anon,
> And pulled his white fetheres everychon,
> And made hym blak, and refte hym al his song,
> And eek hys speche, and out at dore hym slong
> Unto the devel, which I hym betake;   303–7

This violent scene concludes the narrative part of the tale, and to a modern reader it may seem oddly constructed. It has found room for a great deal of material besides the narrative, and the action that does occur is brief and quickly told. This is not an uncommon Chaucerian pattern, for 'The Pardoner's Tale' and 'The Nun's Priest's Tale' both have a slow and digressive development followed by a swift sequence of narration. But this tale shows the mechanics of *amplificatio* much more openly than do those tales, and this seems to be in keeping with the generally meticulous, methodical character of the narrator. Both the openness of the *amplificatio* and the obvious skill of the narrator seem inconsistent with the personality of the Manciple. Severs fought against this conclusion by saying that the rhetoric was not 'purely external and mechanical' but 'functional'.[29] This is based on Manly's quite mistaken view that 'rhetoric' is decoration only and when it is functional it is not 'rhetoric'. In fact it is because the rhetoric is the whole structure of the tale, and overtly so, that we must assume a reasonably learned narrator, albeit one who chooses to appear more 'boystous' than he is. Such a figure is clearly visible in the tale so far, but he is insistently present in the final sequence of the tale.

Now the narrator steps forward firmly to deliver an extensive 'moralitas' of the story we have heard; this is common enough in the middle ages, especially in beast fables, though it is associated with a writer like Henryson more than with Chaucer. The moral is repetitive to a remarkable degree:

> 'My sone, thenk on the crowe, a Goddes name!
> My sone, keep wel thy tonge, and keep thy freened.
> A wikked tonge is worse than a feend;
> My sone, from a feend men may hem blesse.   318–21

Not all of it is as verbally repetitive as this, but the whole is a series of ways of giving the same moral, and the last lines state quite overtly the repetitive nature of the whole passage:

> My sone, be war, and be noon auctour newe
> Of tidynges, wheither they been false or trewe.

Whereso thou come, amonges hye or lowe,
Kepe wel thy tonge, and thenk upon the crowe.' 359-62

The last words return us to the beginning of this 'speech' by the narrator's 'dame'. The passage is an extended elaboration of the one theme, and Geoffrey calls this *interpretatio*. It is the last of the devices of *amplificatio* which are used to fill out this fable. Severs attempts to belittle this last piece of rhetorical elaboration by saying that it is merely 'a stringing together of practical admonitions with which his dame used to school him.'[30] The point seems to be that it is the narrator's mother's learned repetition, not his own ('dame' here clearly means mother; I doubt if Severs intends to suggest 'school-dame' as a meaning, though his comment could be read that way: this meaning seems impossible at this time); the argument is rather forced, especially in the light of all the other devices of *amplificatio* in the tale, which are in no way related to his 'dame'.

In the manner shown here, the narrator has built up an elaborate and informative structure on a very slight story. Interestingly, he has not used two of the devices Geoffrey lists, *collatio occulta*, or metaphor (the metaphor in line 271 is a 'difficult ornament', not a structural figure) and *circuitio*, periphrasis. This may be accidental, but the fact that these are the only two devices of amplification which are, considered as figures of style, classified under the 'difficult ornaments' suggests that they may be omitted because of the generally middle and methodical style of the whole.

The tale has a good deal of character and quality; it begins quietly with modest descriptions, lengthens its stride and grows more incisive with the three *exempla* and from then on offers some forceful amplifications of an idea or a feeling. The action is never given much scope: as we have seen it is skilfully compressed to brusque co-ordination, and the bulk of the tale consists of the methods of *amplificatio*. 'The Manciple's Tale' is, then, something of a performance, and the overt nature of the amplification might induce us to agree with Manly's feeling that the tale is mechanical and 'devoid of life', but there is a good deal of vivid writing in it and a strong personality comes across, giving a dramatic character to the whole poem.

The skilled development of the tale contradicts those critics who think it is early just because it is amateurish, but this by no means indicates that the tale is a late one: there is ample skill in a poem as early as *The Book of the Duchess*, of course, and the forceful presence of a narrator need not imply that the tale was written for a Canterbury pilgrim, as the early poems expertly characterise their narrators (with the exception of *Anelida and Arcite*, as we have seen); there is no closing reference to the circumstances of the pilgrimage and little reference throughout to the audience, and this may further argue—though not very strongly—that the tale existed before being placed here. As far as *The Canterbury Tales* at large is concerned the only conclusions to be drawn from the tale are negative: the rhetorical skills and the sententious character of the narrator do not resemble the Manciple.

In terms of the tale itself what we have is a skilfully developed narrative, notable for its rhetorical development and careful, rather pedantic narrator. There is good poetry in it, for the animal *exempla*, the speeches of Phebus and the crow and the crisp action all show some sign that the poet is moulding his poetry to its meaning; standing on its own the tale must be considered something of a success, though this sort of moralised *exemplum* is hardly to the taste of the modern reader. He looks, in *The Canterbury Tales* at least, for a tale of inherently interesting character which is also part of that understated but curiously powerful unity that we find in the tales as a whole, a unity brought about by setting pilgrim in contrast to pilgrim and making their tales expressive of their personalities. In the first category 'The Manciple's Tale' is quite successful and the more patience the reader has with medieval literary aesthetics the more he will enjoy it. In the second category it offers very little: it seems likely that Chaucer could see the general appropriateness of the tale's moral to the shifty Manicple, and it would seem certain that the prologue was written with this in mind. But the tale was given no direct link with the teller and, so expert was Chaucer at doing this with a few touches, the only likely conclusion is that he did not write it specifically for the Manciple; presumably he saw the possibility of a link between his character and a written tale but did not rewrite the tale to combine prologue and tale into the poetic union that is so impressive in the case of several other tales. 'The Manciple's Prologue and Tale' is not, as it stands, a finished entity; there are qualities in both prologue and tale, but they draw away from each other. In the prologue Chaucer's poetic powers suggest character and conflict as well as anywhere in the entire *Tales;* but in the tale itself the quality of the poetry does not extend outside the confines of the story being told. Consequently, this tale does not build upon the implications of the prologue, and to see the subtle linking of character, prologue and tale that is the finest development of *The Canterbury Tales* we should look elsewhere: 'The Franklin's

Tale' is an excellent example of how, at its best, the poetic skill that Chaucer commanded towards the end of his career can both present a fine story in itself and also lead us to speculate about the nature of the teller of the tale.

II. *'The Franklin's Tale'*

The principal topic in discussion of 'The Franklin's Tale' has been how it reveals the nature of its teller. The tale's concern with 'gentillesse' has been shown to fit with the interests the Franklin expresses in the preliminary link, and a number of critics have seen the tale's action as a covert self-justification by the Franklin, since he demonstrates that 'gentillesse' is not restricted to the nobility, but can be found in squires and clerks as well.[31]

Little attention has been paid to the poetry; the Franklin's opening remarks on rhetoric have been taken as mock-modesty, because of the rhetorical figures to be found later in the tale, but no fuller exposition has been made of the considerable poetic skills that go into the poem.[32] Here I hope to show that it is largely Chaucer's poetic art which creates a convincing personality for the Franklin within his tale and which also (a point too much ignored) shapes the characters and action of the tale itself with considerable subtlety.

The Franklin's first words are addressed to the Squire:

> 'In feith, Squier, thow hast thee wel yquit
> And gentilly. I preise wel thy wit,'
> Quod the Frankeleyn, 'considerynge thy yowthe,
> So feelyngly thou spekest, sire, I allowe the!
> As to my doom, ther is noon that is heere
> Of eloquence that shal be thy peere,
> If that thou lyve; God yeve thee good chaunce,
> And in vertu sende thee continuaunce!   673-80

The praise is good-natured, if a little patronising, but although the speaker offers a judgment on eloquence there is little sign of it in his own speech. The pauses in the first line and, in the second line, the brief run-on phase and the short statement after it all create a jerky effect and this is continued in the third line. There is more fluency from 677 to 679, but the clause 'If that thou lyve' ends the sequence in a clipped manner and reasserts the jerky tone. The overall effect is not a very strong one, but in the light of the Franklin's later speech-style it is interesting, for here there is a certain simplicity, even lameness, about his voice which contrasts with the firm judgment he is giving about eloquence. The style suggests a lack of polish in the speaker and this is supported by the heavy-handed (and heavy sounding) 'If that thou lyve'—not the most sensitive of comments to make when praising a young man.

The effect of this opening is to imply that the speaker is a man of some simplicity, but of some confidence as well; the familiar complaint about his son's evil ways fills out this picture of the Franklin. He has a good deal to say about his son in a sententiously lamenting manner, and though the style is less jerky it still moves in a straightforward way, line by line rather than as a fluent paragraph:

> I have my sone snybbed, and yet shal,
> For he to vertu listeth nat entende;
> But for to pleye at dees, and to despende
> And lese al that he hath, is his usage.
> And he hath levere talken with a page
> Than to comune with any gentil wight
> Where he myghte lerne gentillesse aright.' 688–94

The Host cuts in rudely, so strengthening the implication that the Franklin is prosing on:

> 'Straw for youre gentillesse!' quod oure Hoost. 695

The Franklin's answer shows that he recognises his social position as that of a man liable to the Host's corrections, but it also shows a certain dignity:

> 'That knowe I wel, sire,' quod the Frankeleyn.
> 'I prey yow, haveth me nat in desdeyn,
> Though to this man I speke a word or two.' 699–701

The Host does not accept the Franklin's plea for consideration and remains brusquely dismissive:

> 'Telle on thy tale withouten wordes mo.' 702

But in his answer the Franklin shows that he has not only dignity, but some skill as well:

> 'Gladly, sire Hoost,' quod he, 'I wole obeye
> Unto your wyl; now herkneth what I seye.
> I wol yow nat contrarien in no wyse
> As fer as that my wittes wol suffyse.
> I prey to God that it may plesen yow;
> Thanne woot I wel that it is good ynow.' 703–8

The style is still simple, even flat in its straightforward movement and rhythms, but the answer is not as simple as it might seem; behind the politeness there is a sense of irony in the last lines, as the Franklin appears to pay excessive tribute to the Host's judgment.

The whole sequence begins by imputing simplicity, even gaucheness, to the Franklin, as much by poetic means as by the social context; but he has confidence in his judgments, and by the end of the link he does not seem the shallow bourgeois he at first appeared to be. In the tale as well we find that there is more to the Franklin than we might at first imagine

As he begins to tell his story, we hear again the note of a slightly overweening simplicity:

> But, sires, by cause I am a burel man,
> At my bigynnyng first I yow biseche,
> Have me excused of my rude speche.
> I lerned never rethorik, certeyn;
> Thyng that I speke, it moot be bare and pleyn.
> I sleep nevere on the Mount of Pernaso,
> Ne lerned Marcus Tullius Scithero.
> Colours ne knowe I none, withouten drede,
> But swiche colours as growen in the mede,
> Or elles swiche as men dye or peynte.
> Colours of rethoryk been to me queynte;
> My spirit feeleth noght of swich mateere.
> But if yow list, may tale shul ye heere.   716–28

It is clear that although he calls himself 'burel' the Franklin sees this as the familiar figure of thought called *diminutio:* he presents himself rather like Mark Antony in *Julius Caesar*. Most commentators on the poem have remarked on this passage, finding its view of the narrator's persona in conflict with the reasonably elaborate nature of the poem. Hodgson says that 'the great majority of the recognised tropes and colours can be illustrated from this tale.'[33] Spearing has observed that *The Franklin's Tale* makes use of all the usual rhetorical devices that are found in Chaucer.[34] From the fact that the tale contradicts the man, both critics draw conclusions about the Franklin's character; they differ to some degree but they concur in finding him a little pompous, a man with a certain humble pride in his homespun eloquence, and yet a man by no means negligible as a thinker.[35] I would not disagree with this, but I would like to go further, for if we attend to the stylistic context of these remarks on rhetoric some Chaucerian innuendoes become fairly clear.

In line 721 something has happened to Cicero's name; in his note Robinson suggests that it has been confused with Cythera, but J. J. Murphy favours Mount Cythaeron as the other element in the muddle.[36] Either could be right—or perhaps both are right and it is a multi-named confusion, for, in addition, the first syllable sounds like that of Scipio. All this adds up to a characteristic Chaucerian gibe at ignorant pretension, and the rather simple-minded pun on colour seems, by being spun out at such length, to have a similar implication. The poetry of the passage also gives weight to this implication, and may indeed be a principal agent in transmitting it to us. The style is rather jerky, for the single line is the unit here and there is no enjambement. The first three lines of the passage are the longest syntactical unit in it, but they have no notable fluency, and from then on the passage proceeds with end-stopped lines; the effect is emphasised as the last three lines are all complete statements, firmly end-stopped. This conclusion clinches the overall impression of the passage as one with a broken, jerky rhythm. The poetic style helps to create the homespun effect of the Franklin's ideas as his clumsy notions find a suitably clumsy form of utterance.

But as soon as he turns away from himself and to his story the simplicity of the Franklin's persona is less marked; he fades into the background and, in the first sentence of five lines the style stretches out and flows much more smoothly; enjambement appears twice and there is a fine sense of balance in all of the last three lines of the sentence:

> In Armorik, that called is Britayne,
> Ther was a knyght that loved and dide his payne
> To serve a lady in his beste wise;
> And many a labour, many a greet emprise
> He for his lady wroghte, er she were wonne.   729–33

Having characterised his narrator, Chaucer begins to shape the tale itself and this is the style that he uses for the bulk of the narrative; it is typified by long fluent paragraphs in which the story moves on with assurance. Two such paragraphs follow very shortly:

> But atte laste she, for his worthynesse,
> And namely for his meke obeysaunce,
> Hath swich a pitee caught of his penuance
> That pryvely she fil of his accord
> To take hym for hir housbonde and hir lord,
> Of swich lordshipe as men han over hir wyves.

And for to lede the moore in blisse hir lyves,
Of his free wyl he swoor hire as a knyght
That never in al his lyf he, day ne nyght,
Ne sholde upon hym take no maistrie,
Agayn hir wyl, ne kithehir jalousie,
But hire obeye, and folwe hir wyl in al,
As any lovere to his lady shal,
Save that the name of soveraynetee,
That wolde he have for shame of his degree.   738–52

This passage shows clearly the basic style of this poem, that narrative style in which the large part of *The Canterbury Tales* is written. It is urbane and supple, effective in recounting a story, and there is a clear intelligence at work. The argument in this passage has a lucid flow, threading easily through extended periods filled with relatively complex syntax. There is also an indication that smooth passages like this are not restricted to mere narration, for the poet's controlling mind reveals itself twice, subtly stressed by the modulation of his verse. At the end of the two verse paragraphs in this passage we find a single line, a little slower and heavier than those that have gone before, and each line offers an incisive remark. The first is:

Of swich lordshipe as men han over hir wyves.

And the second reads:

That wolde he have for shame of his degree.

In the pause that follows the end of a paragraph both these lines force us to think again about what has just been said so fluently. The first line casts a quizzical eye over terms like 'hir housebonde and hir lord' and the second probes ironically the nature of Arveragus' 'soveraynetee.' The poet's intelligence is underlined by his metrical delicacy, and to the supple flowing verse is added that slightly astringent tone that is so characteristic of Chaucer.

Once he has established this narrative style in the poem Chaucer reminds us of the different style that he has suggested as being appropriate to the Franklin. There is, though, no sharp break between the progress of the tale and the development of the narrator's personality. Here, as in other tales (the Pardoner's and the Merchant's for example), there is merely a change of emphasis; at times the narrator is more clearly before us than at others, and the style is sensitive to this alteration. At line 761 the sententious narrator steps forward again in his tale:

> For o thyng, sires, saufly dar I seye,
> That freendes everych oother moot obeye,
> If they wol longe holden compaignye.
> Love wol nat been constreyned by maistrye.
> Whan maistrie comth, the God of Love anon
> Beteth his wynges, and farewel, he is gon!
> Love is a thyng as any spirit free.
> Wommen, of kynde, desiren libertee,
> And nat to been constreyned as a thral;
> And so doon men, if I sooth seyen shal.   761–70

The opening sentence is a smooth transition from the fluent narrative to the narrator's voice, for after its relative length the rest of the passage is in the sharp brief style of the Franklin's opening comments and lines 764, 767 and 770 are single line statements of a sententious nature. In fact this speech is notable both for its *sententiae* and for the confident *brevitas* with which these aphorisms are put, as when the Franklin says:

> . . . the God of Love anon
> Beteth his wynges, and farewel, he is gon!

Here he uses a real poetry of brevity, and creates a fine tension, for although the lines contain a learned element which buttresses the *sententia*, the style conveys a general impression of bluntness and thus enforces the *brevitas*. This interplay between *amplificatio* and *abbrevatio* helps to shape character, for although the Franklin may seem slightly foolish in his sententiousness there is also blunt good sense in him that the *brevitas* presses home, and this seems a development of the suggestion made in the dialogue with the Host, that the Franklin has depths that a first impression might miss. The more pretentious side of his character comes out as he concludes; he begins sententiously and then embarks on a truly Polonius-like piece of quibbling, where the patiently elaborate devices of *ratiocinatio, contentio* and *correctio* build up in a passage where little is said; the effect is to suggest a rather fussy and self-admiring speaker:

> Heere may men seen an humble, wys accord;
> Thus hath she take hir servant and hir lord,—
> Servant in love and lord in mariage.
> Thanne was he bothe in lordshipe and servage.
> Servage? nay, but in lordshipe above,
> Sith he hath bothe his lady and his love;
> His lady, certes, and his wyf also,
> The which that lawe of love acordeth to.   791–8

Having reminded us of the Franklin's personality here, Chaucer permits him to move on with the story, but the narrator's penchant for brief *amplificationes* is not forgotten, though it is made less pervasive; another *sententia* comes shortly, but is less extended:

> Who koude telle, but he hadde wedded be,
> The joye, the ese, and the prosperitee
> That is bitwixe an housbonde and his wyf? 803–5

Similarly, as the story turns to Dorigen he cannot resist a comment:

> For his absence wepeth she and siketh,
> As doon thise noble wyves whan hem liketh. 817–18

And a little later he offers a *collatio aperta* to elaborate her friends' attempts to calm her:

> By proces, as ye knowen everichoon,
> Men may so longe graven in a stoon
> Til som figure therinne emprented be.
> So longe han they conforted hire . . . 829–32

But these brief comments seem to mark the fading of the narrator into the background of the story for a lengthy period; now Dorigen occupies the centre of the stage. The phrase the Franklin used in his aside, 'whan hem liketh', carried an implication that the 'noble wyves' were a little self-indulgent, and this is driven into the open by the splendid following line:

> She moorneth, waketh, wayleth, fasteth, pleyneth; 819

This sort of *articulus* (and *similiter cadens* as well) is not rare in Chaucer,[37] but the effect never seems accidental, and this is a flourishing example of it. To have five verbs banked up in this way is clearly extreme, and the excesses of Dorigen's grief are well suggested in this hyperbolic line. The consequent distraction of her thought is also subtly portrayed:

> Desir of his presence hire so destreyneth
> That al this wyde world she sette at noght.
> Hire freendes, whiche that knewe hir hevy thoght,
> Conforten hire in al that ever they may.
> They prechen hire, they telle hire nyght and day
> That causelees she sleeth hirself, allas!
> And every confort possible in this cas
> They doon to hire with al hire bisynesse,
> Al for to make hire leve hire hevynesse. 820–28

This passage has a regular movement in that the first six lines divide into three two-line sentences, and the seventh and eighth lines also form a syntactic unit, this sentence being completed by the ninth line. But this does not give the even rhythms we might expect, because the two-line syntax units are exactly at odds with the two-line rhyme units. Consequently the passage has a disturbing effect. The disruption of rhyme and syntax creates the disturbance of Dorigen's mind that her 'freendes' observe; then, with great skill, Chaucer brings the passage to a close by rhyming at last within the syntactical unit, and the last rhyme—which thus caps the whole passage—is 'hevynesse'. It is a piece of unostentatious stylistic brilliance, and it dramatically captures Dorigen's rather unstable mentality. Her mental equilibrium is easily overthrown by circumstance, her poise is disturbed as the movement of the passage is disturbed, and the only resolution lies in 'hevynesse'. Chaucer's skill lies in directing us with poetic acumen to these elements in Dorigen's character; they are to be vital to the plot, and so he gives added credibility to a narrative whose credibility does not, on the surface, seem its strongest point.

In this desperate state of mind, she is affected deeply by the rocks; they are presented to us in powerful phrases, first as 'grisly rokkes blake' and then, worse yet, as 'grisly feendly rokkes blake'. The weight of the phrases makes more convincing the impact of the rocks on Dorigen's mind. The speech that she gives here is of considerable stylistic interest; it is one of the two speeches that Hodgson concentrates on in giving illustrations of rhetorical figures, and as she analyses it in detail there is no need to do the same here.[38] To be brief, this speech and Dorigen's later lament are the only large gatherings of figures of style in the poem. Hodgson minimises this by saying that it 'is true that the intervening narrative is for the most part simple and direct, yet even here the Franklin introduces tropes'[39] but the issue is clear enough. In this *apostrophe* over the rocks and in her later lament Dorigen is speaking in a loftier style than is common in the poem, and so we find more of the ornamental figures (though the 'difficult ornaments' are largely missing, as they tend to be in the whole of *The Canterbury Tales*). The speech as a whole is rhetorical in structure as well as detail: it develops from *exclamatio* to *interrogatio* and ends with a formal *conclusio* (at line 889). It is more 'rhetorical' than other passages because decorum requires it to be so. The higher style is appropriate because Dorigen is both noble and the agent of high emotion in the poem; sensitive as usual to levels of diction Chaucer creates a fitting utterance for her: a noble and highly wrought personality is embodied in noble and highly wrought poetry. This shows well the variable effect of rhetorical figures. When, as with the Franklin's sententious comments, the figures appear in poetry of little fluency and in a context of slightly pompous comment they can have a mildly comic effect; when, as here, there is nothing to contradict the innate richness of the language they create, they help to project a lofty style:

> 'Eterne God, that thurgh thy purveiaunce
> Ledest the world by certein governaunce,
> In ydel, as men seyn, ye no thyng make.
> But, Lord, thise grisly feendly rokkes blake,
> That semen rather a foul confusion
> Of werk than any fair creacion
> Of swich a parfit wys God and a stable,
> Why han ye wroght this werk unresonable?   865–72

The clustering of rhetorical figures in this long speech is only one aspect (and in my view not a dominating one) of the style: the diction is elaborated with a good deal of Latinate vocabulary, many of the lines run swiftly into each other, the syntax is complex and there is a strong overall balance which leads up to and emphasises the bold question in the last line.

Dorigen's hyperbolic character thus established, the story moves on, in poetry of a fine elaboration—an elaboration which is greater than before in the narrative, and this may well have a reason:

> And this was on the sixte morwe of May,
> Which May hadde peynted with his softe shoures
> This gardyn ful of leves and of floures;
> And craft of mannes hand so curiously
> Arrayed had this garden, trewely,
> That nevere was ther gardyn of swich prys,
> But if it were the verray paradys.
> The odour of floures and the fresshe sighte
> Wolde han maked any herte lighte
> That evere was born, but if to greet siknesse,
> Or to greet sorwe, helde it in distresse;
> So ful it was of beautee with plesaunce.   906–17

The single line of summary which ends the paragraph is a Chaucerian habit we have often seen, but the general effect of this passage is more complicated. The syntax is elaborate, providing a series of qualifications and concessions to give a precise picture of the garden; the

O

descriptio is detailed and ornate from the *translatio* in line 907 to its closing *conclusio*, and this overt 'craft of mannes hand' in the verse, as well as the garden, itself suggests a certain artificiality. The language makes it plain that this is the garden of courtly love: 'curiously Arrayed', 'prys', 'plesauance', 'distresse', and 'odour' are all words familiar in the context of *fin amor;* the language is not very lively—only 'odour' has any rarity, being used only seven times by Chaucer—and this combination of highly complex syntax and the conventional language of the love-garden suggests that these gardens, and what goes on in them, are over-complex, lacking in vitality: the innuendo is given clarification and a moral direction by the line 'But if it were the verray paradys': there is indeed a distance between this garden and Paradise, as we shall see.

The leading figure in the action here is Aurelius; he is a new character and there is vigour in the style and the meaning of his *descriptio:*

> . . . he was, if men sholde hym discryve,
> Oon of the beste farynge man on lyve;
> Yong, strong, right vertuous, and riche, and wys,
> And wel biloved, and holden in greet prys. 931-4

Chaucer heaps qualities upon Aurelius, and at first he seems an impressive figure. There is another touch of hyperbole when we hear what he does:

> Of swiche matere made he manye layes,
> Songes, compleintes, roundels, virelayes, 947-8

But the vigorous note of this *articulus* is contradicted by what has gone before; the plethora of songs is caused by his inability to speak to his beloved:

> . . . no thyng dorste he seye,
> Save in his songes somewhat wolde he wreye
> His wo, as in a general compleynyng; 943-5

This undermining of Aurelius is continued as we hear about him in action; after the driving force of the lines quoted above which described him, it is a great let-down to read the complex syntax that describes his few timorous actions:

> In oother manere than ye heere me seye,
> Ne dorste he nat to hire his wo biwreye,
> Save that, paraventure, somtyme at daunces,

> Ther yonge folk kepen hir observaunces,
> It may wel be he looked on hir face
> In swich a wise as man that asketh grace: 953–8

The suggestion is made, with a sly comic touch, that, chock-full of qualities as he seems to be, when it comes to action he is an unconvincing figure. This revelation is made more explicit when he speaks, and shows himself quite at a loss:

> 'Madame,' quod he, 'by God that this world made,
> So that I wiste it myghte youre herte glade,
> I wolde that day that youre Arveragus
> Wente over the see, that I, Aurelius
> Hadde went ther nevere I sholde have come agayn.   967–71

After this extremely circuitous beginning he warms to his topic and apostrophises Dorigen in the correct manner, though his speech is rather jerky. It comes out in single lines and lacks the fluency of conviction and nobility; this gives it the impression of a parroted lesson, though its jerky haste may also be because, according to him, Aurelius is pressed for time—not the most courtly thing to say to a lady:

> Madame, reweth upon my peynes smerte;
> For with a word ye may me sleen or save.
> Heere at youre feet God wolde that I were grave!
> I ne have as now no leyser moore to seye;
> Have mercy, sweete, or ye wol do me deye!'   974–8

There is a clumsiness about these lines that stresses the impression that Aurelius has a comic inadequacy. But Dorigen (perhaps in character) sees no joke; her reaction is very different from her earlier, lofty speech: its extreme *brevitas* makes it clipped and rather grim:

> She gan to looke upon Aurelius:
> 'Is this youre wyl,' quod she, 'and sey ye thus?
> Nevere erst,' quod she, 'ne wiste I what ye mente.   979–81

This is the terse reaction of her honest wifehood, but it is only one of her reactions to the speech. With that curious emotional mobility that has already been worked into her character, she immediately changes to a different tone. Her second reaction is made *in pley*, and in this she answers Aurelius in the long, flowing and complex syntax that has already been associated with the garden and with Aurelius himself:

> 'Aurelie,' quod she, 'by heighe God above,
> Yet wolde I graunte yow to been youre love,
> Syn I yow se so pitously complayne.
> Looke what day that endelong Britayne
> Ye remoeve alle the rokkes, stoon by stoon,
> That they ne lette ship ne boot to goon,—
> I seye, whan ye han maad the coost so clene
> Of rokkes that ther nys no stoon ysene,
> Thanne wol I love you best of any man,
> Have heer my trouthe, in al that evere I kan.   989–98

Once again, the last line of the paragraph stands rather alone, but the fluent body of the passage is in keeping with the formal vocative of its beginning and contrasts sharply with her initial response to Aurelius. It seems that by its stylistic nature this speech marks Dorigen's momentary adoption of the concepts of the courtly game: she 'plays' with elaborate syntax as she plays with the charming but dangerous notions of *fin amor*—the plot will show the danger. Chaucer's poetic modulation has previously suggested Dorigen's swiftness to plunge into states of emotion, and here there is a similarly swift change of style, as the poetry charts the mobility of her disposition.

Aurelius's response to Dorigen's promise is quite different from his earlier prolixity:

> 'Is ther noon oother grace in yow?' quod he.   999

And a similarly terse style is used to describe his resultant prostration:

> He to his hous is goon with sorweful herte.
> He seeth he may nat fro his deeth asterte;
> Hym semed that he felte his herte colde.   1021–3

The single lines, with the repetitive pattern of *compar* emphasising their clipped nature, stop the action and the poem pauses. This change of style does at one level bring variety into the poem, but it also has meaning; Aurelius's elaborate approaches have, apparently, failed and he is bereft of both his desires and his characteristic style, forced back on bare simplicity. But neither the plot nor Aurelius are finished, despite this reverse, and he finds new life and hope soon enough, rediscovering at the same time his circumlocutory style:

> He seyde, 'Appollo, god and governour
> Of every plaunte, herbe, tree, and flour,

> That yevest, after thy declinacion,
> To ech of hem his tyme and his seson,
> As thyn herberwe chaungeth lowe or heighe,
> Lord Phebus, cast thy merciable eighe
> On wrecche Aurelie, which that am but lorn.   1031–7

The invocation is heavy with subordination, the actual prayer seeming almost lost; as he goes on his style becomes even more elaborate:

>   Youre blisful suster, Lucina the sheene,
> That of the see is chief goddesse and queene
> (Though Neptunus have deitee in the see,
> Yet emperisse aboven hym is she),
> Ye knowen wel, lord, that right as hir desir
> Is to be quyked and lighted of youre fir,
> For which she folweth yow ful bisily,
> Right so the see desireth naturelly
> To folwen hire, as she that is goddesse
> Bothe in the see and ryveres moore and lesse.   1045–54

The parenthesis about Neptune causes a syntactic dislocation in the speech between the second and fifth lines, and this demonstrates the meandering sense of the passage, easily distracted into petty clarifications. The ineffective, over-formal aspect of Aurelius's character is reasserted here, though he sees himself in a quite different light. He imagines that he will, given his prayer, be swift in action, crisp and stern, and in his fantasy he sees himself like some medieval Humphrey Bogart:

> Thanne certes to my lady may I seye,
> 'Holdeth youre heste, the rokkes been aweye.'   1063–4

A similar note is struck in a later scene, when he urges the clerk:

> To bryngen hym out of his peynes smerte,
> Or with a swerd that he wolde slitte his herte.   1259–60

In both remarks alliteration subtly underlines the melodramatic nature of Aurelius's imagination at this stage of the story, and against this fantasy of himself his encounter with Dorigen will seem the more inadequate and comic.

The plot now moves on, and the poem develops the crucial action of the story—the vanishing of the rocks—with great fluency. The emphasis here is on the poem as itself, not as the product of the narrator, but the Franklin is, for all that, not forgotten. He makes

several remarks that remind us of his plain man's attitude (or pose?);
to take them from their full context is to deprive them of the contrast
that stresses their engaging bluntness, but economy requires this to
be done:

> For th'orisonte hath reft the sonne his lyght,—
> This is as muche to seye as it was nyght!—1017–18

> Lete I this woful creature lye;
> Chese he, for me, wheither he wol lyve or dye.   1085–6

> This is to seye, to maken illusioun,
> By swich an apparence or jogelrye—
> I ne kan no termes of astrologye—1264–6

In each of these remarks there is a decided unevenness in the poetry,
a jerky effect which shapes the impact of the remark on the reader.
There are also several less sharp reminders of the narrator, where he
offers a brief sententious comment; none of them is very long, but
they do cluster at times:

> And wel ye knowe that of a sursanure
> In surgerye is perilous the cure,
> But men myghte touche the arwe, or come therby.
> His brother weep and wayled pryvely,
> Til atte laste hym fil in remembraunce,
> That whiles he was at Orliens in Fraunce,
> As yonge clerkes, that been lykerous
> To reden artes that been curious,
> Seken in every halke and every herne
> Particuler sciences for to lerne—
> He hym remembered . . .   1113–23

The opening aside arises out of a medical analogy, and the narrator
confides to us its final development, and then goes on with his story;
but he meanders again, to explain the sort of process these young
clerks go through, and why the brother remembered this particular
book of magic. The narrator is to a certain extent present, and he
does step forward to explain tricky things directly, as here, or to
comment on points of particular note, as when he feels the need to
reassure us about magic:

> . . . swich folye
> As in oure dayes is nat worth a flye,—
> For hooly chirches feith in oure bileve
> Ne suffreth noon illusioun us to greve.   1131–4

But apart from this sort of occasion, in this long central sequence the poem largely exists outside the narrator's personality; exploiting that licence by which he makes the tale both a self-contained entity and also, seen from a different viewpoint, the product of a personality, Chaucer moves on with some passages of enthralling skill.

The working of the plot depends upon magic; first Aurelius's brother reflects on what it can achieve:

> Somtyme hath semed come a grym leoun;
> And somtyme floures sprynge as in a mede;
> Somtyme a vyne, and grapes white and rede;
> Somtyme a castel, al of lym and stoon;
> And whan hem lyked, voyded it anon.   1146–50

And then the magician himself performs, and the passage is a more powerful and extended version of the easier description, using a repetitive series of lines in a speedy passage:

> He shewed hym, er he wente to sopeer,
> Forestes, parkes ful of wilde deer;
> Ther saugh he hertes with hir hornes hye,
> The gretteste that evere were seyne with ye.
> He saugh of hem an hondred slayne with houndes,
> And som with arwes blede of bittre woundes.
> He saugh, whan voyded were thise wilde deer,
> Thise fauconers upon a fair ryver,
> That with hir haukes han the heron slayn.   1189–97

Here the poet builds up the dense and dazzling scene; the lines move quickly, are packed with detail; several of them contain an alliteration which seems to increase the incantatory effect. By these means we are caught up in the poem's enthusiasm for magical powers and, whatever our cooler reactions might be, within the confines of the tale we cannot deny the power of magic: the fine poetry creates a credibility important for the tale as a whole, just as previously the personalities of the main characters have been made the more convincing by the poetic modulation presenting them.

Not all the fine writing is as intimately linked with the mechanics of the poem as this, however. Shortly afterwards we encounter a finely formal passage of *amplificatio* where the winter season is described. But although the passage is not functional in a direct sense, like Chaucer's set-pieces in 'The Knight's Tale' it enriches the poem with a sharply visual imagination and vigorous language, adding greatly to its overall conviction and power to delight:

> Phebus wax old, and hewed lyk laton,
> That in his hoote declynacion
> Shoon as the burned gold with stremes brighte;
> But now in Capricorn adoun he lighte,
> Where as he shoon ful pale, I dar wel seyn.
> The bittre frostes, with the sleet and reyn,
> Destroyed hath the grene in every yerd.
> Janus sit by the fyr, with double berd,
> And drynketh of his bugle horn the wyn;
> Biforn him stant brawen of the tusked swyn,
> And 'Nowel' crieth every lusty man.   1245–55

The passage appeals strongly to the senses; it offers strong colours changed to wintry pallor, heat turned to freezing cold—and then these are answered by a roaring midwinter fire. In the last lines even the senses of hearing and taste are directly invoked. The vigorous imagination of the passage is well matched by the forceful style. Our attention is gripped by stressed monosyllables in 'Phebus wax old', and then the pains of winter are emphasised with strong words, linked in sound in 'bittre frostes' and 'sleet'; similar force is given to the positive side of winter and phrases like 'bugle horn' (linking with the less harsh sounds of 'double berd'), the heavily stressed 'stant brawen' and the prominent 'Nowel'. The selection and ordering of language gives great drive to the passage, and a magnificent set-piece like this helps the poem maintain its firm grasp on the audience's attention and inspire our total confidence in the poet's authority over us and over his material.

The poetic intelligence so plain here is shortly afterwards seen in a different guise, and the processes of the magical art are recounted in an amusing passage of mumbo-jumbo where Chaucer skilfully contrives a sing-song effect:

> His tables Tolletanes forth he brought,
> Ful wel corrected, ne ther lakked nought,
> Neither his collect ne his expans yeeris,
> Ne his rootes, ne his othere geeris,
> As been his centris and his argumentz
> And his proporcioneles convenientz
> For his equacions in every thyng.   1273–9

Several elements help to create the jingling effect: alliteration and springing rhythm in 'tables Tolletanes', the assonance of 'corrected' and 'collect' which makes the lines almost into rhyming half lines, the double rhyme in 'yeeris/geeris', the repetitive use of 'ne' throughout and the skilled placing of the polysyllables so that they assist the speed of the passage. As with much of Chaucer's best work, the closer the passage is examined the more skilful it appears.

These excellent passages move us on with speed and power to the climactic moment when the rocks vanish. Aurelius now hurries to Dorigen and, true to his character, embarks on a speech quite different from the terse command he had fantasised. The speech is superbly convoluted:

> 'My righte lady,' quod this woful man,
> 'Whom I moost drede and love as I best kan,
> And lothest were of al this world displese,
> Nere it that I for yow have swich disese
> That I most dyen heere at youre foot anon,
> Noght wolde I telle how me is wo bigon.   1311–16

Aurelius picks his nervous way through this thicket of subordination only to come to further apologies and verbal footnotes:

> For, madame, wel ye woot what ye han hight—
> Nat that I chalange any thyng of right
> Of yow, my sovereyn lady, but youre grace—
> But in a gardyn yond, at swich a place,
> Ye woot right wel what ye bihighten me;   1323–7

Ten more lines of apology and reassurance follow, till the promised moment arrives:

> . . . have youre biheste in mynde,
> For, quyk or deed, right there ye shal me fynde.
> In yow lith al to do me lyve or deye,—
> But wel I woot the rokkes been aweye.'
> He taketh his leve, and she astoned stood;   1335–9

At the end of his delightfully inept speech he does get out half of the single-line utterance of his earlier imagination. But, apparently overcome by it all, he rushes out: the prominent assonance at the end of line 1339 emphasises the sharp ending of the speech and Dorigen's shock. Not surprisingly, she is stunned. Her reaction contrasts sharply with the *ambages* of the bulk of his speech, for its slow weight is in key with the tone of 'astoned stood':

> In al hir face nas a drope of blood.
> She wende nevere han come in swich a trappe.
> 'Allas,' quod she, 'that evere this sholde happe.'   1340–2

By the modulation of his style Chaucer creates expertly both the comedy that is in Aurelius's uncertain character and the shocked reaction that Dorigen experiences. In these three clipped lines the poem pauses once more, and seems to reflect on her situation. The plight she is in is dramatic indeed, but her reaction to it is, as it was before, so extreme that we do not engage our sympathies with her. The poet observed Dorigen before with a certain amount of irony, and he continues to do so now. Her great lament follows, as she recommends to herself death rather than dishonour; like her previous major speech it is formally rhetorical, being a series of *exempla*, all illustrating the same theme. The detail of the speech is also highly rhetorical, as Hodgson has shown.[40] The fact that it is merely repetitive at considerable length might well lead us to suspect, particularly in such a skilful poem, that Chaucer means us to find Dorigen to be making something of an emotional meal of her situation. This implication grows the stronger as we see that towards the end the *exempla* grow more and more perfunctory and finally tail off with three desultory references:

> The parfit wyfhood of Arthemesie
> Honured is thurgh al the Barbarie,
> O Teuta, queene! thy wyfly chastitee
> To alle wyves may a mirour bee.
> The same thyng I seye of Bilyea,
> Of Rodogone, and eek Valeria.'   1451–6

The reader surely senses here that this lament has gone on far too long, and that the failure is Dorigen's and not the poet's seems clear from the next lines:

> Thus pleyned Dorigen a day or tweye,
> Purposynge evere that she wolde deye.   1457–8

The excessive nature of her behaviour is plainly stated here in the characteristically dry Chaucerian style; she is once more shown to be emotional and given to melodrama. James Sledd, in his article on this speech, feels that the poem here presents 'an attitude of sympathy.'[41] Especially in the light of Dorigen's earlier presentation, this seems to me a limited interpretation; Dorigen is not a foolish figure, as Aurelius is to some extent; but the poem does not, as I see it, accept entirely her own assessment of the situation.

There is a character to judge her by, whose view seems more level-headed, as Arveragus now, for almost the first time in the poem, takes part in the action. Dorigen tells him what has happened, and he at once seems a man of even nature and decisive character:

> This housbonde, with glad chiere, in freendly wyse
> Answerde and seyde as I shal yow devyse:
> 'Is ther oght elles, Dorigen, but this?' 1467–9

And he sees the problem more calmly:

> 'Ye, wyf,' quod he, 'lat slepen that is stille.
> It may be wel, paraventure, yet to day. 1472–3

But as he goes on to say she must keep her word (fulfilling in this way his oath to her that he would not be jealous, cf. lines 747–50), we see that there is real feeling in him:

> Ye shul youre trouthe holden, by my fay!
> For God so wisly have mercy upon me,
> I hadde wel levere ystiked for to be
> For verray love which that I to yow have,
> But if ye sholde youre trouthe kepe and save. 1474–8

The firm opening line is followed by a measured sequence of four lines which leads surely up to 'kepe and save'; the personality of a man of honour and steady nature is well caught in the poetry. He is a man capable of keeping his word but this does not mean he is without emotion: rather it means that his integrity is stronger than his desires:

> Trouthe is the hyeste thyng that man may kepe'—
> But with that word he brast anon to wepe, 1479–80

Here the rhyme boldly links together two ideas that have a very suggestive relation: to keep your word can bring you to weep. After this couplet the syntax sweeps on into Arveragus' next wretched speech, where he asks that Dorigen keep the whole thing secret—again showing his unchanging chararacter as he maintains the concern for the 'shame of his degree' he showed in the opening of the poem—yet this emotional reaction is linked by the rhyme to his previous honourable *sententia*: there is an intimate linking of honour and pain. For the first time in the story a character sets aside self indulgence and for the first time emotion is brief, sharp and painful, where before it has been elaborate, vociferous and rather tedious. The couplet is both bold and successful, for it powerfully marks the watershed of the whole poem.

From this moment on honour is triumphant. Everyone falls into the honourable pattern and the outcome is comic, in the medieval sense. The end of the story is good for everybody and the principal agent of this is Aurelius, as he follows Arveragus's honourable lead. And the style, as we might expect, is sensitive to and indicative of the change in his personality. As soon as Dorigen tells him of the situation, his thoughts are presented in simple syntax:

> Aurelius gan wondren on this cas,
> And in his herte hadde greet compassioun
> Of hire and of hire lamentacioun,
> And of Arveragus, the worthy knyght,
> That bad hire holden al that she had hight,
> So looth hym was his wyf sholde breke her trouthe;   1514–19

His first words to her have some syntactic complexity, as they explain his reasons:

> 'Madame, seyth to youre lord Arveragus,
> That sith I se his grete gentillesse
> To yow, and eek I se wel youre distresse,
> That him were levere han shame (and that were routhe)
> Than ye to me sholde breke thus youre trouthe,
> I have wel levere ever to suffre wo
> Than I departe the love bitwix yow two.   1526–32

Although the syntactical unit is long here, the progress of the sense is straightforward, while in his earlier speeches the sense kept turning back on itself. His last words to her have a manly simplicity:

> . . . and heere I take my leve,
> As of the treweste and the beste wyf
> That evere yet I knew in al my lyf.   1538–40

Aurelius has to face the clerk, of course, and this disturbs him, but his disturbance is far less complex than in his earlier speech to Phebus:

> 'Allas,' quod he, 'allas, that I bihighte
> Of pured gold a thousand pound of wighte
> Unto this philosophre! How shal I do?   1559–61

And, quite changed from his earlier self, he ends with a firm determination, plainly expressed:

> But nathelees, I wole of hym assaye,
> At certeyn dayes, yeer by yeer, to paye,
> And thanke hym of his grete curteisye.
> My trouthe wol I kepe, I wol nat lye.' 1567-70

Unlike his previous plans, this is fulfilled exactly and the new, sensible and capable Aurelius is tellingly presented in a crisp piece of dialogue:

> This philosophre sobrely answerede,
> And seyde thus, whan he thise wordes herde:
> 'Have I nat holden covenant unto thee?'
> 'Yes, certes, wel and trewely,' quod he.
> 'Hastow nat had thy lady as thee liketh?'
> 'No, no,' quod he, and sorwefully he siketh. 1585-90

The speed with which this scene is dispatched may be because the tale is drawing to an end (there is one sign of hasty work in the almost exact repetition of a couplet, lines 1465-6 and 1593-5), but it is also a representation of the change that has come over Aurelius. His last words are especially crisp:

> 'That made me han of hire so greet pitee;
> And right as frely as he sente hire me,
> As frely sente I hire to hym ageyn.
> This al and som; ther is namoore to seyn.' 1603-6

   Aurelius's development has been extensive; at first he appeared a mildly comic character, but the unstable personality of Dorigen threatened to turn the tale into a tragedy and Aurelius into a villain, until the firmness of Arveragus set things on a better course and gave Aurelius a good model for his behaviour. The poem's style has skilfully created these characteristics and gives great vitality to a story which as bare plot is without much credibility. In the direct narrative, especially in the central section of the tale, as similar power is seen at work creating this excellent poem, and we are finally reminded that the teller, also, has been made real for us by Chaucer's dexterous art as the Franklin finally speaks directly in his pausing, thoughtful and rather mundane manner:

> Lordynges, this question, thanne, wol I aske now,
> Which was the mooste fre, as thynketh yow?
> Now telleth me, er that ye ferther wende.
> I kan namoore, my tale is at an ende. 1621-4

Chaucer's skill with the figure of the narrator is as great as with the other aspects of the tale, for although the tale has drifted away from the narrator it finally comes back to him, and we feel no jarring note as he reappears, for little reminders have kept him in our memory throughout. This final sequence relates the thoughtful tale to the Franklin's personality as he gives his own gloss on its meaning, and so it is fitted into the structure—meaningful and technical—of *The Canterbury Tales*. In this tale Chaucer achieves that subtlest of the many effects of the entire tales, the creation of a personality within the tale who yet does not dominate the tale itself. The full union of General Prologue, prologue and tale is seen here, where it was absent in 'The Manciple's Prologue and Tale' and the whole skilful entity links up, through the Squire, the Host and the Franklin's 'gentil' concerns with much of *The Canterbury Tales*. In bringing about this excellent result Chaucer demonstrates amply how good a poet he is, and my judgment would be that the poetry that makes this tale so successful and memorable has a secure claim to be called great.

NOTES

1. 'Chaucer and the Rhetoricians', p. 108, both quotations.
2. P. 108, both quotations.
3. P. 109.
4. P. 15.
5. '*The Canterbury Tales* and their Narrators', *SP*, XLV (1948), 565–7, see p. 576.
6. *Des Haushälters Erzählung aus den Canterbury Geschichten Gottfried Chaucers* (Berlin, 1929), see pp. 160–2.
7. *JEGP*, LXII (1963), 1–31, see p. 3.
8. P. 16.
9. See the excellent criticism by Donaldson, 'The Idiom of Popular Poetry in the Miller's Tale', *Speaking of Chaucer*, pp. 13–29, and A. K. Moore, '*Sir Thopas* as Criticism of Fourteenth-Century Minstrelsy', *JEGP*, LIII (1954), 532–45.
10. 'Is the *Manciple's Tale* a Success?' *JEGP*, LI (1952), 1–16, see p. 10.
11. 'The Unity of Chaucer's Manciple's Fragment', *MLN*, LXX (1951), see p. 249.
12. 'Chaucer's "Gentil" Manciple and his "Gentil" Tale', *NM*, LXI (1960), 257–57 see p. 264.
13. 'Chaucer's Manciple's Tale as Part of a Canterbury Group', *UTQ*, XXII (1953), 147–56, see p. 148.
14. *Medieval Rhetoric to 1400* reprinted ed. (Gloucester, Mass., 1959), 'Synoptic Index', pp. 303–6; for Baldwin's unfavourable view of Geoffrey see pp. 294–6 and his article 'Cicero on Parnassus', *PMLA*, XLIII (1927), 106–12.
15. *Les Arts Poétiques du XIIe et du XIIIe Siècle, Bibliothéque des Études de l'Ecole des Haute Études*, fasc. 238 (Paris, 1924), p. 61.
16. *English Literary Criticism: the Medieval Phase* (Oxford, 1943), see pp. 97 and 102 respectively.
17. Baldwin, p. 188; Kelly, 'The Theory of Composition in Medieval Narrative Poetry and Geoffrey of Vinsauf's *Poetria Nova*', *MS*, XXXI (1969), 117–48.
18. Quotations from the *Poetria Nova* are from the translation by Margaret F. Nims (Toronto, 1967): I have also given line numbers from the Latin text; ll. 204–5, Nims, p. 23. Here Nims translates 'premente figura' as 'keeping to our image', but Jane Baltzell Kopp gives it as 'overall structure being now the consideration stressed'

in her rendering in *Three Medieval Rhetorical Arts*, ed. J. J. Murphy (Los Angeles, 1971), p. 41; Kopp's version seems very speculative to me, though it would suit my argument to adopt it.

19. 'Rhetorical "Amplification" and "Abbreviation" and the Structure of Medieval Narrative', *Pacific Coast Philology*, II (1967), 32–9.

20. Ll. 213–19, Nims, pp. 23–4.

21. Geoffrey separates figures of thought and figures of style in his analysis but immediately afterwards he indicates that he knows this distinction is made only for the purposes of study; his final injunction is:

> Bring together flowers of diction and thought, that the field of discourse may blossom with both sorts of flowers, for a mingled fragrance, blending adornment of both kinds, rises and spreads its sweetness. (ll. 1584–7, Nims, p. 72.)

22. Ll. 81–2, Nims, p. 18.

23. Ll. 1687–9, Nims, p. 40.

24. 'A New Look at Chaucer and the Rhetoricians', *RES*, n.s. XV (1964), 1–20.

25. Matthew of Vendôme says nothing about *amplificatio* and *abbrevatio*, Évrard the German has 43 lines, John of Garland two pages, while Geoffrey offers 470 lines on *amplificatio* and 46 on *abbrevatio*.

26. P. 132. (We are quite without clearly stated rules for the construction of the main part of a poem.

So what is available as instruction would not be altogether informative for us were it not that a section in medieval rhetoric contained detailed references to structural elements, which in their entirety made good that which seems lacking to us. They are the instructions for the use of the devices of Amplification and Abbreviation.)

27. See p. 35; she calls *prosopopoeia*, *apostrophe* and *collatio* 'stylistic' figures, and in discussing *abbrevatio* fails to distinguish between the devices as structural features and the same verbal patterns merely as emphatic elements within a structural pattern—when they are figures of style, of course.

28. P. 25.

29. *TC*, II. 344, 'The Physician's Tale', 223, 'The Prioress's Tale', 609.

30. Chaucer is the first to use 'rakel' of objects, not of people, and it appears eight times, three here and five in *TC*, 'rakelnesse', first used by Chaucer, only appears here and in 'Lenvoy to Scogan'; 'trouble' as an adjective is used thirteen times, but ten of them are in *Boece*, 'The Parson's Tale' and *RR*, a trio notable for learned and ornate terminology; 'unavysed' only appears four times, *TC*, *RR* and 'The Parson's Tale' being the other locations.

31. P. 14.

32. P. 14.

33. The issues raised by the best criticism of 'The Franklin's Tale' have been conveniently brought together in the thorough introductions to two separate editions of it, Phyllis Hodgson's *The Franklin's Tale* (London, 1960) and A. C. Spearing's *The Franklin's Prologue and Tale* (Cambridge, 1966).

34. For specific discussions see Hodgson, pp. 73–6, Spearing, pp. 16–22, B. S. Harrison, 'The Rhetorical Inconsistency of Chaucer's Franklin', *SP*, XXXIII (1935), 55–65 and Baldwin, 'Cicero on Parnassus', cf. note 14 above.

35. P. 75.

36. P. 19.

37. Hodgson, pp. 10–16 and Spearing, pp. 22–4 and 33–8.

38. 'A New Look at Chaucer and the Rhetoricians', p. 10.

39. For less extreme examples, see lines 221, 390 and 640 of 'The Franklin's Tale'.

40. P. 75.

41. P. 75.

42. P. 75.

43. 'Dorigen's Complaint', *MP*, XLV (1947), 36–45, see p. 42.

5. The Nun's Priest's Tale

Most critical accounts of 'the Nun's Priest's Tale' have been fairly limited in range; they usually praise its mock-heroic wit and its breadth of reference, but hesitate to investigate more deeply its possible meaning or the details of its construction. Two well-known critics have, however, gone further and have imputed a specific meaning to the tale. J. Leslie Hotson has expounded it as a political allegory about Chaucer's contemporaries, but he does recognise the mock-heroic character of the tale as well, and says that the contemporary references would add:

> ... a subtlety of touch-and-go allusion to contemporary events of the first order, and give the matchless tale a new zest.

In a more single-minded reading Mortimer J. Donovan regards the tale as a Christian allegory; he takes the animal plot as a pure fable and allows little value to the mock-heroic interpretation of the poem, saying firmly that as a whole it is 'a sermon on alertness to moral obligation.'[2] In comparison with other tales, relatively little has been said about the story-teller; this may be partly because the priest is barely mentioned outside his tale and its links, and so Arthur T. Broes and R. M. Lumiansky have had to depend on internal evidence for what light they have cast on this issue. As a result both have based their findings on rather speculative and thin arguments.[3]

Since the tale has been so widely praised, it is surprising that so little has been said about its mechanics. The structure has not been discussed at all; this seems especially odd since its similarities to 'The Pardoner's Tale'—a long theoretical discussion and then brisk action—and the clear juxtaposition of views at the end would seem to invite structural analysis, especially in the light of R. M. Jordan's stimulating book on Chaucerian structure.[4]

Several writers have discussed topics close to an assessment of the poem's style, without dealing directly with it. Karl Young and Robert A. Pratt have investigated the sources of the rhetorical references and Manly used the tale as an opening *exemplum* in his famous lecture.[5] He felt that in it Chaucer showed the natural conclusion of his 'gradual release' from the rhetoricians; C. S. Baldwin took a sterner view of the author's treatment of his authorities, saying that he 'pillories' Geoffrey of Vinsauf.[6] Recent critics have seen Chaucer's relationship with his rhetorical masters as more complex than this. Dorothy Everett has reminded her readers of Chaucer's enigmatic character,[7] and E. T. Donaldson suggests that rhetoric is, in a way, the true topic of the tale.[8] I shall return to these two critics later, for their comments are important and should be considered in the light of what is to be argued here.

Only a few critics speak in any detail about the poem's style and none of these says very much. Muscatine treats this tale last of all in his discussion of *The Canterbury Tales* and while he does describe the stylistic changes that occur in it, he gives none of the detailed comment that is so impressive in his handling of *Troilus and Criseyde* and 'The Miller's Tale'. He treats the tale as an epitome of the mixed style that he has previously explicated in Chaucer, and consequently much of his comment is general.[9] The remarks that Speirs makes are also general, but this is in keeping with his approach, tending as he does to sum up a passage's tone and effect without any extensive detailed analysis; more detailed comments on the tale are given by D. J. Brindley in an article which follows fairly closely Speirs's methods with Chaucer, and which makes some perceptive comments.[10] R. W. V. Elliott gives a brief but lucid summary of the poem's style in his account of this and 'The Pardoner's Tale'.[11] All of these writers state or imply that at certain points Chaucer does exploit his stylistic powers to create or emphasise his effects, but none of them, with the partial exception of Donaldson, attempts to offer a critique that could be summarised. Rather they make a series of interesting points, and these will be referred to as they become relevant in the course of this chapter.

The fact that these critics have said little about the poetics of this tale might suggest that there is little to say, and this would seem to be confirmed by those who have edited it most fully. Kenneth Sisam makes a few shrewd comments on Chaucer's tags and line-fillers;[12] Coghill and Tolkien appreciate some high points and discuss some of the commoner rhetorical figures.[13] The most recent editor, Maurice Hussey, speaks more directly about his view of the tale 'as poetry'. He notes several simple effects of repetition and some

P

characteristics of orally-delivered poetry, mentions some apparently irregular lines and then says that now '. . . we are to consider the wider effects of the poetry, since we have seen that the verse is not devised to yield the utmost only to close critical scrutiny.'[14] In Hussey's view the nature of the poetry here is the same as that summed up by A. C. Spearing in *Criticism and Medieval Poetry* when he describes the characteristics of *The Book of the Duchess*:[15]

> The 'poetry', one might say, is not even noticeable locally; by calling attention to single lines in the passage I have maltreated it. That is not how it works; its most important effects are cumulative.

I have been arguing in these chapters, often explicitly and always implicitly, that Chaucer does frequently write with close attention to the detailed effects of his poetry, and so it would seem necessary to contradict this view of 'The Nun's Priest's Tale', especially as it is widely held to be among the most expert pieces of Chaucer's later poetry. Happily, it is very easy to assert that a close reading does not, to use Spearing's word, 'maltreat' the poem: there is a good deal of highly skilled detailed writing that has either gone unnoticed or has not been fully appreciated.

'The Nun's Priest's Tale' is the last in a wonderfully varied group. Before it come 'The Shipman's Tale', 'The Prioress's Tale', Chaucer's tales of Sir Thopas and Melibee and 'The Monk's Tale'. Apart from the sign of uncompleted revision in 'The Shipman's Tale' (where he speaks like the Wife of Bath, lines 12–19) it is a finished and varied group. The coarse vigour of the Shipman is answered by the elegant religiosity of the Prioress; Chaucer's own tales are in fine contrast with each other and his serious tale seems to expose a moral threadbareness in both the Monk and the Prioress. The Nun's Priest to some extent 'quites' the Monk, as several critics have shown.[16] In its highly aware intelligence and assured reference to practically every literary genre in medieval England 'The Nun's Priest's Tale' is a worthy end to this brilliant and subtly related sequence.

The link before the tale is short, but in it we find both the sense of interplay and tension that is created in the group as a whole and also the stylistic subtlety of Chaucer's most artful poetry. The Knight begins by interrupting the Monk, though he seems to have waited for a decent moment to speak—the Monk's analysis of tragedy with regard to Croesus makes a reasonably apt conclusion to his gloomy discourse, though he clearly does not mean it as one. The Knight's opening words demonstrate a tone that is clearly appropriate for interrupting a pilgrim of some importance:

> 'Hoo!' quod the Knyght, 'good sire, namoore of this!
> That ye han seyd is right ynough, ywis,
> And muchel moore; for litel hevynesse
> Is right ynough to muche folk, I gesse.
> I seye for me, it is a greet disese,
> Whereas men han been in greet welthe and ese,
> To heeren of hire sodeyn fal, allas!   2767-73

Caution and tact are suggested by the many pauses as well as by the oblique syntax; with great politeness the Knight blames himself for finding the tale oppressive. The tactful style implies much about the Knight himself, and about the respect due to the Monk. As the Knight goes on, though, he describes a more positive type of story without pause or qualification:

> And the contrarie is joye and greet solas,
> As whan a man hath been in povre estaat,
> And clymbeth up and wexeth fortunat,
> And there abideth in prosperitee.
> Swich thyng is gladsom, as it thynketh me,
> And of swich thyng were goodly for to telle.'   2774-9

In the context of this firm and flowing passage the parenthetic 'as it thynketh me' is a statement of confidence, not one of cautious qualification, and the passage shows how the Knight, typically, has managed to assert his quiet but forceful personality.

The Host, a less polite assessor of personalities, now speaks with less tact and less fluency:

> 'Ye,' quod oure Hooste, 'by seinte Poules belle!
> Ye seye right sooth; this Monk he clappeth lowde.
> He spak how Fortune covered with a clowde
> I noot nevere what; and als of a tragedie
> Right now ye herde, and, pardee, no remedie
> It is for to biwaille ne compleyne
> That that is doon, and als it is a peyne,
> As ye han seyd, to heere of hevynesse.   2780-7

As in his remarks to the Monk before his tale, the Host does not judge him worthy of much politness—his tone to the Prioress is very different, for example. The word 'clappeth' is bluntly rude, and the effect of the run-on 'I noot nevere what' is damningly dismissive. The

Host's frequent use of enjambement here does not give an ornate tone as it can in some other speakers; rather, as in Ector's use of it, the effect is to break up the ordered quality that regular verse can have (cf. p. 56 above). The pauses and the varying rhythms of the lines help to create the colloquial effect. In keeping, the syntax is very simple, for there is no subtle subordination here. The repeated 'and als' and the colloquial running-on of the lines create an effect very like that of the sequences of loosely linked co-ordinate clauses typical of much medieval English prose.

So the Host dismisses the Monk in a speech-style which proclaims a plain man having little patience with folly, especially when it is contrasted with that of the Knight. The Host rambles on into another loosely connected sentence:

> Wherfore, sire Monk, or daun Piers by your name,
> I pray yow hertely telle us somwhat elles;
> For sikerly, nere clynkyng of youre belles,
> That on youre bridel hange on every syde,
> By hevene kyng, that for us alle dyde,
> I sholde er this han fallen doun for sleep,
> Although the slough had never been so deep;
> Thanne hadde your tale al be toold in veyn.   2792–9

He has need of the summarising final line here, for the sentence has maundered to a rather obscure close—it is a passage that students often find tricky to translate into the 'good modern English prose' of examination rubrics. The Host here shows none of the crisp organisation and forceful vocabulary of the Knight at his most fluent, and none of the tact of him at his most pausing; but the Host is not being as rude as he is elsewhere (to the Franklin, for example), and the following lines show an attempt to placate the Monk:

> For certeinly, as that thise clerkes seyn,
> Whereas a man may have noon audience,
> Noght helpeth it to tellen his sentence.
>   And wel I woot the substance is in me,
> If any thyng shal wel reported be.
> Sir, sey somwhat of huntyng, I yow preye.'   2800–5

The Host fits in a few learned terms—'sentence', 'audience' and 'substance'—presumably to humour the Monk, and tries to move him on to a topic he ought to describe well.[17] The Monk briskly refuses and so the Host turns to another cleric; here he feels no need for persuasion and adopts a different tone, forceful and imperative singular:[18]

> 'Com neer, thou preest, com hyder, thou sir John!
> Telle us swich thyng as may oure hertes glade.
> Be blithe, though thou ryde upon a jade.
> What thogh thyn hors be bothe foul and lene?
> If he wol serve thee, rekke nat a bene.
> Looke that thyn herte be murie everemo.'   2810–15

The Priest assents; he strikes a humble note:

> 'Yis, sir,' quod he, 'yis, Hoost, so moot I go,
> But I be myrie, ywis I wol be blamed.'   2816–17

He accepts the Host's authority so readily and offers so much servile agreement in two lines that, in the light of the tale to follow, it is hard to avoid thinking that his words imply a judgment on the Host's bossy manner. This may be to read a lot into the link, but Chaucer invites such reading. This link, like so many others, is rich with implication; the speeches indicate that the pilgrims are constantly making judgments about each other, and these judgments are subtly implied in the manner in which they speak. The Host's style of speech is many-sided, and his assessment of a person is shown in several aspects of his style, not merely in the well-known variation between 'ye' and 'thow'. But other characters also participate in these little dramas, and their speech can also imply judgments. These links are the most advanced form of Chaucer's mimetic art; there is very little direct description—here we are just told that the Host is 'rude and boold' in speech to the Priest and we are given a final assessment of the Priest as 'sweete' and 'goodly.' Both characters demonstrate these qualities in their styles of speech.

A lot goes on in the links of this group of tales, and this one is typical of the general effect of them; they emphasise the tension between the pilgrims and, consequently, between the tales. Without them it would be hard to say whether Chaucer really meant the tales to interact, but on the evidence of the links this is plainly his purpose, though it may not be his only purpose—the tales are at the same time self-sufficient. But after a link like this one we are prepared to look for effects deriving from the juxtaposition of the tales and, important to this study, our ears are attuned to different styles of speaking and we expect different styles to have differing implications. As in all the links where we find this 'roadside drama,' so well described a good time ago by Kittredge,[19] the style of the speaker is central to his meaning, and this should bring us to read—or listen to—'The Nun's Priest's Tale' itself with heightened awareness and expectation.

The tale opens in a simple manner, giving us undecorated information:

> A povre wydwe, somdeel stape in age
> Was whilom dwellyng in a narwe cotage,
> Biside a grove, stondynge in a dale.
> This wydwe, of which I telle yow my tale,
> Syn thilke day that she was last a wyf,
> In pacience ladde a ful symple lyf,
> For litel was hir catel and hir rente.   2821–7

The lines move along steadily, notable neither for fluency nor jerkiness; the diction is not ornate, but nor is it brusque in manner, for there is a reasonable number of two-syllable words and French-derived terms. In the last line the narrator pauses over the widow's income: the word 'catel' is a little surprising in this humble context, for its normal uses are different. It and 'rente' are generally used of a more elaborate system of life. Though both are French, they are reasonably common in Chaucer and in earlier texts, though the fact that about half the occurrences of 'catel' are from 'The Parson's Tale' and *The Romaunt of the Rose* may imply a learned ambience. But any possible irony in this slightly elaborate description is, for the moment, muted, for the narrator goes on to speak about the widow's simple mode of life in a simple style:

> By housbondrie of swich as God hire sente
> She foond hirself and eek hir doghtren two.
> Thre large sowes hadde she, and namo,
> Three keen, and eek a sheep that highte Malle.   2828–31

This is rather plainer than the opening lines; the style now creates more fully the simplicity of this humble scene as the narrator lists the animals with scrupulous care. The fact that it is the sheep who is named may prepare us subliminally for a beast-fable, but the basic effect is that these lines are fully in sympathy with the widow's life. The scene might be being set for a story of moral virtue, like the opening of 'The Clerk's Tale'. In this context the use of the words 'catel' and 'rente' might seem a little odder than before, and as the narrator continues the reason for their use becomes clear. If it is to be a moral tale, it is not to be a simple, low-key one, for in the next lines the possible ironies of 'catel' and 'rente' are reinforced by a series of words whose ambience is more clearly inappropriate to this scene:

> Ful sooty was hire bour and eek hir halle,
> In which she eet ful many a sklendre meel.   2832–3

The words 'bour' and 'halle' belong to a type of building quite different from humble cottages. The hall is, of course, the great hall of the medieval house and the 'bour' is the ladies withdrawing room which, at this time, would only be found in really large houses: the grandeur the words imply is well seen in a house like Penshurst Place. The irony here is clear enough, but a number of editors have missed the important point that it is a one-room cottage—bower and hall are one. We would expect this of a humble cottage at this time in any case, but the fact that both 'rooms' are sooty clarifies the point—a real 'bour' would not contain a fire. To add weight to this joke, in Chaucer the word 'bour' has a genteel connotation, and the same appears true of the word 'sklendre'.[20] The humility of the window's state is treated ironically in the vocabulary, and in this context 'catel' and 'rente' seem to have taken on an ironic quality as well. The narrator now raises this little joke into a major motif, for the next passage showers us with a series of elaborate gastronomical terms:

> Of poynaunt sauce hir neded never a deel.
> No deyntee morsel passed thurgh hir throte;
> Hir diete was accordaunt to hir cote.   2834–6

The account found in all the histories of the language, that elegant foods bear French names, here springs into poetic life, and the setting of the food terms in the same place in each line stresses the effect with an easy skill. The following lines enlarge the joke, pointing out that if you use French names for fine foods you also have to use French names for the physical problems they cause:

> Repleccioun ne made hire nevere sik;
> Attempree diete was al hir phisik,
> And exercise, and hertes suffisaunce.
> The goute lette hir nothyng for to daunce,
> N'apoplexie shente nat hir heed.   2837–41

Again the lines are skilfully constructed; the French names for disorders tend to come early in the line and a good balance is maintained between the two halves of the line. This gives a firm clarity to the negative-positive balance in the argument. The skilled jesting with language is now dropped for a while, but it has had an important effect. Not only has this been an interesting and lively description of country simplicity, it has also introduced the mock-heroic to the tale; the language used has directed a certain amount of mockery at the areas where these elaborate words are used without being inappropriate—here, on the other hand, is not only simplicity, but health as well.

The final sequence of this description returns to the simple style:

> No wyn ne drank she, neither whit ne reed;
> Hir bord was served moost with whit and blak,—
> Milk and broun breed, in which she foond no lak,
> Seynd bacoun, and somtyme an ey or tweye;
> For she was, as it were, a maner deye. 2842–6

The mild note of mockery towards courtliness is maintained, as we are told that the widow is quite satisfied with this diet, and the style of the lines very satisfyingly acts out the plainness of her life. There is no enjambement, no elaborate diction, and here we do find that simple monosyllabic note which was not present in the opening lines of the description. The simple rhyme words press the point— 'blak'/'lak' and 'tweye'/'deye' and the extra pause and rather bathetic comment of the final line bring the whole description to a slow and fading close. The whole passage is just one more example of the remarkable richness Chaucer can produce from a formal description: it is not as dense with implication as the description of Alisoun in 'The Miller's Tale' but it is a little masterpiece. The poor widow is convincingly created. Muscatine remarks on 'the husbanding of sensory effect' in this passage and Brindley talks of the 'unassuming realism of the widow's style',[21] but there is more than this here. Within the description there is an indication of, and a preparation for the varying tones the tale is to demonstrate. This is brought about by the subtle modulation of the style throughout this passage and by the manipulation of the vocabulary in particular.

The narrator moves on to another description which is to be, in visual terms, very different, but the ground-bass of which has already been sounded in the ironic use of ornate language in the widow's description. First we read simply:

> A yeerd she hadde, enclosed al aboute
> With stikkes, and a drye dych withoute,
> In which she hadde a cok, hight Chauntecleer. 2847–9

Reading the tale for a second time, it sounds very like a farmyard equivalent of a defended position—this may be an accident, but if so it is a happy one, for this selection of detail fits in well with Chauntecleer's chivalric presentation. At first his description is merely hyperbolic:

> In al the land, of crowyng nas his peer.
> His voys was murier than the murie orgon
> On messe-dayes that in the chirche gon.   2850–2

But the simile is not only a *superlatio*: it is a most dignified sort of simile and the word 'orgon' is itself a lofty term to use.[22] The next couplet continues this note:

> Wel sikerer was his crowyng in his logge
> Than is a clokke or an abbey orlogge.   2853–4

As so often in Chaucer, the similes do not merely state a comparison; the object used in comparison implies something about the subject of the simile. To describe Chauntecleer we need a union of the grandeurs of the medieval church and the subtleties of medieval technology—and ornate language is a *sine qua non*. Even a 'clokke' will not do: the word 'orlogge' is enlisted for a more fitting comparison—and Chauntecleer still overgoes it. The word 'logge' also appears to dignify Chauntecleer, for it probably has a chivalric connotation.[23] The rest of the discussion of Chauntecleer's crowing continues the *superlatio*, of thought and of style:

> By nature he knew ech ascencioun
> Of the equynoxial in thilke toun;
> For whan degrees fiftene weren ascended,
> Thanne crew he, that it myghte nat been amended.   2855–8

The confidence and vigour of his crowing are finely expressed: after the elaborate language the blunt 'Thanne crew he' is delightfully judged, and the rest of the line seems to have rather a lot of stresses, asserting in its firm sound just what it says.

The physical description of Chauntecleer that follows also shows this high humour and uses more ironic language to characterise this magnificent cock:

> His coomb was redder than the fyn coral,
> And batailled as it were a castel wal;
> His byle was blak, and as the jeet it shoon;
> Lyk asure were his legges and his toon;
> His nayles whitter than the lylye flour,
> And lyk the burned gold was his colour.   2859–64

The description has been discussed elsewhere and critics have explained the multiple joke—the elegance of the similes and the rhetorical correctness of the *effictio*.[24] That the language is so grand and the organisation so decorous is one side of the joke: that it is, apparently, an accurate picture of the most gorgeous of farmyard birds is the other side.[25] It is one of the high moments of Chaucer's work, and the effect derives largely from the witty selection of epithet and simile. But, especially in the light of this study, it is interesting to note the suggestion of dignity and formality that is given as the lines group into something very close to a *repetitio* with *compar*. There is a brief stiffening and elevation in the sound of the verse which brings out finely the excellent joke.

The language of romance is sustained as the narrator moves on to the rest of the household:

> This gentil cok hadde in his governaunce
> Seven hennes for to doon al his plesaunce,
> Whiche were his sustres and his paramours,
> And wonder lyk to hym, as of colours;　2865–8

The mock-heroic language is plain enough, but here we also have a trick which is to recur in the tale and whose effect depends upon poetic subtlety. Embedded in this passage is one piece of information which subverts the whole edifice of lofty language—the hens were his sisters as well as his paramours. But this reference is skated over, the narrator runs on quickly in the only three-line sentence we have had for about twenty lines; he seems to want only to tell us about the colour of the hens. The organisation of the lines throws the emphasis quite away from the startlingly animal detail that Chauntecleer's court—and we must by now call it that—was incestuous. This teasing effect recurs almost at once.

Pertelote is, as has frequently been noted, a properly courtly lady:

> Curteys she was, discreet, and debonaire,
> And compaignable, and bar hyrself so faire,
> Syn thilke day that she was seven nyght oold,
> That trewely she hath the herte in hoold
> Of Chauntecleer, loken in every lith;　2871–5

The sentence builds up grandly to the climactic enjambement and the closing conventional phrase 'loken in every lith.' But again, a deflatingly realistic piece of chicken-life has been hurried over. A week is young indeed for a courtly lady to be beloved, but more acceptable for a chicken. As before, the narrator plants the jolting fact in the middle of his grand sentence, and the effect is to prevent the lofty language from asserting its nobility: the style remains mock-heroic because of this, and the poem is not allowed to assume the sort of seriousness that this style might lead us to expect. The characters may be described like lords and ladies and may act a little like lords and ladies, but we are prompted to remember that they are nothing but chickens. The issue seems important to the poet at this early stage, for after a few lines he makes the point again. We hear of the two lovers singing, in the proper language of the lyrics:

> But swich a joye was it to here hem synge,
> Whan that the brighte sonne gan to sprynge,
> In sweete accord, 'My lief is faren in londe!'   2877–9

But then the narrator says:

> For thilke tyme, as I have understonde,
> Beestes and briddes koude speke and synge.   2880–1

The remark breaks the fantasy of the story once more. An ingenious commentator could impute it to that well-known naïve narrator whom Chaucer often uses as a stalking-horse; I think it is not necessary to be so complicated. The remark fits in with the other references that specify the mock-heroic tone of the poem and it may well serve another fairly simple function; it is quite common for the narrator of a tale to speak in his own voice at the end of a section. This presumably had a lot to do with the exigencies of reading aloud a long story—both 'The Knight's Tale' and *Troilus and Criseyde* have many of these moments. And this point does mark the end of the opening sequence of the tale, for now there is to be some action.

The poetic skills that have been quite clear in this opening are still to be found in the next sequence, though I think they are shown differently. So far, the main weight of the poetic subtlety has been in the imaginative choice of language, though sometimes the organisation of the lines has given added point to this and sometimes effects have been implied by the prosody alone. In the following sequence I believe Chaucer uses a subtle modulation of style in a major way, to give Chauntecleer and Pertelote contrasting personalities.

When Pertelote hears Chauntecleer groaning in his sleep her reaction is affectionate, but crisp:

> She was agast, and seyde, 'Herte deere,
> What eyleth yow, to grone in this manere?
> Ye been a verray sleper; fy, for shame!'   2889–91

His reply is a little different:

> And he answerde, and seyde thus: 'Madame,
> I pray yow that ye take it nat agrief.
> By God, me mette I was in swich meschief
> Right now, that yet myn herte is soore afright.   2892–95

Both speakers use the polite plural and both begin with a lofty
vocative. 'Herte deere' and 'Madame' are both firmly stressed and
provide the rhyme, so drawing our attention to the extreme politeness of these birds. But Chauntecleer lacks the sharp tone and brisk
style of Pertelote; this difference is first seen in the contrast between
'She was agast, and seyde' and the slacker 'And he answerde and
seyde', and the longer syntactical units of Chauntecleer's lines
continue the same note. He uses one enjambement, where the ends
of her lines fall heavily. It would be an adventurous criticism which
confidently found a marked character difference in these two short
passages alone, but as the tale continues we find that the contrast
sketched here is made stronger.

As Chauntecleer goes on, enjambement seems a motif of his style:

> Now God,' quod he, 'my swevene recche aright,
> And kepe my body out of foul prisoun!
> Me mette how that I romed up and doun
> Withinne our yeerd, wheer as I saugh a beest
> Was lyk an hound, and wolde han maad areest
> Upon my body, and wolde han had me deed.   2896–901

The opening two lines are reasonably crisp, though the comma at
the end of the first line represents a light pause at most, but then the
lines are strongly run on; this no doubt makes more emphatic the
final monosyllabic 'wolde han had me deed' but also gives a curious
fluency, perhaps a volubility to the lines. But Chauntecleer does not
always speak in this way; the dramatic ending to this passage is
pursued in the next lines where he gives a vivid account of the
mysterious 'beest':

> His colour was bitwixe yelow and reed,
> And tipped was his tayl and bothe his eeris
> With blak, unlyk the remenaunt of his heeris;
> His snowte smal, with glowynge eyen tweye.
> Yet of his look for feere almoost I deye: 2902–6

There is one enjambement here, but the effect of the run-on 'With
blak' is rather crisp and cannot be said to continue the flowingly

run-on effect of the previous passage.[26] Throughout Chauntecleer's speech we will find these two tones; sometimes he speaks in a general and fluent manner, moving with grace and speed, while at other times he is more dramatic and impressive: he uses both styles skilfully to be a convincing speaker. But even at his most dramatic and forceful his tone is different from Pertelote's normal style. He is always elegant and poised, but her verse is more broken up by pauses, is not run on, and she conveys a business-like, common-sense note:

> 'Avoy!'; quod she, 'fy on yow, hertelees!
> Allas!' quod she, 'for, by that God above,
> Now han ye lost myn herte and al my love.
> I kan nat love a coward, by my faith!
> For certes, what so any womman seith,
> We alle desiren, if it myghte bee,
> To han housbondes hardy, wise, and free,
> And secree, and no nygard, ne no fool,
> Ne hym that is agast of every tool,
> Ne noon avauntour, by that God above!   2908–17

Each line ends firmly, and very few of them are without some pause. The pauses fall differently in each line and so we do not get a measured, repetitive effect; instead it is a direct, forceful and rather pungent style—clear, straight speaking to match the strong feelings that she has on the topic. She has firm opinions, crisply expressed, and they are informative and factual. They may be *sententiae*, but they are not sententious, in the modern sense of the word. As she goes on the style remains forceful. The lines are still end-stopped, full of specific nouns and clear adjectives and the rhythms are constantly changing. The speech cannot be intoned: it has to be punched out, just as she punches out clear opinions and reams of information:

> Swevenes engendren of replecciouns,
> And ofte of fume and of complecciouns,
> Whan humours been to habundant in a wight.
> Certes this dreem, which ye han met to-nyght,
> Cometh of the greete superfluytee
> Of youre rede colera, pardee,
> Which causeth folk to dreden in hir dremes
> Of arwes, and of fyr with rede lemes,
> Of rede beestes, that they wol hem byte,
> Of contek, and of whelpes, grete and lyte;   2923–2

There is one enjambement here, as line 2930 runs on to 'Of arwes', but this does not establish a fluid tone as does enjambement in Chauntecleer's speech; the run-on phrase is short and the effect is to emphasise this beginning of Pertelote's list of the contents of choleric dreams. There is some complex language here, for she is learned and controls the vocabulary of dream lore. The speech continues in this way, full of good sense and information, ending with a charmingly detailed account of medieval laxatives:

> A day or two ye shul have digestyves
> Of wormes, er ye take youre laxatyves
> Of lawriol, centaure, and fumetere,
> Or elles of ellebor, that groweth there,
> Of katapuce, or of gaitrys beryis,
> Of herbe yve, growynge in oure yeerd, there mery is;
> Pekke hem up right as they growe and ete hem yn.   2961–7

Once again a few lines are run on, and once again the effect is to stress the pauses in this careful, packed speech (just previously, lines 2946–7 are another example of this); the rugged rhythms of the lines emphasise the firm effect—the last two lines are especially deliberate.

In tone, then, Pertelote's long speech is forceful, even aggressive; it masses information and advice in crisp language, learned when it needs to be but never anywhere near high style. Her Latinisms are particular and necessary, not general and decorative. In total concord with this style is the fact that her speech has a closely worked argument. She states: (1) You have acted in a cowardly manner, fearing a dream. (2) Dreams are not to be feared. (3) This is because they derive from disordered humours. (4) Treatment is available for this condition. (5) Therefore, taking the treatment, 'Dredeth no dreem' (line 2969).

Speirs has summed up Pertelote:[27]

> Pertelote is the practical wife. She ascribes a purely physio-
> logical cause and significance to dreams and advises a laxative.
> She has a wealth of knowledge of medicine, of remedies and
> herbs, at her finger-tips.

This is true, but Speirs does not note that it is the driving, blunt style of her speech that creates this impression as much as anything else; if she spoke differently we would read her personality differently. The speech she has made seems in many ways to conflict

with the description of her as 'Curteys,' 'discreet, and debonaire'
and makes these terms seem even more ironically unfitting. Of course,
the heroine of romance is often presented as a healer—it is the one
act of which she seems capable, in many romances—but she heals
by laying on of hands and by mixing unspecified magical potions.
Pertelote is a very down-to-earth version of this—and here may be
yet another joke in the tale. If it is, the poetic control of the tale
helps to make the joke, as it helps to shape her whole personality.

Chauntecleer seems to have experienced this sort of thing before,
because he is neither daunted nor persuaded by her; he replies with
great politeness:

> 'Madame,' quod he, 'graunt mercy of youre loore.   2970

And he embarks on a refutation. That it is necessary to quote his
opening words at length immediately suggests something about the
type of answer he is making:

> But nathelees, as touching daun Catoun,
> That hath of wysdom swich a greet renoun,
> Though that he bad no dremes for to drede,
> By God, men may in olde bookes rede
> Of many a man moore of auctorite
> Than evere Caton was, so moot I thee,
> That al the revers seyn of this sentence,
> And han wel founden by experience
> That dremes ben significaciouns
> As wel of joye as of tribulaciouns
> That folk enduren in this lif present.   2971–81

It is one long elaborate sentence, with subordinate phrases and
clauses running here and there. The elaborate syntax and the
extended utterance are quite opposed to Pertelote's style. Another
marked difference is that where she used Latinisms as the specific
names of objects, Chauntecleer uses them as abstract nouns, and
they tend to fall as rhyme words to stress their elaborate nature. Her
long words were functional parts of her lines, his advertise themselves more. The complex language is in keeping with his scholarly—
even scholastic—approach: he immediately takes up her one
'auctorite' and refutes it. But his refutation needs examining: she
referred to Cato and quoted briefly from him. Chauntecleer in
reply gives the opinion of a number of unspecified authorities, and
gives it in indirect speech—he is neither exact nor convincing. The
argument of this opening sentence is vague and the fluent floridities

of its style seem to have little content. But Chauntecleer is satisfied
that the point has been nailed down, for he goes on:

> Ther nedeth make of this noon argument;
> The verray preeve sheweth it in dede. 2982–3

These assured lines lead into his *exempla*, and his confidence sounds
quite hollow against the swift-moving scholarly banalities of his
opening refutation. It is a simple enough joke—the husband assumes
his pretensions to knowledge will satisfy the little woman. It is
Chaucer's control of poetic style that shapes the joke so well; the
narrator does not have to prompt the reader, for character is
created in speech here just as it was in the link before the tale.

We would associate long-windedness with the bombastic opening
Chauntecleer has given us, and he does not disappoint. He embarks
on his 'verray preeve' (which incidentally has nothing to do with
dreams of joy, though he has just raised this topic in line 2980). His
opening line has a note of imprecise scholarship in it, but he is now
in his dramatic mode and moves quickly on:

> Oon of the grettesste auctor that men rede
> Seith thus: that whilom two felawes wente
> On pilgrimage, in a ful good entente;
> And happed so, they coomen in a toun
> Wher as ther was swich congregacioun
> Of peple, and eek so streit of herbergage,
> That they ne founde as muche as o cotage
> In which they bothe myghte ylogged bee. 2984–91

The syntax is still extended, but the effect of subordination is not as
marked as it was in his general opening remarks. The passage starts
off with a good deal of enjambement, but this does not have as
convoluted an effect as before because here there is a narrative moving
onwards and a series of active verbs.

The muted enjambement we find here would seem to be a
transitional device, for as the *exemplum* continues it settles down into a
purely end-stopped style. This may be because it would be hard
indeed to tell a direct and straightforward *exemplum* in an elaborate
and roundabout style, but Chaucer does let Chauntecleer begin to
speak in a florid style and only then makes him talk simply. We
have seen already that Chauntecleer can talk with directness—he
is not all hot air, as the story will finally show, or perhaps we should
say he commands a variety of hot airs. This change of style demon-

strates that he has more than one way of impressing his audience, for now he starts on a skilfully told, gripping *exemplum*.

Elsewhere we have seen Chaucer merging one style into another, and this is what he seems to be doing here. The effect is to show that Chauctecleer can be persuasive and dominating, though the validity of this domination will be questioned by another change of style before long. Perhaps another effect—and it may be an important one to Chaucer the craftsman—is to vary the stylistic surface of this poem again. The full effect of this change may be hard to assess, but it is there, for now Chauntecleer leaves his vague and general manner and falls quickly into the dramatic recounting of his story, straightforward and speedy: the movement is simple and there is at least one active verb in every line:

> And so bifel that, longe er it were day,
> This man mette in his bed, ther as he lay,
> How that his felawe gan upon hym calle,
> And seyde, 'Allas! for in an oxes stalle
> This nyght I shal be mordred ther I lye.
> Now helpe me, deere brother, or I dye. 3001-6

The *exemplum* proceeds in this manner, seeming to speed up as it goes along; the syntax becomes extended at times, though never convoluted, for the movement is a quick one from line to line and enjambement is used only twice and then for stress. The first instance of this illustrates the speed of movement as well:

> This man gan fallen in suspecioun,
> Remembrynge on his dremes that he mette,
> And forth he gooth—no lenger wolde he lette—
> Unto the west gate of the toun, and fond
> A dong-carte, 3032-6

The grisly aspect of the murder is thus stressed and enjambement is used again for this effect shortly afterwards:

> The people out sterte and caste the cart to grounde,
> And in the myddel of the dong they founde
> The dede man, that mordred was al newe. 3047-9

This climax of the *exemplum* epitomises its direct swift style. But if we are impressed by this, we are soon checked: immediately Chauntecleer switches styles and we are reminded of his bombastic side. He offers a rhetorical *conclusio*:

Q

> O blisful God, that art so just and trewe,
> Lo, how that thou biwreyest mordre alway!
> Mordre wol out, that se we day by day.
> Mordre is so wlatsom and abhomynable
> To God, that is so just and resonable,
> That he ne wol nat suffre it heled be,
> Though it abyde a yeer, or two, or thre.
> Mordre wol out, this my conclusion.   3050–7

Chauntecleer is aware of this as a formal conclusion and he makes the style appropriate. He opens with *exclamatio* and moves on with *sententiae;* he multiplies epithets in an elevated manner—'just and resonable', 'just and trewe'—and offers a pair of really ornate epithets in 'wlatsom and abhomynable': according to the dictionaries the Germanic word would have been quite as rare as the Latinate one at this time.[28] The second line opens with a vowel assonance that almost amounts to a hoot in 'Lo, how that thou', the word 'Mordre' is used in *traductio* here, and it is the subject of a fine *sententia* in line 3052 that is repeated in the closing line. There is *repetitio* in the placing of 'Mordre' three times at the head of the line, and there is a stylish control in the line 'Though it abyde a yeer,or two, or three'. It is a well-modelled piece of verse; a seventeenth century printer might have been tempted to put one of those disembodied pointing hands in the margin, and perhaps the improving rubric 'Sentence' beside it as well.

The preceding passages should have advised us to be cautious about what Chauntecleer is saying—is it really as important as it sounds? And if we consider for a moment, this high point has an implicit comic quality. The finely presented conclusion has, in fact, only a tangential relevance to the topic, for he has been talking about dreams, not murders, and his floridity leads him astray here. The point is made clearer when Chauntecleer returns to his story; he races though the final events in a totally contrasting style and ends with an anti-climactic, but fully relevant conclusion:

> And right anon, ministres of that toun
> Han hent the carter and so soore hym pyned,
> And eek the hostiler so soore engyned,
> That they biknewe hire wikkednesse anon,
> And were anhanged by the nekke-bon.
> Heere may men seen that dremes been to drede.   3058–63

Chauntecleer has previously carried himself away with his party-piece on murder and here has to return jerkily to his topic. His stylistic powers seem fine, but his conceptual control is not so good. There may well be another irony, in support of this, in the next lines. He goes on with another story, saying:

> And certes in the same booke I rede,
> Right in the nexte chapitre after this—
> I gabbe nat, so have I joye or blis— 3064–6

His insistence that he tells the truth makes it all the more likely that this is another indication of his shaky scholarship and his willingness to cast up a cloud of words, for as Coghill and Tolkien remark this story does not follow the previous one in the source. It would be a recherché point, but then in many ways it is a recherché tale and Chaucer does seem to draw attention to the assertion.

The second *exemplum* is a reworking of the theme of the first, and it similarly begins with a long, flowing sentence:

> Two men that wolde han passed over see,
> For certeyn cause, into a fer contree,
> If that the wynd ne hadde been contrarie,
> That made hem in a citee for to tarie
> That stood ful myrie upon an haven-syde; 3067–71

Then the *exemplum* simplifies its style and continues in a quick and compact manner. The change from an extended to a simple syntax is not perhaps as marked as it is in the first *exemplum*, but it is there and it does to some extent support the tonal characterisation of Chauntecleer as a naturally long-winded person who can 'perform' dramatically at times. The third *exemplum* is on the same theme, and although these *exempla* do not advance the argument at all this in itself should not make us question their validity. The building up of exemplary proof is a perfectly acceptable form of medieval argument, and because it seems like a move from the very particular to the very general a modern reader should not therefore assume Chaucer has no time for it. Manly's description of exemplary argument as an 'astonishing fad' is too peremptory,[29] but Chaucer does seem sensitive to the possible misuse of exemplary argument— the Pardoner is one example, in 'The Franklin's Tale' he shows Dorigen going nowhere at great length with a series of *exempla*, and here he chooses to give this method of arguing to the wordy Chauntecleer and a different method to the clear-headed Pertelote.

The stylistic nature of the third *exemplum* strengthens this impression; in it Chauntecleer's bombastic nature emerges very clearly. This *exemplum* is not told in the swift, rather objective style of the other two. It is heavy with enjambement, a motif of Chauntecleer's florid style:

> His norice hym expowned every deel
> His sweven, and bad hym for to kepe hym weel
> For traisoun; but he nas but seven yeer old,
> And therfore litel tale hath he toold
> Of any dreem, so hooly was his herte.   3115–19

The learned condescension of Chauntecleer is obvious:

> By God! I hadde levere than my sherte
> That ye hadde rad his legende, as have I.   3120–1

The reference to his 'sherte' brings back all the ludicrous aspect of the learned cock, and a specifically comic context is recreated—if we have forgotten it—to enrich the moment as Chauntecleer reels of a list of learned authorities in his support.

It seems then, that although *exempla* may be perfectly acceptable, as in 'The Tale of Melibee', there is a possibility of abuse and there may be a comic aspect to them. The first leads into flowery irrelevance, the second reminds us of this briefly and the third demonstrates clearly the speaker's pretentious personality. His conclusion has a similar note:

> Shortly I seye, as for conclusioun,
> That I shal han of this avisioun
> Adversitee; and I seye forthermoor,
> That I ne telle of laxatyves no stoor,
> For they been venymous, I woot it weel;
> I hem diffye, I love hem never a deel!   3151–6

Chauntecleer's words are formal and stylish in construction. The placing of the word 'Adversitee' is especially artistic, and Naunin identifies *contrarietas* in line 3156.[30] It is a formal 'defiance', and the speaker shows learning and nobility. The fact that it is laxatives he faces so nobly is in itself comic enough—Chaucer seems to have found the whole topic of excretion as funny as English comedians still find it—and the whole joke is summed up in the ambiguous word 'diffye,' meaning both the lofty challenge and the simple act of digestion. Once more the comedy is given its fine point by the delicate modulation of the style and the skilled selection of language.

In the following sequence the comedy develops strongly, setting out more boldly in action the comic implications made so far. In spite of his lengthy arguments, Chauntecleer ignores his dream and flies down, because Pertelote transmits courage to him. The lines that summarise this have a real comic vigour:

> For whan I see the beautee of youre face,
> Ye been so scarlet reed aboute youre yen,
> It maketh al my drede for to dyen; 3160–2

And Chauntecleer's explanation demonstrates his shoddy scholarship and his confident bombast:

> For al so siker as *In principio*,
> *Mulier est hominis confusio*,—
> Madame, the sentence of this Latyn is,
> 'Womman is mannes joye and al his blis.' 3163–6

Where Pertelote used her learning in a practical way, Chauntecleer uses his—it is less than he pretends—to assert his dominance. Donaldson says that 'rhetoric here is regarded as the inadequate defence that mankind erects against an inscrutable reality.'[31] I feel this is to be too serious, as I shall argue later, but Donaldson certainly sees the effect of the rhetoric that Chaucer places in the rooster's mouth.

This strongly marked sequence of comic implication is followed by action which creates physically the mock-heroic follies so far only stated in description and revealed in speech:

> And with that word he fley doun fro the beem,
> For it was day, and eke his hennes alle,
> And with a chuk he gan hem for to calle,
> For he hadde founde a corn, lay in the yerd.
> Real he was, he was namoore aferd.
> He fethered Pertelote twenty tyme,
> And trad hire eke as ofte, er it was pryme,
> He looketh as it were a grym leoun,
> And on his toos he rometh up and doun;
> Hym deigned nat to sette his foot to grounde. 3172–81

The regal notions that Chauntecleer has of himself are objictified in the farmyard; it is a brilliantly funny piece of observation, and the narrator mulls over the joke pleasantly:

> Thus roial, as a prince is in his halle,
> Leve I this Chauntecleer in his pasture,
> And after wol I telle his aventure. 3184–6

Like the 'leoun' simile, the word 'halle' calls up the ironic effects of the opening part of the poem, 'pasture' is a dignified name to give to running round after 'a corn' and 'aventure' itself is a word from the chivalric context. We are reminded of the verbal play that has gone before, but this passage is not notable for its poetic effects: its achievements are those of the comic imagination and they do not depend on poetic modulation to imply effect. The style is supple and polished, and the stressed repetition of 'He' and 'hym' assists the note of *superlatio*, but the mainspring of the comedy here is not prosodic.

The Nun's Priest has said that he will now get down to the story, but he continues it in that teasing manner that runs strongly throughout this tale (Sisam has commented very sensibly on this[32]), for Chauntecleer's morning crow is approached with a wonderfully elaborate passage. Like the previous action, it is the working-out of an element in the original description of him. The whole passage has to be quoted to show the effect:

> Whan that the month in which the world bigan,
> That highte March, whan God first maked man,
> Was compleet, and passed were also,
> Syn March bigan, thritty dayes and two,
> Bifel that Chauntecleer in al his pryde,
> His sevene wyves walkynge by his syde,
> Caste up his eyen to the bright sonne,
> That in the signe of Taurus hadde yronne
> Twenty degrees and oon, and somwhat moore,
> And knew by kynde, and by noon oother loore,
> That it was pryme, and crew with blisful stevene.   3187–97

If you read the passage aloud it is a test of breath control; 'caste' is the first verb of any weight, in the seventh line, and the construction of the sentence will not allow you to pause properly until the end. The structural figure of *circuitio* is excellently illustrated here (the figure of *amplificatio* that is missing in 'The Manciple's Tale') and the joke expands with this complication: only a massively elaborated sentence will do to explain the circumstances under which *this* cock will give his morning crow.

The action slowly gets under way: the narrator frequently turns aside to comment to his audience in an ironic manner, and the variety of tone that he can encompass makes these moments the sharper. Thus he sombrely remarks:

> For evere the latter end of joye is wo.
> God woot that worldly joye is soone ago;   3205–6

And he mockingly adds that a 'rethor' might 'saufly' write this down as a 'sovereyn notabilitee'—the elaborate phrase contrasts vividly with the mournful stresses of the *sententia* itself and suggests just that learned pomposity that is the topic of the joke.

The fluency of the narrator's comments strengthens the joke when he stops to make a rhetorical mountain out of a fox lying in some cabbages:

> O false mordrour, lurkynge in thy den!
> O newe Scariot, newe Genylon,
> False dissymulour, of Greek Synon,
> That broghtest Troye al outrely to sorwe!   3226–9

It is not startling stuff; we know Chaucer can write like this, and the effect is not as complex as some of the earlier poetry in this tale where the rhythms and diction were prompting us towards attitudes to the speaker. The stylistic powers used towards the end of this tale are those of a great writer on holiday. Chaucer spreads himself; he makes fun of most sorts of medieval literature from romance to theology, and his poetry flows quickly and unostentatiously along as the narrator moves from joke to joke, from ironic reference to ironic reference. But if Chaucer is on holiday he is still a great poet, and a clear sign of this is that he provides us with two magnificent set-pieces.

In the first he amplifies the joke we have already seen, the idea of which is to build a rhetorical monument to an incident in this farmyard narrative. Chauntecleer approaches his doom and a sober moral is immediately drawn:

> This Chauntecleer his wynges gan to bete,
> As man that koude his traysoun nat espie,
> So was he ravysshed with his flaterie.   3322–4

The point is driven home with all the pausing, weighty elaboration of the 'Allegoria' at the end of a medieval fable:

> Allas! ye lordes, many a fals flatour
> Is in youre courtes, and many a losengeour,
> That plesen yow wel moore, by my feith,
> Than he that soothfastnesse unto yow seith.
> Redeth Ecclesiaste of flaterye;
> Beth war, ye lordes, of hir trecherye.   3325–30

The final, crucial action in this sequence races past in co-ordinate clauses:

> This Chauntecleer stood hye upon his toos,
> Strecchynge his nekke, and heeld his eyen cloos,
> And gan to crowe loude for the nones.
> And daun Russell the fox stirte up atones,
> And by the gargat hente Chauntecleer
> And on his bak toward the wode hym beer,
> For yet ne was ther no man that hym sewed.   3331–7

At the end the monosyllabic subordinate clause breaks the chain of action and gives a momentary pause.[33] After it, the storm of rhetoric breaks. The series of apostrophes opens with *exclamatio* and *repetitio* and there follows, as Naunin engagingly describes it, 'ein ganze Kette von Apostrophen':[34]

> O destinee that mayst nat been eschewed!
> Allas, that Chauntecleer fleigh fro the bemes!
> Allas, his wyf ne roghte nat of dremes!
> And on a Friday fil al this meschaunce.   3338–41

The last line here is now elaborated in an apostrophe to Venus, filled with ornate language, which builds up to an *interrogatio* in the last line:

> O Venus, that art goddesse of pleasaunce,
> Syn that thy servant was this Chauntecleer,
> And in thy servyce dide al his poweer,
> Moore for delit than world to multiplye,
> Why woldestow suffre hym on thy day to dye?   3342–6

The diction is appropriately elaborate and the syntax extended—the style of the paragraph rises to the height decorous for an address to Venus, and its elaboration seems fully in key with its ingenious discussion about the motivation of Chauntecleer's sexuality. The style is just what is needed for the joke to be an excellent one, and building upon this flourishing passage is the charming reference to 'Gaufred, deere maister sovereyn' in the following lines.

Dorothy Everett has said ' . . . if, as we read the *Nun's Priest's Tale*, we laugh too heartily and unthinkingly at the rhetoricians, there is a danger that Chaucer may be laughing at us.'[35] The tone of this passage shows the wisdom of her remark; Chaucer is not mocking Geoffrey, rather he is self-indulgently flourishing rhetorical language in a holiday mood. If the style here were crude and limping, making 'rhetoric' seem banal or bathetic, we might well say this was a determine of satire on the rhetoricians. But the style is easy, confident: the playfulness is that of a master. And indeed, he does not spend too long using his best rhetorical style in a comic cause, for as this long *apostrophe* continues the comedy is more of imagination and action than of language. The *apostrophe* to Geoffrey is widely regarded as the rhetorical sensation of the tale, but in fact it is not very ornate. There is a little elevated diction in it—'sovereyn', 'compleynedest', 'sentence'—and there is an *interrogatio* in line 3346. But if we are looking for a parody of rhetoric this will disappoint, and this may well be why Speirs said this apostrophe 'anticlimaxed' the others, though he does not give reasons.[36]

This muted tone is maintained in the next *apostrophe*: the hens are presented as classical matrons, but the language is quite restrained. The style is flowing, it is true, but there is little decoration:

> But sovereynly dame Pertelote shrighte
> Ful louder than dide Hasdrubales wyf,
> Whan that hir housbonde hadde lost hys lyf,
> And that the Romayns hadde brend Cartage.
> She was so ful of torment and of rage
> That wilfully into the fyr she sterte,
> And brende hirselven with a stedefast herte.   3562–8

The word 'sovereynly' is witty, for it means both that she shrieked the most and implies that she did it in queenly fashion, and the passage moves swiftly along, so swiftly that many an inattentive student has thought it is Pertelote who immolates herself. Chaucer's playing with high rhetorical style here has been brief; at first the style is carefully modelled to make the joke, but he feels no need to sustain the elaborate style once the point is established.

A longer passage of bravura poetry follows, when the farmyard chase occurs. This has often been discussed as a masterpiece of vigour and speed, and little comment is needed here.[37] Not only stylistic brilliance is shown, but also that imaginative humour and subtlety that have typified the whole tale:

> Ran Colle our dogge, and Talbot and Gerland,
> And Malkyn, with a dystaf in her hand;
> Ran cow and calf, and eek the verray hogges,
> So fered for the berkyng of the dogges
> And shoutyng of the men and wommen eeke,
> They ronne so hem thoughte hir herte breeke.   3383–88

Talbot and Gerland are rather aristocratic dogs' names, traditional for hunting dogs, and set against the humble name Colle they touch lightly the mock-heroic note again; the narrative sleight of hand of 'oure dogge' strengthens the immediacy of the scene, and not only is the animal world of the farmyard mobilised, but we actually see into their thoughts: the narrator is suddenly empowered to tell us what the pigs were feeling. A lightly carried, but very real skill makes the scene intensely vivid. Chaucer's power to embody the meaning of a scene in the poetry is well illustrated in the final lines:

> Of bras they broghten bemes, and of box,
> Of horn, of boon, in whiche they blewe and powped,
> And therwithal they skriked and they howped.
> It semed as that hevene sholde falle.   3398–401

After these spectacularly noisy lines Chaucer moves easily and undemonstratively to the end; the *conclusio* of the tale is a muted and thoughtful one, as varying interpretations of the tale are offered. Cock and Fox see it as a simply moral lesson advising them to cautious action in the world; the Priest himself speculates quizzically about its doctrinal possibilities; the Host's limited capacity has only grasped the vulgar bits—although the validity of this final link has been questioned,[38] its effect is clear enough as the tale stands. None of these views is given prominence, neither by direct statement nor by tonal implication, and most commentators have agreed that Chaucer saw an enigma as the only fit way of ending this most subtle of tales.

This quiet ending is, of course, in itself a piece of poetic modulation: the absence of spectacular effects here might tell us as much as the silence of the dog in the night-time told Holmes in 'Silver Blaze'. I believe this quiet close and the fading of spectacular rhetoric in the famous series of apostrophes show that Donaldson was over-serious when the argued the thematic importance of rhetoric in the tale, saying that here we find that:[39]

> . . . rhetoric enables man to find significance both in his desires and in his fate, and to pretend to himself that the universe takes him seriously.

It is an appealing argument, and a well-presented one; he goes on to say 'And rhetoric has a habit, too, of collapsing in the presence of simple common sense', which could be taken as an explanation of the quiet end (though Donaldson does not say this). But the fading of the rhetoric in the mock apostrophes and the quiet end of the tale make me believe that rhetorical writing is just one of the aspects of learning that Chaucer gently mocks in this festival tale, and I cannot see that this play anywhere has an implicitly moral side, except to warn us not to take ourselves too seriously.

The quiet ending is in part a return to normality after the pyrotechnics of the tale and partly a plain assertion that a story can be allegorised in a number of ways: there is a knowing simplicity in the Priest's tone as he finally speaks that makes the learned complexities the tale has presented seem hollow. In this respect the poetry at the end of this tale is as subtly evocative of the whole meaning of the tale as is the grand close to *Troilus and Criseyde* and the complex mixture of tones which ends *The Parlement of Foules* and 'The Knight's Tale'.

Not all of Chaucer's poems are, in stylistic terms, as complex and as successful as are these, nor does Chaucer always seek to create a highly-wrought poetry where meaning and style are inextricably united. That he does often do so has been the thesis of this study, and it is because I would value this type of poetry so highly that I would judge *Troilus and Criseyde* as Chaucer's finest work, and one of the finest in the language: in it extended and subtle meaning is transmitted in exquisitely judged and finely modulated poetry. But such a judgment starts from the premise that meaning-implying poetic modulation is the finest type of poetry, and this premise is not absolute. When we have shown that Chaucer can write like this and can satisfy the most exacting taste in this type of poetry, we should then note that he does not always write in this way. Just as to ignore Chaucer's poetic art has been, in the past, an error, it would be equally foolish to imagine that the poetic mastery outlined here is the only important thing about his work. It is all too easy to be obsessed by one's own arguments and one's own inclinations, and to believe no more needs to be said. Having this in mind, I would finally like to suggest that with a full understanding of Chaucer's power as a poet we can go on and see the other fine things his work has to offer, and we can go on more confidently because a comprehension of this basic and pervasive poetic skill will help us to understand and evaluate the many other aspects of his expansive genius.

NOTES

1. 'Colfax *vs.* Chauntecleer', *PMLA*, XXXIX (1924), 762–81; see p. 781.
2. 'The *moralite* of the Nun's Priest's Sermon', *JEPG*, LII (1953), 498–508; see p. 498.
3. In 'Chaucer's Disgruntled Cleric: *The Nun's Priest's Tale*', *PMLA*, LXXVIII (1963), 156–62, Broes argues that the Priest mocks the Prioress throughout his tale; Lumiansky 'The Nun's Priest in *The Canterbury Tales*', *PMLA*, LXVIII (1953), 896–906, feels the basis of the tale to be the difference between the Priest's real personality and the one the Host imputes to him.

4. *Chaucer and the Shape of Creation* (Cambridge, Mass., 1967).
5. Young, 'Chaucer and Geoffrey of Vinsauf', *MP*, XLI (1943-4), 172-82; Pratt, 'The Classical Lamentations in the *Nun's Priest's Tale*', *MLN*, LXVIV (1949), 77-8; Manly, p. 97.
6. In 'Cicero on Parnassus', (cf. note 14, p. 204), p. 110.
7. P. 174.
8. *Speaking of Chaucer*, pp. 146-50.
9. Pp. 237-43.
10. Speirs, pp. 185-93; Brindley, 'The Mixed Style of the *Nun's Priest's Tale*', *English Studies in Africa*, VII (1964), 148-56.
11. *The Nun's Priest's Tale and the Pardoner's Tale* (Oxford, 1965); see pp. 19-25.
12. *The Nun's Priest's Tale* (Oxford, 1927), pp. 30-1.
13. *The Nun's Priest's Tale* (London, 1959); see the Introduction, pp. 7-30 *passim* and the appendix on rhetoric, pp. 46-50.
14. *The Nun's Priest's Prologue and Tale* (Cambridge, 1965); see p. 32.
15. P. 16.
16. This issue has been examined recently by Charles S. Watson, 'The Relationship of the *Monk's Tale* and the *Nun's Priest's Tale*', *Studies in Short Fiction*, I (1964), 277-88.
17. The word 'reported' may also be a learned term here; Chaucer only uses the verb five times and the noun 'reporter' once. The OED records him as the first to use it in English.
18. Lumiansky notes 'the patronizing tone and content of this speech', p. 901.
19. *Chaucer and His Poetry*, reprinted ed. (Cambridge, Mass., 1951); see pp. 146-218 *passim.*
20. Although of OE origin, the word 'bour' is not common in Chaucer; it appears in the conventional phrases 'bright in bour' (S. Thop. 1932) and 'byrde in bour' (RR., 1014); it appears three other times in collocation with 'halle'; it is used twice in 'The Miller's Tale' with apparent ironic effect (cf. Donaldson's remarks on this in the tale) and once in 'The Wife of Bath's Tale' (line 300) where it also appears to have a genteel connotation.

     The word 'sklendre' occurs six times, three of them referring to a lady's slimness (Cl. 1198, Mch. 1602, RR. 858). When the Reeve is described as a 'sclendre colerik man' this may point towards the Miller's questioning of his masculinity. The other reference, Mk. 3147, seems neither to support nor contradict the notion that the word has a romance connotation.
21. Muscatine, p. 239; Brindley, p. 149.
22. In addition to the editorial notes on 'orgon' also see Fritz Karpf, *Studien zur Syntax in den Werken Geoffrey Chaucers*, I, *Weiner Beiträge zur Englischen Philologie*, LV (1930), 1-148; on pp. 124-7 he discusses 'orgon' and establishes its exotic character.
23. At the time of writing the MED has not inched its way as far as 'logge'; the existing dictionaries suggest a general sense of 'rough shelter' which would seem, *prima facie*, appropriate enough for a cock. But the OED also lists 'hut, booth, tent, arbour' as meanings. These tend towards the chivalric, and on several occasions the word is used in romances to mean the rough shelter the hero makes in the forest for his lady and himself. It is of French origin and Chaucer only uses it once (the verb 'logge' appears four times, but it has no notion of 'roughness' or chivalry, and it has its own noun, 'loggynge' appearing once). The word may well have chivalric connotations, then, and if this were so it would give point to the only word in this passage without a specific implication,
24. See Muscatine, p. 239, Elliott, p. 21 and the notes on the passage by Hussey and by Coghill and Tolkien.
25. See Lalia P. Boone, 'Chauntecleer and Partlet Identified', *MLN*, LXIV (1949), 78-81.
26. Kökeritz sees *rime riche* in 2903-4 (see p. 946), but it hardly gives the sequence an ornate tone.
27. P. 187.

28. Chaucer only uses 'wlatsom' twice, here and in 'The Monk's Tale'—perhaps another touch of parody.
29. P. 104.
30. P. 42.
31. *Speaking of Chaucer*, p. 149.
32. P. xxx: 'For he is both entertaining them and teasing them with suspense and irrelevance: he keeps an eye on them all the time, gauging to a nicety how far he can go without spoiling their pleasure, cajoling them with a promise, or muffling a protest by protesting first'.
33. Chaucer only uses 'gargat' here; it also appears in *Kyng Alisaundre* and as a knightly surname. The word seems to be of exotic origin—OED suggests Italian or Spanish—and so this is one more dignification of Chauntecleer.
34. P. 38.
35. P. 174.
36. P. 191.
37. See Brindley, pp. 154–5, Ian Robinson, p. 146, Muscatine, p. 240 and the notes by Hussey and by Coghill and Tolkien.
38. See Robinson's note, Lumiansky argues, convincingly I think, for the validity of the end-link.
39. *Speaking of Chaucer*, p. 149.

The Figures of Style

When we talk of 'medieval rhetorical treatises' the phrase suggests something arcane and sterile; the titles the authors themselves used show that they, at least, did not see their work in that light. Geoffrey of Vinsauf wrote the *Poetria Nova*, John of Garland the *Poetria*, Gervase de Melkley the *Ars Versificaris* and Matthew of Vendôme the *Ars Versficatoria*. Other treatises, some by the same authors, had other titles, but these indicate well how the authors thought of the contents; the works are a thorough analysis of poetry as medieval men saw it, written so that the reader would understand the art and how to practise it. This approach often seems extremely programmatic to modern people, filled as we are with Romantic ideas about inspiration as the essence of poetry. Modern sensibilities are reluctant to embark on the detailed analysis of the verbal and conceptual structure of poetry, but a study of the manuscripts of Yeats and Eliot will soon show that modern poets are as concerned as medieval writers were with the arduous mechanics of fit expression.

Geoffrey de Vinsauf, whom I take here as typical since he was the most influential of the rhetoricians and, apparently, the one Chaucer knew most about, offers an analysis of various aspects of the poem. He talks about strategies of beginning, about structuring the poem (see the discussion of *amplificatio* above, with regard to 'The Manciple's Tale'), about the conceptual elements of the whole (the 'Figures of Thought'), about images of various sorts (the 'Difficult Ornaments'), and about types of verbal complexity and emphasis (the 'Easy Ornaments'); these last two areas are both described as the Figures of Style. As the interest of this study has been in the meaningful aspects of Chaucer's style, I have not employed the terms referring to the Figures of Thought, but this should not suggest that I think them unimportant: an analysis of Chaucer's use of them to shape his meaning needs very much to be written, but this has not been the place to speculate on such a topic. The 'Difficult Ornaments' have also been little discussed here, and this is caused by the nature of Chaucer's poetry. These 'high style' features occur little in his work: metaphor does appear in invocations and in highly emotional speeches, and *pronominatio* is sometimes found. It has not seemed necessary to illustrate or gloss the 'Difficult Ornaments' here because they are explained in the text on the few occasions when they are relevant. The 'Easy Ornaments' appear frequently in Chaucer, however, and definitions and illustrations follow.

The Figures of Style: the 'Easy Ornaments'

The figures appear in alphabetical order for easier reference; I cannot see any consistent rationale behind the order Geoffrey uses, and as he works the figures into a sample speech, rather than tabulating them, there may well be a random element in the order. Chaucer uses most of the Easy Ornaments, but because he is writing in English, and in rhyme as well, some of the figures which depend on the flexibility of Latin word-order appear in a rather attenuated form in his work: *conversio, complexio, adjunctio, conjunctio* and *disjunctio* are examples of this. It should also be noted that no two rhetoricians agree exactly on the terminology of the figures or on their definition; here I set out Geoffrey's analysis as a working tool, and am not aiming at a synoptic account of the rhetorical figures.

adjunctio—placing a verb either at the beginning or the end of two successive clauses, controlling them both:

> Criseyde also, right in the same wyse,
> Of Troilus gan in hire herte shette
> His worthynesse, his lust, his dedes wise,
> His gentilesse, and how she with hym mette,
>
> *TC*, III. 1548–51.

adnominatio—world-play depending on a change in the word:

> So whan this Calkas knew by calkulynge, *TC*, I.71

articulus—a series of single words without grammatical links:

> She moorneth, waketh, wayleth, fasteth, pleyneth; *FT*, 819

commutatio—repeating the words or structure of the first half of the line in the second half of the line, with the order reversed:

> For y am sorwe, and sorwe ys y. *BD*, 597

compar—clauses or phrases with similar length and structure:

> The juge dremeth how his plees been sped;
> The carter dremeth how his cartes gon;
> The riche, of gold; the knyght fyght with his fon;
> The syke met he drynketh of the tonne;
> The lovere met he hath his lady wonne.   *PF*, 101–5

complexio—repetition of the first and last words of successive clauses (i.e. *conversio* and *repetitio* combined):

> I cannot find this figure; rhyme means that Chaucer cannot use identical words to end lines (though *rime riche* is close to it) and he seems not to end clauses within the lines with the same word. An effect very like *complexio* occurs within formal passages of *repetitio* (see below), when the first word in each line is the same and the lines rhyme—the effect is especially marked in a rhyme royal stanza.

conclusio—pithy statement in conclusion:

> Pekke hem up right as they growe and ete hem yn.
> Be myrie, housbonde, for youre fader kyn!
> Dredeth no dreem, I kan sey yow namoore.'   *NPT*, 2967–9

conduplicatio—repeating a word or words for emphasis:

> O wynd, o wynd, the weder gynneth clere;   *TC*, II.2

conjunctio—placing a single verb between two clauses, linking them:

> And whiche eyen my lady hadde!
> Debonaire, goode, glade, and sadde,
> Symple, of good mochel, noght to wyde.   *BD*, 859–61

contentio—a statement depending on contraries:

> Myn hele ys turned into seknesse,
> In drede ys al my sykernesse;
> To derke ys turned al my lyght,
> My wyt ys foly, my day ys nyght,   *BD*, 607–10

continuatio—a short group of words expressing a thought in a pithy manner:

> Thyn is affeccioun of hoolynesse,
> And myn is love, as to a creature;   *KT*, 1158–9

contrarium—arguing by contraries:

'Right as ther dyed nevere man,' quod he,
'That he ne lyvede in erthe in some degree,
Right so ther lyvede never man,' he seyde
'In al this world, that som tyme he ne deyde.   *KT*, 2843–6

conversio—repetition of a word at the end of successive clauses:

see note under *complexio*

correctio—withdrawing a word and substituting a better one:

Ful blisfully in prison maistow dure,—
In prison? certes nay, but in paradys!   *KT*, 1236–7

definitio—crisp summary:

Syngeres with harpes, baudes, wafereres,
Whiche ben the verray develes officeres
To kyndle and blowe the fyr of lecherye,
That is annexed unto glotonye.   *PT*, 479–82

disjunctio—placing verbs at the end of two or more successive clauses:

With myghty maces the bones they tobreste.
He thurgh the thikkeste of the throng gan threste;
                                   KT, 2611–12

dissolutio—a series of clauses or phrases without connecting words:

. . . in the taas they founde,
Thurgh-girt with many a grevous blody wounde,
Two yonge kynghtes, liggynge by and by,
Bothe in oon armes, wroght ful richely,   *KT*, 1009–12

dubitatio—stating a doubt about what to say:

'But which a visage had she thertoo!
Allas! myn herte ys wonder woo
That I ne kan discryven hyt!
Me lakketh both Englyssh and wit
For to undo hyt at the fulle;   *BD*, 895–9

exclamatio—expression of grief or indignation:

Allas, the wo! allas, the peynes stronge,
That I for yow have suffred, and so longe!
Allas, the deeth! allas, myn Emelye!
Allas, departynge of oure compaigynye!   *KT*, 2771–4

R

expeditio—stating several choices and rejecting all but one:

> For every heer on hir hed,
> Soth to seyne, hyt was not red,
> Ne nouther yelowe, ne broun hyt nas,
> Me thoghte most lyk gold hyt was.   *BD*, 855–8

gradatio—repeating the last word of a clause or phrase as the first word of the next:
> As shryfte without repentaunce.'
> 'Repentaunce! nay, fy!' quod he,   *BD*, 1114–15

interpretatio—repeating an idea in different words:

> Til that the brighte sonne loste his hewe;
> For th'orisonte hath reft the sonne his lyght,—
> This is as muche to seye as it was nyght!—   *FT*, 1016–18

interrogatio—use of a question:

> Who koude telle, but he hadde wedded be,
> The joye, the ese and the prosperitee
> That is bitwixe an housbonde and his wyf?   *FT*, 803–5

membrum—two or three short clauses or phrases, each complete in itself, but together expressing a meaning:

> They yolleden as feendes doon in helle;
> The dokes cryden as men wolde hem quelle;
> The gees for feere flowen over the trees;
> Out of the hyve cam the swarm of bees.   *NPT*, 3389–92

occupatio—describing something while apparently refusing to describe it:

> But it were al to longe for to devyse
> The grete clamour and the waymentynge
> That the ladyes made at the brennynge
> Of the bodies, and the grete honour
> That Theseus, the noble conquerour,
> Dooth to the ladyes, whan they from hym wente;
> > *KT*, 994–9

permissio—seeking direction from another person, a divinity or the audience:

> My konnyng is so wayk, o blisful Queene,
> For to declare thy grete worthynesse

That I ne may the weighte nat susteene;
But as a child of twelf month oold, or lesse,
That kan unnethes any word expresse,
Right só fare I, amd therfore I yow preye,
Gydeth my song that I shal of yow seye.'   *PrT*, 481–87

praecisio—breaking off a phrase or clause for emphasis
    Nay! rather deth then do so foul a dede!
    And axe merci, gilteles,—what nede?   *AA*, 300–1

ratiocinatio—an extended argument using question and answer:
    See *FT*, 1364 *et seq.*

repetitio—repeating a word at the opening of successive clauses:

Myn is the drenchyng in the see so wan;
Myn is the prison in the derke cote;
Myn is the stranglyng and hangyng by the throte,

KT, 2456–8

sententia—a statement of what is generally regarded to be true, a maxim:

Ek though I speeke of love unfelyngly,
No wondre is, for it nothyng of newe is;
A blynd man kan nat juggen wel in hewis.   *TC*, II.19–21

similiter cadens—two or three words in a clause with the same endings; Baldwin describes this as 'rhyme on inflections'. It is obviously easier in Latin than in English, but the illustration under *articulus* is an example.

similiter desinens—two or three indeclinable words with the same endings in one clause or phrase; Baldwin says this is *rime riche*. It could also be used to describe assonance like that employed to characterise Calchas. Neither this figure nor *similiter cadens* seems of much importance in Chaucer.

subjectio—a question posed and answered by the same speaker:

'Endeth thanne love in wo? Ye, or men lieth!   *TC*, IV.834

traductio—repetition of the same word with different meanings:

The best example in Chaucer is the play on the word 'hende' in 'The Miller's Tale', cf. Donaldson's 'The Idiom of Popular Poetry in "The Miller's Tale" ' for a full discussion.

R*

transitio—a resumé of what has been said and a statement of what will follow:

> And thus in joy and blisse I lete hem dwelle,
> And of the sike Aurelius wol I telle.   *FT*, 1099–100

Abbreviations used in this Appendix:

AA	*Anelida and Arcite*
BD	*The Book of the Duchess*
FT	'The Franklin's Tale'
KT	'The Knight's Tale'
MT	'The Miller's Tale'
NPT	'The Nun's Priest's Tale'
PF	*The Parlement of Foules*
PrT	'The Prioress's Tale'
PT	'The Pardoner's Tale'
TC	*Troilus and Criseyde*

Index

abbrevatio, 170, 178, 188
adjunctio, 237
adnominatio, 50, 55, 78, 237
alliteration, in 'The Franklin's Tale', 195, 197, 198
  in 'The Knight's Tale', 127, 148, 154, 155–6
  in *The Parliament of Foules*, 31, 35, 40–1
  in *Troilus and Criseyde*, 51, 92
amplificatio, 22, 93, 143, 168–72, 176, 178, 180, 181, 188, 189, 197–8, 228, 236
anacoluthon, 133
Anelida and Arcite, characterisation in, 11, 19–20, 21, 22, 46
  Complaint, 2, 16, 17–23, 24
  critical opinion on, 2–3, 161
  dating, 1
  invocations in, 4–6, 16, 24, 26
  metaphor in, 14, 15, 17, 18, 21, 22
  metre of, 22–3, 46
  middle style in, 14, 24
  narrative, 6–16, 182
  plain style in, 10–11, 16, 24
  uneveness of, 23–4
apostrophe, 84, 87, 108, 110, 120, 121, 163, 170, 178, 179, 190, 230–1, 232
Ars Versificaris, 236
Ars Versificatoria, 236
Arthuriad, Malory's, 137
articulus, 14, 21, 71, 85, 108, 121, 189, 192, 237
assonance, 30, 53, 54, 199, 224
Atkins, J. W. H., 169
Austen, Jane, 49

Baldwin, C. S., 169, 207, 241
Barbour, John, 126
Bateson, F. W., xv, 25–6, 27, 34–5
Baum, Paul F., 50, 100
beast fables, 180, 212
Bennett, J. A. W., 24, 25, 33, 37
Benoît de Sainte-Maure, 55, 75
Birney, Earle, 164–5, 177
Bloomfield, M. W., 83

Boccaccio, Giovanni, 55, 74, 85–6, 88, 99, 143
Boece, 105, 110, 133
Boethius, 133, 157
Book of the Duchess, The, xiii, 22, 33, 52, 181, 208
Borthwick, Sister, 62, 64
brevitas, 163, 188
Brewer, D. S., 24, 25
Brindley, D. J., 207, 214
Broes, Arthur T., 206

Chatman, Seymour B., xv
Cherniss, Michael D., 3
chiasmus, 25
circuitio, 171, 181, 228
Clemen, Wolfgang, 2, 20
'Clerk's Tale', 'The', 175, 212
Coghill, Neville, 207, 225
collatio, 17, 32, 170, 171
  aperta, 174, 189
  occulta, 172, 181
commutatio, 60, 68, 94, 102, 118, 237
compar, xvii, 7, 9, 18, 21, 57, 74, 84–5, 86, 91, 94, 108, 110, 118, 121, 124, 130, 133–4, 139, 144, 146–7, 177, 194, 216, 237–8
complexio, 238
conclusio, 85, 86, 175, 190, 192, 223–4, 232, 238
conduplicatio, 80, 126, 238
conjunctio, 238
contentio, 25, 60, 94, 188, 238
continuatio, 138, 238
contrarietas, 226
contrarium, 93, 238–9
conversio, 239
correctio, 18, 188, 239
courtly love, conventional poetry of, 102–103, 192, 194
Criticism and Medieval Poetry, xiii, 208

Dean, Christopher, 100
definitio, 119, 239

Delasanta, Rodney, 99, 135
demonstratio, 162
descriptio, 99, 102–3, 115, 125–6, 147, 158, 170, 172, 173, 192
Dickens, Charles, 49
digressio, 170, 173, 174, 176, 177
diminutio, 185
disjunctio, 239
dissolutio, 122, 239
Donaldson, E. Talbot, xiv, 64, 74, 77, 92, 100, 207, 227, 232, 241
Donner, Morton, 164
Donovan, Mortimer J., 206
Double Sorrow of Troilus, The, 70
dreams, in *Parlement of Foules*, 31–45, 46
vocabulary of, 220
dubitatio, 78, 82, 102, 113, 120, 137, 138, 239

Edmunds, Paul, 76
effictio, 71, 149, 151–2, 216
Eliot, T. S., 236
Elliott, R. W. V., 207
emblems, 125–6, 149
enjambement, in *Anelida and Arcite*, 12, 14
in 'The Franklin's Tale', 186
in 'The Knight's Tale', 104, 113, 124, 125, 127, 149, 155
in 'The Nun's Priest's Tale', 211, 216, 218, 220, 222, 223, 226
in *The Parlement of Foules*, 29, 35, 44, 46
in *Troilus and Criseyde*, 56, 57, 59, 61, 67, 72, 79
envoi, 90, 93–4
Everett, Dorothy, xiv, 51, 77, 207
exclamatio, 13, 18, 80, 81, 91, 116, 120, 121, 129, 140, 162, 163, 178, 179, 190, 224, 230, 239
exempla, 162, 174–5, 181, 182, 200, 222–3, 225–6
expeditio, 240

Faerie Queene, The, 51
Faral, E., 169
Fielding, Henry, as narrator, 145
'Figures of Style', 236, 237–42
'Figures of Thought', 236
Foster, Edward E., 100
Fowler, Roger, xv
Frank, Robert W. Jr, 24
'Franklin's Tale, 'The', 14, 39, 63, 131, 161, 225
character of narrator, 183–5, 186, 187–9, 195–7, 203–204
characterisation of Arveragus, 201

development of the tale, 185, 186, 191, 194–5, 197, 199, 201–3
and 'gentillesse', 183
jingling descriptive language in, 198–9
narrative style, 186–7, 191–2, 197
set piece description, 197–8
style and characterisation of Aurelius, 192–3, 194–5, 199, 202–203
style and characterisation of Dorigen, 189–91, 193–4, 199–201
French, W. H., 98
Frost, William, 98, 126, 144, 157

Geoffrey of Vinsauf, 17, 168–72, 174, 181, 207, 230, 236
Gordon, Ida L., 70
Gower, John, 9, 31
gradatio, 240
Granson, Sir Otes de, 2
Green, A. Wigfall, 3
Guido da Colonna, 55

Haller, R. S., 100, 140
Halverson, John, 98
Harrington, D. V., 99–100, 136
Hazelton, Richard, 163–4
Henryson, Robert, 180
Hill, A. M., 75
Hodgson, Phyllis, 185, 190, 200
Hotson, J. Leslie, 206
Hough, Graham, xvi
Hous of Fame, The, 22, 33
Hulbert, J. R., 162, 171
Huppé, B. F., 50
Hussey, Maurice, 207–208
hyperbaton, 77

Iliad, The, 77
interpretatio, 32, 61, 63, 84, 85, 115, 120, 124, 171, 181, 240
interrogatio, 66, 113, 116, 129, 141, 190, 230, 231, 240
invocatio, 78
irony, in 'The Franklin's Tale', 200
in 'The Manciple's Tale', 175
in 'The Nun's Priest's Tale', 212–13, 215, 221, 228
in *The Parlement of Foules*, 31
in *Troilus and Criseyde*, 64, 65, 70, 88

Jakobson, Roman, xv
John of Garland, 236
Jordan, R. M., 100, 206

Kaske, R. E., 64
Kean, P. M., 63
Kelly Douglas, 169
Ker, W. P., 2
Kittredge, G. L., 61, 210
'Knight's Tale', 'The', 4, 6, 7, 164, 171, 217
  characterisation in, 98, 151
  critical opinion on, 98–100
  elevated style in, 99, 101–3, 105, 108,
    110, 115–16, 119–20, 123–4, 125, 126,
    128, 134, 135, 143–4, 153, 158
  imagery, 100, 107, 108–109, 110–11,
    115, 116, 117, 123, 124, 137, 139, 140,
    148
  major set pieces in, 145–59, 197
  meaning of, 98
  motif of balance in, 102, 104, 117–18,
    123, 141, 155, 157
  the narrator, 136–45
  Palamon and Arcite, 101–24
  plain style in, 105
  prayers in, 119–23, 142
  structure, 98, 100, 126, 150–1, 158, 233
  style of disputation, 133–4
  Theseus, 124–36
Kökeritz, Helge, 50, 52, 55, 60, 78, 100
Kopp, Jane Baltzell, 169, 172

Leech, G. N., xv
Levin, S. R., xv
lists, in *Parlement of Foules*, 35, 36–7, 38
  in *Troilus and Criseyde*, 85
Lumiansky, R. M., 55, 71, 206

Machaut, Guillaume de, 61
Malory, Sir Thomas, 88, 137
'Manciple's Tale', 'The', and concept of
  '*amplificatio*', 168–72, 236
  critical opinion on, 161–5
  the development of the tale, 172–80, 181,
    182
  high style in, 179
  middle style in, 173, 174, 178, 181
  moral of the tale, 180–1
  narrator, 174, 175, 176–7, 178, 179, 181
  Prologue to, 165–8, 182, 204
Manly, J. M., 2, 20, 162, 180, 207, 225
Marckwardt, A. H., 99
Matthew of Vendôme, 236
McDonald, Charles, 24
Measure for Measure, 134
Meech, S. B., 74, 75–6
Melkley, Gervase de, 236
membrum, 240
'Merchant's Tale', 'The', 187
metaphors, 17, 70, 80, 83, 91, 124, 137, 237

'Miller's Tale', 'The', xiv, 163, 176, 207,
  214
'Monk's Tale, 'The', 208
Morte Arthure, alliterative, 156
Murphy, J. J., 171, 186
Muscatine, Charles, xiv, 49, 83, 98, 99,
  100, 101, 121, 126, 133, 152–3, 207,
  214

Naunin, T., 226, 230
'Nun's Priest's Tale', 'The', 139, 170, 171,
  180
  characterisation of animals in, 217–26,
    227
  contemporary references in, 206, 229
  and critical opinion, 206–8
  development of the tale, 210, 214, 227,
    228–30, 232–3
  the farmyard chase, 231–2
  linking passages, 208–9
  mock-heroic aspects of, 206, 213–14,
    215–17, 224, 226, 227, 229, 231–2

occupatio, 99, 136–7, 138, 143–4, 145, 146,
  158, 163, 240
oppositio, 93, 170, 172–3
oratio obliqua, 67
'ornaments', 'difficult', 236–7
  'easy', 236, 237–42
Ovid, 2
oxymoron, 25

Paradis d'Amour, Le, 61
Paradise Lost, 171
'Pardoner's Tale', 'The', 164, 180, 187,
  206, 207
Parlement of Foules, The, 1, 46–7, 55–6, 233
  critical opinion on, 24–5
  dating of, 1
  invocations in, 32–3, 38
  metaphors, 34
  middle style in, 32
  narrative sections of, 28–45
  plain style in, 11, 28, 30, 44–5
  rhetorical opening of, 25–8
  speech styles in, 39–44
  verisimilitude of, 44
parody, 163–4
'Parson's Tale', 'The', 133, 165, 212
Payne, Robert O., 77
permissio, 240–1
personification, 85, 88, 149
Petrarch, 17
Piehler, Paul, 64
Piers Plowman, 50, 156

Plessow, Gustav, 163, 172
Poetria, of John of Garland, 236
Poetria Nova, 236
praecisio, 63, 119, 241
Pratt, Robert A., 207
prayers, Arcite's in 'The Knight's Tale', 121–2
　　Aurelius's in 'The Franklin's Tale', 194–5
　　bidding prayer in *Troilus and Criseyde*, 78, 90
　　closing prayer in *Troilus and Criseyde*, 93, 94–5
　　Emily's in 'The Knight's Tale', 121, 142
　　Palamon's in 'The Knight's Tale', 119–21
'Prioress's Tale', 'The', 29, 208
pronominatio, 4, 32, 61, 63, 84, 120, 178, 237
prosecutio, 79
prosecutio cum proverbiis, 70
prosopopoeia, 170, 177–8
proverbs, 70–1
puns, 50–1

rallentando, 92, 130
ratiocinatio, 178, 188, 241
repetitio, xvii, 7, 13, 18, 21, 57, 60, 61, 66, 74, 78, 86, 91, 108, 113, 118, 124, 129, 130, 133–4, 139, 141, 144, 149, 177, 216, 224, 230, 241
'Retracciouns', 'The', 165
rhetorical treatises, 236
　　and see Geoffrey de Vinsauf
rhyme royal, 1, 4, 6, 8, 16, 24, 29, 59, 77
rime riche, 15, 55, 60, 67, 68, 92, 241
Robertson, D. W., 64
Robinson, F. N., 2, 50, 67, 106, 132, 162–3, 171, 186
Robinson, Ian, 100, 146
Romaunt of the Rose, The, 7, 38, 110, 153, 212
Root, R. K., 57, 65, 67, 78, 80, 85, 98
roundel, 45
Ruggiers, Paul G., 99

Salter, Elizabeth, 98, 99, 100, 154–5
sententia, 25, 27, 31–2, 41, 79, 82, 102, 162, 170, 174, 188, 189, 201, 219, 224, 229, 241
sermocinatio, 162
Severs, J. Burke, 164, 177, 180, 181
Shakespeare, William, 17, 49, 158
'Shipman's Tale', 'The', 208
Shumaker, William, 165
significatio, 50, 55, 110, 140

'Silver Blaze', 232
similes, 17, 34, 57, 92, 107, 108–109, 110, 117, 123, 139, 140, 174, 216
　　and see, Troilus and Criseyde
similiter cadens, 189, 241
similiter desinens, 241
similitudo, 83, 86
Sir Gawaine and the Green Knight, 127, 137, 153, 170
'Sir Thopas', 'Tale of', 6, 163, 208
Sisam, Kenneth, 207, 228
Skelton, John, 22
Sledd, James, 200
Spearing, A. C., xiii, xv, 99, 100, 101, 103, 125, 132, 140, 155, 156, 185, 208
Speirs, John, xiii, 71, 100, 207, 220, 231
Spenser, Edmund, 51, 88
Spitzer, Leo, xvi
Statius, 6–7
Style and Stylistics, xvi
subjectio, 241
superlatio, 8, 126, 215, 228
suspensio, 25
syntax, complex, 80, 87, 90, 132, 187, 191–3
　　co-ordinate, 112–13, 121, 125, 144, 153, 229–30
　　extended, 105, 106, 108, 109, 114, 129, 147, 221, 222, 223, 230

'Tale of Lancelot and Guinevere', 88
'Tale of Melibee', 'The', 226
Tatlock, John S. P., 55, 76
Teseida, 99
Thackery, W. M., as narrator, 145
Tolkein, J. R. R., 207, 225
traductio, 50, 55, 224, 241
transitio, 242
translatio, 14, 80, 115, 172, 178, 192
Troilus and Criseyde, xiv, xvii, 1, 15, 17, 29, 32, 207, 217, 233
　　animal imagery in, 15, 64
　　Antigone, 59–65, 76
　　Chalcas, 50–6, 76
　　character of Troilus, 66, 71–2, 83
　　Diomede, 65–76
　　Ector, 56–9, 76
　　ending of, 46, 92–5
　　expansive images in, 62, 63
　　high style in, 80, 81, 83, 84–5, 86, 87, 93, 95, 120
　　invocations in, 4, 38, 77
　　middle style in, 78
　　the narrator, 49, 64, 76–95, 137, 139
　　plain style in, 81, 83
　　prohemia, 77–89

similes in, 58, 83, 91, 92
song of Antigone, 60, 61-2, 64

Van, Thomas A., 100
vocabulary, 81
  French, 105, 153, 212, 213
  Germanic, 224
  Latin, 191, 220, 221, 224
  Norse, 153
  Romance, 72, 110, 126, 178-9

Whittock, Trevor, 100, 136
Wimsatt, James I., 2-3
'Wife of Bath's Prologue', 58
word play, 50-2, 53
Wyatt, Thomas, 17
Wyclif, John, 178

Yeats, W. B., 236
Young, Karl, 207